Big Data

PRINCIPLES AND BEST PRACTICES OF SCALABLE REAL-TIME DATA SYSTEMS

NATHAN MARZ
JAMES WARREN

MANNING

This edition has been published by arrangement with the **Manning Publications Co., USA.** and published in India by **Dreamtech Press, 19-A, Ansari Road, Daryaganj, New Delhi-110002.**

Limits of Liability/disclaimer of Warranty : The author and publisher have used their best efforts in preparing this book. Manning Publications Co., USA and The author makes no representation or warranties with respect to the accuracy or completeness of the contents of this book, and specifically disclaim any implied warranties of merchantability or fitness for any particular purpose. There are no warranties which extend beyond the descriptions contained in this paragraph. No warranty may be created or extended by sales representatives or written sales materials. The accuracy and completeness of the information provided herein and the opinions stated herein are not guaranteed or warranted to produce any particular results, and the advice and strategies contained herein may not be suitable for every individual. Neither Manning Publications Co., USA, nor the author shall be liable for any loss of profit or any other commercial damages, including but not limited to special, incidental, consequential, or other damages.

Trademarks : All brand names and product names used in this book are trademarks, registered trademarks, or trade names of their respective holders. Manning Publications Co., USA is not associated with any product or vendor mentioned in this book.

ISBN: 978-93-5119-806-2

Edition : 2017

Printed at : N. K. Book Binder, Delhi.

brief contents

iii

contents

v

preface

When I first entered the world of Big Data, it felt like the Wild West of software development. Many were abandoning the relational database and its familiar comforts for NoSQL databases with highly restricted data models designed to scale to thousands of machines. The number of NoSQL databases, many of them with only minor differences between them, became overwhelming. A new project called *Hadoop* began to make waves, promising the ability to do deep analyses on huge amounts of data. Making sense of how to use these new tools was bewildering.

At the time, I was trying to handle the scaling problems we were faced with at the company at which I worked. The architecture was intimidatingly complex—a web of sharded relational databases, queues, workers, masters, and slaves. Corruption had worked its way into the databases, and special code existed in the application to handle the corruption. Slaves were always behind. I decided to explore alternative Big Data technologies to see if there was a better design for our data architecture.

One experience from my early software-engineering career deeply shaped my view of how systems should be architected. A coworker of mine had spent a few weeks collecting data from the internet onto a shared filesystem. He was waiting to collect enough data so that he could perform an analysis on it. One day while doing some routine maintenance, I accidentally deleted all of my coworker's data, setting him behind weeks on his project.

I knew I had made a big mistake, but as a new software engineer I didn't know what the consequences would be. Was I going to get fired for being so careless? I sent out an email to the team apologizing profusely—and to my great surprise, everyone was very sympathetic. I'll never forget when a coworker came to my desk, patted my back, and said "Congratulations. You're now a professional software engineer."

In his joking statement lay a deep unspoken truism in software development: we don't know how to make perfect software. Bugs can and do get deployed to production. If the application can write to the database, a bug can write to the database as well. When I set about redesigning our data architecture, this experience profoundly affected me. I knew our new architecture not only had to be scalable, tolerant to machine failure, and easy to reason about—but tolerant of human mistakes as well.

My experience re-architecting that system led me down a path that caused me to question everything I thought was true about databases and data management. I came up with an architecture based on immutable data and batch computation, and I was astonished by how much simpler the new system was compared to one based solely on incremental computation. Everything became easier, including operations, evolving the system to support new features, recovering from human mistakes, and doing performance optimization. The approach was so generic that it seemed like it could be used for any data system.

Something confused me though. When I looked at the rest of the industry, I saw that hardly anyone was using similar techniques. Instead, daunting amounts of complexity were embraced in the use of architectures based on huge clusters of incrementally updated databases. So many of the complexities in those architectures were either completely avoided or greatly softened by the approach I had developed.

Over the next few years, I expanded on the approach and formalized it into what I dubbed the *Lambda Architecture.* When working on a startup called BackType, our team of five built a social media analytics product that provided a diverse set of realtime analytics on over 100 TB of data. Our small team also managed deployment, operations, and monitoring of the system on a cluster of hundreds of machines. When we showed people our product, they were astonished that we were a team of only five people. They would often ask "How can so few people do so much?" My answer was simple: "It's not what we're doing, but what we're not doing." By using the Lambda Architecture, we avoided the complexities that plague traditional architectures. By avoiding those complexities, we became dramatically more productive.

The Big Data movement has only magnified the complexities that have existed in data architectures for decades. Any architecture based primarily on large databases that are updated incrementally will suffer from these complexities, causing bugs, burdensome operations, and hampered productivity. Although SQL and NoSQL databases are often painted as opposites or as duals of each other, at a fundamental level they are really the same. They encourage this same architecture with its inevitable complexities. Complexity is a vicious beast, and it will bite you regardless of whether you acknowledge it or not.

This book is the result of my desire to spread the knowledge of the Lambda Architecture and how it avoids the complexities of traditional architectures. It is the book I wish I had when I started working with Big Data. I hope you treat this book as a journey—a journey to challenge what you thought you knew about data systems, and to discover that working with Big Data can be elegant, simple, and fun.

NATHAN MARZ

acknowledgments

This book would not have been possible without the help and support of so many individuals around the world. I must start with my parents, who instilled in me from a young age a love of learning and exploring the world around me. They always encouraged me in all my career pursuits.

Likewise, my brother Iorav encouraged my intellectual interests from a young age. I still remember when he taught me Algebra while I was in elementary school. He was the one to introduce me to programming for the first time—he taught me Visual Basic as he was taking a class on it in high school. Those lessons sparked a passion for programming that led to my career.

I am enormously grateful to Michael Montano and Christopher Golda, the founders of BackType. From the moment they brought me on as their first employee, I was given an extraordinary amount of freedom to make decisions. That freedom was essential for me to explore and exploit the Lambda Architecture to its fullest. They never questioned the value of open source and allowed me to open source our technology liberally. Getting deeply involved with open source has been one of the great privileges of my life.

Many of my professors from my time as a student at Stanford deserve special thanks. Tim Roughgarden is the best teacher I've ever had—he radically improved my ability to rigorously analyze, deconstruct, and solve difficult problems. Taking as many classes as possible with him was one of the best decisions of my life. I also give thanks to Monica Lam for instilling within me an appreciation for the elegance of Datalog. Many years later I married Datalog with MapReduce to produce my first significant open source project, Cascalog.

Chris Wensel was the first one to show me that processing data at scale could be elegant and performant. His Cascading library changed the way I looked at Big Data processing.

None of my work would have been possible without the pioneers of the Big Data field. Special thanks to Jeffrey Dean and Sanjay Ghemawat for the original MapReduce paper, Giuseppe DeCandia, Deniz Hastorun, Madan Jampani, Gunavardhan Kakulapati, Avinash Lakshman, Alex Pilchin, Swaminathan Sivasubramanian, Peter Vosshall and Werner Vogels for the original Dynamo paper, and Michael Cafarella and Doug Cutting for founding the Apache Hadoop project.

Rich Hickey has been one of my biggest inspirations during my programming career. Clojure is the best language I have ever used, and I've become a better programmer having learned it. I appreciate its practicality and focus on simplicity. Rich's philosophy on state and complexity in programming has influenced me deeply.

When I started writing this book, I was not nearly the writer I am now. Renae Gregoire, one of my development editors at Manning, deserves special thanks for helping me improve as a writer. She drilled into me the importance of using examples to lead into general concepts, and she set off many light bulbs for me on how to effectively structure technical writing. The skills she taught me apply not only to writing technical books, but to blogging, giving talks, and communication in general. For gaining an important life skill, I am forever grateful.

This book would not be nearly of the same quality without the efforts of my co-author James Warren. He did a phenomenal job absorbing the theoretical concepts and finding even better ways to present the material. Much of the clarity of the book comes from his great communication skills.

My publisher, Manning, was a pleasure to work with. They were patient with me and understood that finding the right way to write on such a big topic takes time. Through the whole process they were supportive and helpful, and they always gave me the resources I needed to be successful. Thanks to Marjan Bace and Michael Stephens for all the support, and to all the other staff for their help and guidance along the way.

I try to learn as much as possible about writing from studying other writers. Bradford Cross, Clayton Christensen, Paul Graham, Carl Sagan, and Derek Sivers have been particularly influential.

Finally, I can't give enough thanks to the hundreds of people who reviewed, commented, and gave feedback on our book as it was being written. That feedback led us to revise, rewrite, and restructure numerous times until we found ways to present the material effectively. Special thanks to Aaron Colcord, Aaron Crow, Alex Holmes, Arun Jacob, Asif Jan, Ayon Sinha, Bill Graham, Charles Brophy, David Beckwith, Derrick Burns, Douglas Duncan, Hugo Garza, Jason Courcoux, Jonathan Esterhazy, Karl Kuntz, Kevin Martin, Leo Polovets, Mark Fisher, Massimo Ilario, Michael Fogus, Michael G. Noll, Patrick Dennis, Pedro Ferrera Bertran, Philipp Janert, Rodrigo Abreu, Rudy Bonefas, Sam Ritchie, Siva Kalagarla, Soren Macbeth, Timothy Chklovski, Walid Farid, and Zhenhua Guo.

NATHAN MARZ

I'm astounded when I consider everyone who contributed in some manner to this book. Unfortunately, I can't provide an exhaustive list, but that doesn't lessen my appreciation. Nonetheless, there are individuals to whom I wish to explicitly express my gratitude:

- My wife, Wen-Ying Feng—for your love, encouragement and support, not only for this book but for everything we do together.
- My parents, James and Gretta Warren—for your endless faith in me and the sacrifices you made to provide me with every opportunity.
- My sister, Julia Warren-Ulanch—for setting a shining example so I could follow in your footsteps.
- My professors and mentors, Ellen Toby and Sue Geller—for your willingness to answer my every question and for demonstrating the joy in sharing knowledge, not just acquiring it.
- Chuck Lam—for saying "Hey, have you heard of this thing called Hadoop?" to me so many years ago.
- My friends and colleagues at RockYou!, Storm8, and Bina—for the experiences we shared together and the opportunity to put theory into practice.
- Marjan Bace, Michael Stephens, Jennifer Stout, Renae Gregoire, and the entire Manning editorial and publishing staff—for your guidance and patience in seeing this book to completion.
- The reviewers and early readers of this book—for your comments and critiques that pushed us to clarify our words; the end result is so much better for it.

Finally, I want to convey my greatest appreciation to Nathan for inviting me to come along on this journey. I was already a great admirer of your work before joining this venture, and working with you has only deepened my respect for your ideas and philosophy. It has been an honor and a privilege.

JAMES WARREN

about this book

Services like social networks, web analytics, and intelligent e-commerce often need to manage data at a scale too big for a traditional database. Complexity increases with scale and demand, and handling Big Data is not as simple as just doubling down on your RDBMS or rolling out some trendy new technology. Fortunately, scalability and simplicity are not mutually exclusive—you just need to take a different approach. Big Data systems use many machines working in parallel to store and process data, which introduces fundamental challenges unfamiliar to most developers.

Big Data teaches you to build these systems using an architecture that takes advantage of clustered hardware along with new tools designed specifically to capture and analyze web-scale data. It describes a scalable, easy-to-understand approach to Big Data systems that can be built and run by a small team. Following a realistic example, this book guides readers through the theory of Big Data systems and how to implement them in practice.

Big Data requires no previous exposure to large-scale data analysis or NoSQL tools. Familiarity with traditional databases is helpful, though not required. The goal of the book is to teach you how to think about data systems and how to break down difficult problems into simple solutions. We start from first principles and from those deduce the necessary properties for each component of an architecture.

Roadmap

An overview of the 18 chapters in this book follows.

Chapter 1 introduces the principles of data systems and gives an overview of the Lambda Architecture: a generalized approach to building any data system. Chapters 2 through 17 dive into all the pieces of the Lambda Architecture, with chapters alternating between *theory* and *illustration* chapters. Theory chapters demonstrate the concepts that hold true regardless of existing tools, while illustration chapters use real-world tools to demonstrate the concepts. Don't let the names fool you, though—all chapters are highly example-driven.

Chapters 2 through 9 focus on the *batch layer* of the Lambda Architecture. Here you will learn about modeling your master dataset, using batch processing to create arbitrary views of your data, and the trade-offs between incremental and batch processing.

Chapters 10 and 11 focus on the *serving layer*, which provides low latency access to the views produced by the batch layer. Here you will learn about specialized databases that are only written to in bulk. You will discover that these databases are dramatically simpler than traditional databases, giving them excellent performance, operational, and robustness properties.

Chapters 12 through 17 focus on the *speed layer*, which compensates for the batch layer's high latency to provide up-to-date results for all queries. Here you will learn about NoSQL databases, stream processing, and managing the complexities of incremental computation.

Chapter 18 uses your new-found knowledge to review the Lambda Architecture once more and fill in any remaining gaps. You'll learn about incremental batch processing, variants of the basic Lambda Architecture, and how to get the most out of your resources.

Code downloads and conventions

The source code for the book can be found at https://github.com/Big-Data-Manning. We have provided source code for the running example SuperWebAnalytics.com.

Much of the source code is shown in numbered listings. These listings are meant to provide complete segments of code. Some listings are annotated to help highlight or explain certain parts of the code. In other places throughout the text, code fragments are used when necessary. Courier typeface is used to denote code for Java. In both the listings and fragments, we make use of a **bold code font** to help identify key parts of the code that are being explained in the text.

Author Online

Purchase of *Big Data* includes free access to a private web forum run by Manning Publications where you can make comments about the book, ask technical questions, and receive help from the authors and other users. To access the forum and subscribe to it, point your web browser to www.manning.com/BigData. This Author Online (AO) page provides information on how to get on the forum once you're registered, what kind of help is available, and the rules of conduct on the forum.

Manning's commitment to our readers is to provide a venue where a meaningful dialog among individual readers and between readers and the authors can take place. It's not a commitment to any specific amount of participation on the part of the authors, whose contribution to the AO forum remains voluntary (and unpaid). We suggest you try asking the authors some challenging questions, lest their interest stray!

The AO forum and the archives of previous discussions will be accessible from the publisher's website as long as the book is in print.

About the cover illustration

The figure on the cover of *Big Data* is captioned "Le Raccommodeur de Fiance," which means a mender of clayware. His special talent was mending broken or chipped pots, plates, cups, and bowls, and he traveled through the countryside, visiting the towns and villages of France, plying his trade.

The illustration is taken from a nineteenth-century edition of Sylvain Maréchal's four-volume compendium of regional dress customs published in France. Each illustration is finely drawn and colored by hand. The rich variety of Maréchal's collection reminds us vividly of how culturally apart the world's towns and regions were just 200 years ago. Isolated from each other, people spoke different dialects and languages. In the streets or in the countryside, it was easy to identify where they lived and what their trade or station in life was just by their dress.

Dress codes have changed since then, and the diversity by region, so rich at the time, has faded away. It is now hard to tell apart the inhabitants of different continents, let alone different towns or regions. Perhaps we have traded cultural diversity for a more varied personal life—certainly for a more varied and fast-paced technological life.

At a time when it is hard to tell one computer book from another, Manning celebrates the inventiveness and initiative of the computer business with book covers based on the rich diversity of regional life of two centuries ago, brought back to life by Maréchal's pictures.

A new
paradigm for Big Data

This chapter covers

- Typical problems encountered when scaling a traditional database
- Why NoSQL is not a panacea
- Thinking about Big Data systems from first principles
- Landscape of Big Data tools
- Introducing SuperWebAnalytics.com

In the past decade the amount of data being created has skyrocketed. More than 30,000 gigabytes of data are generated *every second*, and the rate of data creation is only accelerating.

The data we deal with is diverse. Users create content like blog posts, tweets, social network interactions, and photos. Servers continuously log messages about what they're doing. Scientists create detailed measurements of the world around us. The internet, the ultimate source of data, is almost incomprehensibly large.

This astonishing growth in data has profoundly affected businesses. Traditional database systems, such as relational databases, have been pushed to the limit. In an increasing number of cases these systems are breaking under the pressures of "Big Data." Traditional systems, and the data management techniques associated with them, have failed to scale to Big Data.

To tackle the challenges of Big Data, a new breed of technologies has emerged. Many of these new technologies have been grouped under the term *NoSQL*. In some ways, these new technologies are more complex than traditional databases, and in other ways they're simpler. These systems can scale to vastly larger sets of data, but using these technologies effectively requires a fundamentally new set of techniques. They aren't one-size-fits-all solutions.

Many of these Big Data systems were pioneered by Google, including distributed filesystems, the MapReduce computation framework, and distributed locking services. Another notable pioneer in the space was Amazon, which created an innovative distributed key/value store called Dynamo. The open source community responded in the years following with Hadoop, HBase, MongoDB, Cassandra, RabbitMQ, and countless other projects.

This book is about complexity as much as it is about scalability. In order to meet the challenges of Big Data, we'll rethink data systems from the ground up. You'll discover that some of the most basic ways people manage data in traditional systems like relational database management systems (RDBMSs) are too complex for Big Data systems. The simpler, alternative approach is the new paradigm for Big Data that you'll explore. We have dubbed this approach the *Lambda Architecture*.

In this first chapter, you'll explore the "Big Data problem" and why a new paradigm for Big Data is needed. You'll see the perils of some of the traditional techniques for scaling and discover some deep flaws in the traditional way of building data systems. By starting from first principles of data systems, we'll formulate a different way to build data systems that avoids the complexity of traditional techniques. You'll take a look at how recent trends in technology encourage the use of new kinds of systems, and finally you'll take a look at an example Big Data system that we'll build throughout this book to illustrate the key concepts.

1.1   How this book is structured

You should think of this book as primarily a theory book, focusing on how to approach building a solution to any Big Data problem. The principles you'll learn hold true regardless of the tooling in the current landscape, and you can use these principles to rigorously choose what tools are appropriate for your application.

This book is not a survey of database, computation, and other related technologies. Although you'll learn how to use many of these tools throughout this book, such as Hadoop, Cassandra, Storm, and Thrift, the goal of this book is not to learn those tools as an end in themselves. Rather, the tools are a means of learning the underlying principles of architecting robust and scalable data systems. Doing an involved compare-and-contrast between the tools would not do you justice, as that just distracts from learning the underlying principles. Put another way, you're going to learn how to fish, not just how to use a particular fishing rod.

In that vein, we have structured the book into *theory* and *illustration* chapters. You can read just the theory chapters and gain a full understanding of how to build Big Data systems—but we think the process of mapping that theory onto specific tools in the illustration chapters will give you a richer, more nuanced understanding of the material.

Don't be fooled by the names though—the theory chapters are very much example-driven. The overarching example in the book—SuperWebAnalytics.com—is used in both the theory and illustration chapters. In the theory chapters you'll see the algorithms, index designs, and architecture for SuperWebAnalytics.com. The illustration chapters will take those designs and map them onto functioning code with specific tools.

1.2 Scaling with a traditional database

Let's begin our exploration of Big Data by starting from where many developers start: hitting the limits of traditional database technologies.

Suppose your boss asks you to build a simple web analytics application. The application should track the number of pageviews for any URL a customer wishes to track. The customer's web page pings the application's web server with its URL every time a pageview is received. Additionally, the application should be able to tell you at any point what the top 100 URLs are by number of pageviews.

You start with a traditional relational schema for the pageviews that looks something like figure 1.1. Your back end consists of an RDBMS with a table of that schema and a web server. Whenever someone loads a web page being tracked by your application, the web page pings your web server with the pageview, and your web server increments the corresponding row in the database.

Column name	Type
id	integer
user_id	integer
url	varchar(255)
pageviews	bigint

Figure 1.1 Relational schema for simple analytics application

Let's see what problems emerge as you evolve the application. As you're about to see, you'll run into problems with both scalability and complexity.

1.2.1 Scaling with a queue

The web analytics product is a huge success, and traffic to your application is growing like wildfire. Your company throws a big party, but in the middle of the celebration you start getting lots of emails from your monitoring system. They all say the same thing: "Timeout error on inserting to the database."

You look at the logs and the problem is obvious. The database can't keep up with the load, so write requests to increment pageviews are timing out.

You need to do something to fix the problem, and you need to do something quickly. You realize that it's wasteful to only perform a single increment at a time to the database. It can be more efficient if you batch many increments in a single request. So you re-architect your back end to make this possible.

Instead of having the web server hit the database directly, you insert a queue between the web server and the database. Whenever you receive a new pageview, that event is added to the queue. You then create a worker process that reads 100 events at a time off the queue, and batches them into a single database update. This is illustrated in figure 1.2.

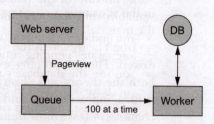

Figure 1.2   Batching updates with queue and worker

This scheme works well, and it resolves the timeout issues you were getting. It even has the added bonus that if the database ever gets overloaded again, the queue will just get bigger instead of timing out to the web server and potentially losing data.

1.2.2   *Scaling by sharding the database*

Unfortunately, adding a queue and doing batch updates was only a band-aid for the scaling problem. Your application continues to get more and more popular, and again the database gets overloaded. Your worker can't keep up with the writes, so you try adding more workers to parallelize the updates. Unfortunately that doesn't help; the database is clearly the bottleneck.

You do some Google searches for how to scale a write-heavy relational database. You find that the best approach is to use multiple database servers and spread the table across all the servers. Each server will have a subset of the data for the table. This is known as *horizontal partitioning* or *sharding*. This technique spreads the write load across multiple machines.

The sharding technique you use is to choose the shard for each key by taking the hash of the key modded by the number of shards. Mapping keys to shards using a hash function causes the keys to be uniformly distributed across the shards. You write a script to map over all the rows in your single database instance, and split the data into four shards. It takes a while to run, so you turn off the worker that increments pageviews to let it finish. Otherwise you'd lose increments during the transition.

Finally, all of your application code needs to know how to find the shard for each key. So you wrap a library around your database-handling code that reads the number of shards from a configuration file, and you redeploy all of your application code. You have to modify your top-100-URLs query to get the top 100 URLs from each shard and merge those together for the global top 100 URLs.

As the application gets more and more popular, you keep having to reshard the database into more shards to keep up with the write load. Each time gets more and more painful because there's so much more work to coordinate. And you can't just run one script to do the resharding, as that would be too slow. You have to do all the resharding in parallel and manage many active worker scripts at once. You forget to update the application code with the new number of shards, and it causes many of the increments to be written to the wrong shards. So you have to write a one-off script to manually go through the data and move whatever was misplaced.

1.2.3 Fault-tolerance issues begin

Eventually you have so many shards that it becomes a not-infrequent occurrence for the disk on one of the database machines to go bad. That portion of the data is unavailable while that machine is down. You do a couple of things to address this:

- You update your queue/worker system to put increments for unavailable shards on a separate "pending" queue that you attempt to flush once every five minutes.
- You use the database's replication capabilities to add a slave to each shard so you have a backup in case the master goes down. You don't write to the slave, but at least customers can still view the stats in the application.

You think to yourself, "In the early days I spent my time building new features for customers. Now it seems I'm spending all my time just dealing with problems reading and writing the data."

1.2.4 Corruption issues

While working on the queue/worker code, you accidentally deploy a bug to production that increments the number of pageviews by two, instead of by one, for every URL. You don't notice until 24 hours later, but by then the damage is done. Your weekly backups don't help because there's no way of knowing which data got corrupted. After all this work trying to make your system scalable and tolerant of machine failures, your system has no resilience to a human making a mistake. And if there's one guarantee in software, it's that bugs inevitably make it to production, no matter how hard you try to prevent it.

1.2.5 What went wrong?

As the simple web analytics application evolved, the system continued to get more and more complex: queues, shards, replicas, resharding scripts, and so on. Developing applications on the data requires a lot more than just knowing the database schema. Your code needs to know how to talk to the right shards, and if you make a mistake, there's nothing preventing you from reading from or writing to the wrong shard.

One problem is that your database is not self-aware of its distributed nature, so it can't help you deal with shards, replication, and distributed queries. All that complexity got pushed to you both in operating the database and developing the application code.

But the worst problem is that the system is not engineered for human mistakes. Quite the opposite, actually: the system keeps getting more and more complex, making it more and more likely that a mistake will be made. Mistakes in software are inevitable, and if you're not engineering for it, you might as well be writing scripts that randomly corrupt data. Backups are not enough; the system must be carefully thought out to limit the damage a human mistake can cause. Human-fault tolerance is not optional. It's essential, especially when Big Data adds so many more complexities to building applications.

1.2.6   *How will Big Data techniques help?*

The Big Data techniques you're going to learn will address these scalability and complexity issues in a dramatic fashion. First of all, the databases and computation systems you use for Big Data are aware of their distributed nature. So things like sharding and replication are handled for you. You'll never get into a situation where you accidentally query the wrong shard, because that logic is internalized in the database. When it comes to scaling, you'll just add nodes, and the systems will automatically rebalance onto the new nodes.

Another core technique you'll learn about is making your data immutable. Instead of storing the pageview counts as your core dataset, which you continuously mutate as new pageviews come in, you store the raw pageview information. That raw pageview information is never modified. So when you make a mistake, you might write bad data, but at least you won't destroy good data. This is a much stronger human-fault tolerance guarantee than in a traditional system based on mutation. With traditional databases, you'd be wary of using immutable data because of how fast such a dataset would grow. But because Big Data techniques can scale to so much data, you have the ability to design systems in different ways.

1.3   *NoSQL is not a panacea*

The past decade has seen a huge amount of innovation in scalable data systems. These include large-scale computation systems like Hadoop and databases such as Cassandra and Riak. These systems can handle very large amounts of data, but with serious trade-offs.

Hadoop, for example, can parallelize large-scale batch computations on very large amounts of data, but the computations have high latency. You don't use Hadoop for anything where you need low-latency results.

NoSQL databases like Cassandra achieve their scalability by offering you a much more limited data model than you're used to with something like SQL. Squeezing your application into these limited data models can be very complex. And because the databases are mutable, they're not human-fault tolerant.

These tools on their own are not a panacea. But when intelligently used in conjunction with one another, you can produce scalable systems for arbitrary data problems with human-fault tolerance and a minimum of complexity. This is the Lambda Architecture you'll learn throughout the book.

1.4   *First principles*

To figure out how to properly build data systems, you must go back to first principles. At the most fundamental level, what does a data system do?

Let's start with an intuitive definition: *A data system answers questions based on information that was acquired in the past up to the present.* So a social network profile answers questions like "What is this person's name?" and "How many friends does this person have?" A bank account web page answers questions like "What is my current balance?" and "What transactions have occurred on my account recently?"

Data systems don't just memorize and regurgitate information. They combine bits and pieces together to produce their answers. A bank account balance, for example, is based on combining the information about all the transactions on the account.

Another crucial observation is that not all bits of information are equal. Some information is derived from other pieces of information. A bank account balance is derived from a transaction history. A friend count is derived from a friend list, and a friend list is derived from all the times a user added and removed friends from their profile.

When you keep tracing back where information is derived from, you eventually end up at information that's not derived from anything. This is the rawest information you have: information you hold to be true simply because it exists. Let's call this information *data*.

You may have a different conception of what the word *data* means. Data is often used interchangeably with the word *information*. But for the remainder of this book, when we use the word *data,* we're referring to that special information from which everything else is derived.

If a data system answers questions by looking at past data, then the most general-purpose data system answers questions by looking at the *entire* dataset. So the most general-purpose definition we can give for a data system is the following:

query = function(all data)

Anything you could ever imagine doing with data can be expressed as a function that takes in all the data you have as input. Remember this equation, because it's the crux of everything you'll learn. We'll refer to this equation over and over.

The Lambda Architecture provides a general-purpose approach to implementing an arbitrary function on an arbitrary dataset and having the function return its results with low latency. That doesn't mean you'll always use the exact same technologies every time you implement a data system. The specific technologies you use might change depending on your requirements. But the Lambda Architecture defines a consistent approach to choosing those technologies and to wiring them together to meet your requirements.

Let's now discuss the properties a data system must exhibit.

1.5   Desired properties of a Big Data system

The properties you should strive for in Big Data systems are as much about complexity as they are about scalability. Not only must a Big Data system perform well and be resource-efficient, it must be easy to reason about as well. Let's go over each property one by one.

1.5.1   Robustness and fault tolerance

Building systems that "do the right thing" is difficult in the face of the challenges of distributed systems. Systems need to behave correctly despite machines going down randomly, the complex semantics of consistency in distributed databases, duplicated data, concurrency, and more. These challenges make it difficult even to reason about what a system is doing. Part of making a Big Data system robust is avoiding these complexities so that you can easily reason about the system.

As discussed before, it's imperative for systems to be *human-fault tolerant*. This is an oft-overlooked property of systems that we're not going to ignore. In a production system, it's inevitable that someone will make a mistake sometime, such as by deploying incorrect code that corrupts values in a database. If you build immutability and recomputation into the core of a Big Data system, the system will be innately resilient to human error by providing a clear and simple mechanism for recovery. This is described in depth in chapters 2 through 7.

1.5.2 Low latency reads and updates

The vast majority of applications require reads to be satisfied with very low latency, typically between a few milliseconds to a few hundred milliseconds. On the other hand, the update latency requirements vary a great deal between applications. Some applications require updates to propagate immediately, but in other applications a latency of a few hours is fine. Regardless, you need to be able to achieve low latency updates *when you need them* in your Big Data systems. More importantly, you need to be able to achieve low latency reads and updates without compromising the robustness of the system. You'll learn how to achieve low latency updates in the discussion of the speed layer, starting in chapter 12.

1.5.3 Scalability

Scalability is the ability to maintain performance in the face of increasing data or load by adding resources to the system. The Lambda Architecture is horizontally scalable across all layers of the system stack: scaling is accomplished by adding more machines.

1.5.4 Generalization

A general system can support a wide range of applications. Indeed, this book wouldn't be very useful if it didn't generalize to a wide range of applications! Because the Lambda Architecture is based on functions of all data, it generalizes to all applications, whether financial management systems, social media analytics, scientific applications, social networking, or anything else.

1.5.5 Extensibility

You don't want to have to reinvent the wheel each time you add a related feature or make a change to how your system works. Extensible systems allow functionality to be added with a minimal development cost.

Oftentimes a new feature or a change to an existing feature requires a migration of old data into a new format. Part of making a system extensible is making it easy to do large-scale migrations. Being able to do big migrations quickly and easily is core to the approach you'll learn.

1.5.6 Ad hoc queries

Being able to do ad hoc queries on your data is extremely important. Nearly every large dataset has unanticipated value within it. Being able to mine a dataset arbitrarily gives opportunities for business optimization and new applications. Ultimately, you can't discover interesting things to do with your data unless you can ask arbitrary questions of it. You'll learn how to do ad hoc queries in chapters 6 and 7 when we discuss batch processing.

1.5.7 Minimal maintenance

Maintenance is a tax on developers. Maintenance is the work required to keep a system running smoothly. This includes anticipating when to add machines to scale, keeping processes up and running, and debugging anything that goes wrong in production.

An important part of minimizing maintenance is choosing components that have as little *implementation complexity* as possible. You want to rely on components that have simple mechanisms underlying them. In particular, distributed databases tend to have very complicated internals. The more complex a system, the more likely something will go wrong, and the more you need to understand about the system to debug and tune it.

You combat implementation complexity by relying on simple algorithms and simple components. A trick employed in the Lambda Architecture is to push complexity out of the core components and into pieces of the system whose outputs are discardable after a few hours. The most complex components used, like read/write distributed databases, are in this layer where outputs are eventually discardable. We'll discuss this technique in depth when we discuss the speed layer in chapter 12.

1.5.8 Debuggability

A Big Data system must provide the information necessary to debug the system when things go wrong. The key is to be able to trace, for each value in the system, exactly what caused it to have that value.

"Debuggability" is accomplished in the Lambda Architecture through the functional nature of the batch layer and by preferring to use recomputation algorithms when possible.

Achieving all these properties together in one system may seem like a daunting challenge. But by starting from first principles, as the Lambda Architecture does, these properties emerge naturally from the resulting system design.

Before diving into the Lambda Architecture, let's take a look at more traditional architectures—characterized by a reliance on incremental computation—and at why they're unable to satisfy many of these properties.

1.6 The problems with fully incremental architectures

At the highest level, traditional architectures look like figure 1.3. What characterizes these architectures is the use of read/write databases and maintaining the state in those databases incrementally as new data is seen. For example, an incremental approach to counting pageviews would be to process a new pageview by adding one to the counter for its URL. This characterization of architectures is a

Figure 1.3 Fully incremental architecture

lot more fundamental than just relational versus non-relational—in fact, the vast majority of both relational and non-relational database deployments are done as fully incremental architectures. This has been true for many decades.

It's worth emphasizing that fully incremental architectures are so widespread that many people don't realize it's possible to avoid their problems with a different architecture. These are great examples of *familiar complexity*—complexity that's so ingrained, you don't even think to find a way to avoid it.

The problems with fully incremental architectures are significant. We'll begin our exploration of this topic by looking at the general complexities brought on by any fully incremental architecture. Then we'll look at two contrasting solutions for the same problem: one using the best possible fully incremental solution, and one using a Lambda Architecture. You'll see that the fully incremental version is significantly worse in every respect.

1.6.1 *Operational complexity*

There are many complexities inherent in fully incremental architectures that create difficulties in operating production infrastructure. Here we'll focus on one: the need for read/write databases to perform online compaction, and what you have to do operationally to keep things running smoothly.

In a read/write database, as a disk index is incrementally added to and modified, parts of the index become unused. These unused parts take up space and eventually need to be reclaimed to prevent the disk from filling up. Reclaiming space as soon as it becomes unused is too expensive, so the space is occasionally reclaimed in bulk in a process called *compaction*.

Compaction is an intensive operation. The server places substantially higher demand on the CPU and disks during compaction, which dramatically lowers the performance of that machine during that time period. Databases such as HBase and Cassandra are well-known for requiring careful configuration and management to avoid problems or server lockups during compaction. The performance loss during compaction is a complexity that can even cause cascading failure—if too many machines compact at the same time, the load they were supporting will have to be handled by other machines in the cluster. This can potentially overload the rest of your cluster, causing total failure. We have seen this failure mode happen many times.

To manage compaction correctly, you have to schedule compactions on each node so that not too many nodes are affected at once. You have to be aware of how long a compaction takes—as well as the variance—to avoid having more nodes undergoing compaction than you intended. You have to make sure you have enough disk capacity on your nodes to last them between compactions. In addition, you have to make sure you have enough capacity on your cluster so that it doesn't become overloaded when resources are lost during compactions.

All of this can be managed by a competent operational staff, but it's our contention that the best way to deal with any sort of complexity is to get rid of that complexity altogether. The fewer failure modes you have in your system, the less likely it is that you'll suffer unexpected downtime. Dealing with online compaction is a complexity inherent to fully incremental architectures, but in a Lambda Architecture the primary databases don't require any online compaction.

1.6.2 *Extreme complexity of achieving eventual consistency*

Another complexity of incremental architectures results when trying to make systems highly available. A highly available system allows for queries and updates even in the presence of machine or partial network failure.

It turns out that achieving high availability competes directly with another important property called *consistency*. A consistent system returns results that take into account all previous writes. A theorem called the CAP theorem has shown that it's impossible to achieve both high availability and consistency in the same system in the presence of network partitions. So a highly available system sometimes returns stale results during a network partition.

The CAP theorem is discussed in depth in chapter 12—here we wish to focus on how the inability to achieve full consistency and high availability at all times affects your ability to construct systems. It turns out that if your business requirements demand high availability over full consistency, there is a huge amount of complexity you have to deal with.

In order for a highly available system to return to consistency once a network partition ends (known as *eventual consistency*), a lot of help is required from your application. Take, for example, the basic use case of maintaining a count in a database. The obvious way to go about this is to store a number in the database and increment that number whenever an event is received that requires the count to go up. You may be surprised that if you were to take this approach, you'd suffer massive data loss during network partitions.

The reason for this is due to the way distributed databases achieve high availability by keeping multiple replicas of all information stored. When you keep many copies of the same information, that information is still available even if a machine goes down or the network gets partitioned, as shown in figure 1.4. During a network partition, a system that chooses to be highly available has clients update whatever replicas are reachable to them. This causes replicas to diverge and receive different sets of updates. Only when the partition goes away can the replicas be merged together into a common value.

Suppose you have two replicas with a count of 10 when a network partition begins. Suppose the first replica gets two increments and the second gets one increment. When it comes time to merge these replicas together, with values of 12 and 11, what should the merged value be? Although the correct answer is 13, there's no way to know just by looking at the numbers 12 and 11. They could have diverged at 11 (in which case the answer would be 12), or they could have diverged at 0 (in which case the answer would be 23).

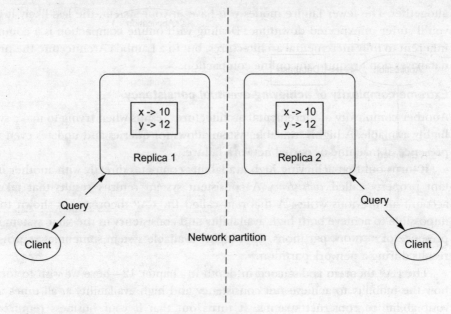

Figure 1.4   Using replication to increase availability

To do highly available counting correctly, it's not enough to just store a count. You need a data structure that's amenable to merging when values diverge, and you need to implement the code that will repair values once partitions end. This is an amazing amount of complexity you have to deal with just to maintain a simple count.

In general, handling eventual consistency in incremental, highly available systems is unintuitive and prone to error. This complexity is innate to highly available, fully incremental systems. You'll see later how the Lambda Architecture structures itself in a different way that greatly lessens the burdens of achieving highly available, eventually consistent systems.

1.6.3   *Lack of human-fault tolerance*

The last problem with fully incremental architectures we wish to point out is their inherent lack of human-fault tolerance. An incremental system is constantly modifying the state it keeps in the database, which means a mistake can also modify the state in the database. Because mistakes are inevitable, the database in a fully incremental architecture is guaranteed to be corrupted.

It's important to note that this is one of the few complexities of fully incremental architectures that can be resolved without a complete rethinking of the architecture. Consider the two architectures shown in figure 1.5: a synchronous architecture, where the application makes updates directly to the database, and an asynchronous architecture, where events go to a queue before updating the database in the background. In both cases, every event is permanently logged to an events datastore. By keeping every event, if a human mistake causes database corruption, you can go back

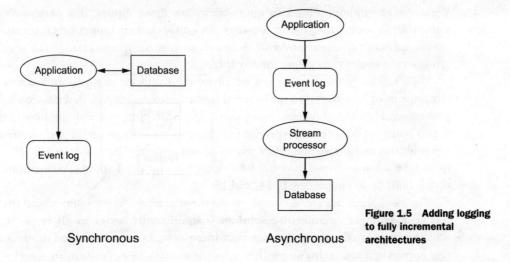

Synchronous   Asynchronous

Figure 1.5 Adding logging to fully incremental architectures

to the events store and reconstruct the proper state for the database. Because the events store is immutable and constantly growing, redundant checks, like permissions, can be put in to make it highly unlikely for a mistake to trample over the events store. This technique is also core to the Lambda Architecture and is discussed in depth in chapters 2 and 3.

Although fully incremental architectures with logging can overcome the human-fault tolerance deficiencies of fully incremental architectures without logging, the logging does nothing to handle the other complexities that have been discussed. And as you'll see in the next section, any architecture based purely on fully incremental computation, including those with logging, will struggle to solve many problems.

1.6.4 Fully incremental solution vs. Lambda Architecture solution

One of the example queries that is implemented throughout the book serves as a great contrast between fully incremental and Lambda architectures. There's nothing contrived about this query—in fact, it's based on real-world problems we have faced in our careers multiple times. The query has to do with pageview analytics and is done on two kinds of data coming in:

- *Pageviews*, which contain a user ID, URL, and timestamp.
- *Equivs*, which contain two user IDs. An equiv indicates the two user IDs refer to the same person. For example, you might have an equiv between the email *sally@gmail.com* and the username *sally*. If sally@gmail.com also registers for the username *sally2*, then you would have an equiv between sally@gmail.com and sally2. By transitivity, you know that the usernames *sally* and *sally2* refer to the same person.

The goal of the query is to compute the number of unique visitors to a URL over a range of time. Queries should be up to date with all data and respond with minimal latency (less than 100 milliseconds). Here's the interface for the query:

```
long uniquesOverTime(String url, int startHour, int endHour)
```

What makes implementing this query tricky are those equivs. If a person visits the same URL in a time range with two user IDs connected via equivs (even transitively), that should only count as one visit. A new equiv coming in can change the results for any query over any time range for any URL.

We'll refrain from showing the details of the solutions at this point, as too many concepts must be covered to understand them: indexing, distributed databases, batch processing, HyperLogLog, and many more. Overwhelming you with all these concepts at this point would be counterproductive. Instead, we'll focus on the characteristics of the solutions and the striking differences between them. The best possible fully incremental solution is shown in detail in chapter 10, and the Lambda Architecture solution is built up in chapters 8, 9, 14, and 15.

The two solutions can be compared on three axes: accuracy, latency, and throughput. The Lambda Architecture solution is significantly better in all respects. Both must make approximations, but the fully incremental version is forced to use an inferior approximation technique with a 3–5x worse error rate. Performing queries is significantly more expensive in the fully incremental version, affecting both latency and throughput. But the most striking difference between the two approaches is the fully incremental version's need to use special hardware to achieve anywhere close to reasonable throughput. Because the fully incremental version must do many random access lookups to resolve queries, it's practically required to use solid state drives to avoid becoming bottlenecked on disk seeks.

That a Lambda Architecture can produce solutions with higher performance in every respect, while also avoiding the complexity that plagues fully incremental architectures, shows that something very fundamental is going on. The key is escaping the shackles of fully incremental computation and embracing different techniques. Let's now see how to do that.

1.7   Lambda Architecture

Computing arbitrary functions on an arbitrary dataset in real time is a daunting problem. There's no single tool that provides a complete solution. Instead, you have to use a variety of tools and techniques to build a complete Big Data system.

The main idea of the Lambda Architecture is to build Big Data systems as a series of layers, as shown in figure 1.6. Each layer satisfies a subset of the properties and builds upon the functionality provided by the layers beneath it. You'll spend the whole book learning how to design, implement, and deploy each layer, but the high-level ideas of how the whole system fits together are fairly easy to understand.

Everything starts from the *query = function(all data)* equation. Ideally, you could run the functions on the fly to get the results. Unfortunately, even if this were possible, it would take a huge amount of resources to do and would be unreasonably expensive.

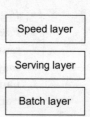

Figure 1.6   Lambda Architecture

Imagine having to read a petabyte dataset every time you wanted to answer the query of someone's current location.

The most obvious alternative approach is to precompute the query function. Let's call the precomputed query function the *batch view*. Instead of computing the query on the fly, you read the results from the precomputed view. The precomputed view is indexed so that it can be accessed with random reads. This system looks like this:

batch view = function(all data)
   query = function(batch view)

In this system, you run a function on all the data to get the batch view. Then, when you want to know the value for a query, you run a function on that batch view. The batch view makes it possible to get the values you need from it very quickly, without having to scan everything in it.

Because this discussion is somewhat abstract, let's ground it with an example. Suppose you're building a web analytics application (again), and you want to query the number of pageviews for a URL on any range of days. If you were computing the query as a function of all the data, you'd scan the dataset for pageviews for that URL within that time range, and return the count of those results.

The batch view approach instead runs a function on all the pageviews to precompute an index from a key of [url, day] to the count of the number of pageviews for that URL for that day. Then, to resolve the query, you retrieve all values from that view for all days within that time range, and sum up the counts to get the result. This approach is shown in figure 1.7.

It should be clear that there's something missing from this approach, as described so far. Creating the batch view is clearly going to be a high-latency operation, because it's running a function on all the data you have. By the time it finishes, a lot of new data will have collected that's not represented in the batch views, and the queries will be out of date by many hours. But let's ignore this issue for the moment, because we'll

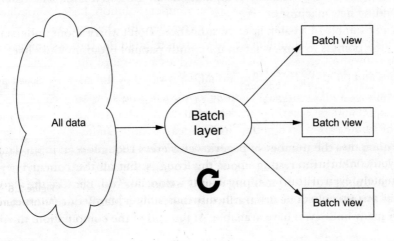

**Figure 1.7
Architecture of
the batch layer**

be able to fix it. Let's pretend that it's okay for queries to be out of date by a few hours and continue exploring this idea of precomputing a batch view by running a function on the complete dataset.

1.7.1   *Batch layer*

The portion of the Lambda Architecture that implements the *batch view = function(all data)* equation is called the *batch layer*. The batch layer stores the master copy of the dataset and precomputes batch views on that master dataset (see figure 1.8). The master dataset can be thought of as a very large list of records.

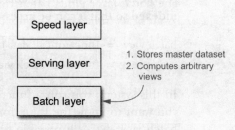

1. Stores master dataset
2. Computes arbitrary views

Figure 1.8   Batch layer

The batch layer needs to be able to do two things: store an immutable, constantly growing master dataset, and compute arbitrary functions on that dataset. This type of processing is best done using batch-processing systems. Hadoop is the canonical example of a batch-processing system, and Hadoop is what we'll use in this book to demonstrate the concepts of the batch layer.

The simplest form of the batch layer can be represented in pseudo-code like this:

```
function runBatchLayer():
  while(true):
   recomputeBatchViews()
```

The batch layer runs in a while(true) loop and continuously recomputes the batch views from scratch. In reality, the batch layer is a little more involved, but we'll come to that later in the book. This is the best way to think about the batch layer at the moment.

The nice thing about the batch layer is that it's so simple to use. Batch computations are written like single-threaded programs, and you get parallelism for free. It's easy to write robust, highly scalable computations on the batch layer. The batch layer scales by adding new machines.

Here's an example of a batch layer computation. Don't worry about understanding this code—the point is to show what an inherently parallel program looks like:

```
Api.execute(Api.hfsSeqfile("/tmp/pageview-counts"),
    new Subquery("?url", "?count")
        .predicate(Api.hfsSeqfile("/data/pageviews"),
           "?url", "?user", "?timestamp")
        .predicate(new Count(), "?count");
```

This code computes the number of pageviews for every URL given an input dataset of raw pageviews. What's interesting about this code is that all the concurrency challenges of scheduling work and merging results is done for you. Because the algorithm is written in this way, it can be arbitrarily distributed on a MapReduce cluster, scaling to however many nodes you have available. At the end of the computation, the output directory will contain some number of files with the results. You'll learn how to write programs like this in chapter 7.

1.7.2 Serving layer

The batch layer emits batch views as the result of its functions. The next step is to load the views somewhere so that they can be queried. This is where the serving layer comes in. The serving layer is a specialized distributed database that loads in a batch view and makes it possible to do random reads on it (see figure 1.9). When new batch views are available, the serving layer automatically swaps those in so that more up-to-date results are available.

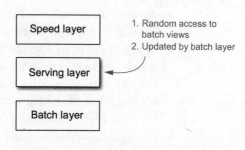

Figure 1.9   Serving layer

A serving layer database supports batch updates and random reads. Most notably, it doesn't need to support random writes. This is a very important point, as random writes cause most of the complexity in databases. By not supporting random writes, these databases are extremely simple. That simplicity makes them robust, predictable, easy to configure, and easy to operate. ElephantDB, the serving layer database you'll learn to use in this book, is only a few thousand lines of code.

1.7.3 Batch and serving layers satisfy almost all properties

The batch and serving layers support arbitrary queries on an arbitrary dataset with the trade-off that queries will be out of date by a few hours. It takes a new piece of data a few hours to propagate through the batch layer into the serving layer where it can be queried. The important thing to notice is that other than low latency updates, the batch and serving layers satisfy every property desired in a Big Data system, as outlined in section 1.5. Let's go through them one by one:

- *Robustness and fault tolerance*—Hadoop handles failover when machines go down. The serving layer uses replication under the hood to ensure availability when servers go down. The batch and serving layers are also human-fault tolerant, because when a mistake is made, you can fix your algorithm or remove the bad data and recompute the views from scratch.

- *Scalability*—Both the batch and serving layers are easily scalable. They're both fully distributed systems, and scaling them is as easy as adding new machines.

- *Generalization*—The architecture described is as general as it gets. You can compute and update arbitrary views of an arbitrary dataset.

- *Extensibility*—Adding a new view is as easy as adding a new function of the master dataset. Because the master dataset can contain arbitrary data, new types of data can be easily added. If you want to tweak a view, you don't have to worry about supporting multiple versions of the view in the application. You can simply recompute the entire view from scratch.

- *Ad hoc queries*—The batch layer supports ad hoc queries innately. All the data is conveniently available in one location.

- *Minimal maintenance*—The main component to maintain in this system is Hadoop. Hadoop requires some administration knowledge, but it's fairly straightforward to operate. As explained before, the serving layer databases are simple because they don't do random writes. Because a serving layer database has so few moving parts, there's lots less that can go wrong. As a consequence, it's much less likely that anything *will* go wrong with a serving layer database, so they're easier to maintain.

- *Debuggability*—You'll always have the inputs and outputs of computations run on the batch layer. In a traditional database, an output can replace the original input—such as when incrementing a value. In the batch and serving layers, the input is the master dataset and the output is the views. Likewise, you have the inputs and outputs for all the intermediate steps. Having the inputs and outputs gives you all the information you need to debug when something goes wrong.

The beauty of the batch and serving layers is that they satisfy almost all the properties you want with a simple and easy-to-understand approach. There are no concurrency issues to deal with, and it scales trivially. The only property missing is low latency updates. The final layer, the speed layer, fixes this problem.

1.7.4   *Speed layer*

The serving layer updates whenever the batch layer finishes precomputing a batch view. This means that the only data not represented in the batch view is the data that came in while the precomputation was running. All that's left to do to have a fully real-time data system—that is, to have arbitrary functions computed on arbitrary data in real time—is to compensate for those last few hours of data. This is the purpose of the speed layer. As its name suggests, its goal is to ensure new data is represented in query functions as quickly as needed for the application requirements (see figure 1.10).

You can think of the speed layer as being similar to the batch layer in that it produces views based on data it receives. One big difference is that the speed layer only looks at recent data, whereas the batch layer looks at all the data at once. Another big difference is that in order to achieve the smallest latencies possible, the speed layer doesn't look at all the new data at once. Instead, it updates the realtime views as it receives new data instead of recomputing the views from scratch like the batch layer does. The speed layer does incremental computation instead of the recomputation done in the batch layer.

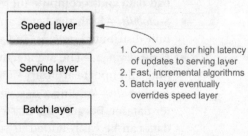

1. Compensate for high latency of updates to serving layer
2. Fast, incremental algorithms
3. Batch layer eventually overrides speed layer

Figure 1.10   Speed layer

We can formalize the data flow on the speed layer with the following equation:

realtime view = function(realtime view, new data)

A realtime view is updated based on new data and the existing realtime view.

The Lambda Architecture in full is summarized by these three equations:

batch view = function(all data)

realtime view = function(realtime view, new data)

query = function(batch view. realtime view)

A pictorial representation of these ideas is shown in figure 1.11. Instead of resolving queries by just doing a function of the batch view, you resolve queries by looking at both the batch and realtime views and merging the results together.

The speed layer uses databases that support random reads and random writes. Because these databases support random writes, they're orders of magnitude more complex than the databases you use in the serving layer, both in terms of implementation and operation.

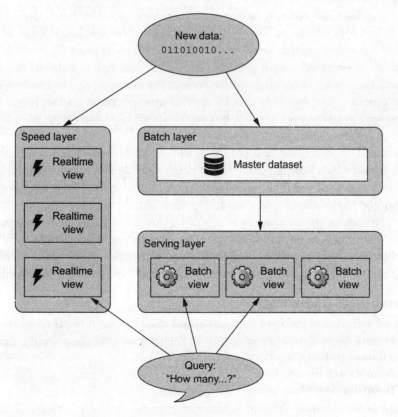

Figure 1.11   Lambda Architecture diagram

The beauty of the Lambda Architecture is that once data makes it through the batch layer into the serving layer, the corresponding results in the realtime views *are no longer needed.* This means you can discard pieces of the realtime view as they're no longer needed. This is a wonderful result, because the speed layer is far more complex than the batch and serving layers. This property of the Lambda Architecture is called *complexity isolation,* meaning that complexity is pushed into a layer whose results are only temporary. If anything ever goes wrong, you can discard the state for the entire speed layer, and everything will be back to normal within a few hours.

Let's continue the example of building a web analytics application that supports queries about the number of pageviews over a range of days. Recall that the batch layer produces batch views from [url, day] to the number of pageviews.

The speed layer keeps its own separate view of [url, day] to number of pageviews. Whereas the batch layer recomputes its views by literally counting the pageviews, the speed layer updates its views by incrementing the count in the view whenever it receives new data. To resolve a query, you query both the batch and realtime views as necessary to satisfy the range of dates specified, and you sum up the results to get the final count. There's a little work that needs to be done to properly synchronize the results, but we'll cover that in a future chapter.

Some algorithms are difficult to compute incrementally. The batch/speed layer split gives you the flexibility to use the exact algorithm on the batch layer and an approximate algorithm on the speed layer. The batch layer repeatedly overrides the speed layer, so the approximation gets corrected and your system exhibits the property of *eventual accuracy.* Computing unique counts, for example, can be challenging if the sets of uniques get large. It's easy to do the unique count on the batch layer, because you look at all the data at once, but on the speed layer you might use a Hyper-LogLog set as an approximation.

What you end up with is the best of both worlds of performance and robustness. A system that does the exact computation in the batch layer and an approximate computation in the speed layer exhibits eventual accuracy, because the batch layer corrects what's computed in the speed layer. You still get low latency updates, but because the speed layer is transient, the complexity of achieving this doesn't affect the robustness of your results. The transient nature of the speed layer gives you the flexibility to be very aggressive when it comes to making trade-offs for performance. Of course, for computations that can be done exactly in an incremental fashion, the system is fully accurate.

1.8   Recent trends in technology

It's helpful to understand the background behind the tools we'll use throughout this book. There have been a number of trends in technology that deeply influence the ways in which you can build Big Data systems.

1.8.1   CPUs aren't getting faster

We've started to hit the physical limits of how fast a single CPU can go. That means that if you want to scale to more data, you must be able to parallelize your computation.

This has led to the rise of shared-nothing parallel algorithms and their corresponding systems, such as MapReduce. Instead of just trying to scale by buying a better machine, known as *vertical scaling,* systems scale by adding more machines, known as *horizontal scaling.*

1.8.2 *Elastic clouds*

Another trend in technology has been the rise of elastic clouds, also known as *Infrastructure as a Service.* Amazon Web Services (AWS) is the most notable elastic cloud. Elastic clouds allow you to rent hardware on demand rather than own your own hardware in your own location. Elastic clouds let you increase or decrease the size of your cluster nearly instantaneously, so if you have a big job you want to run, you can allocate the hardware temporarily.

Elastic clouds dramatically simplify system administration. They also provide additional storage and hardware allocation options that can significantly drive down the price of your infrastructure. For example, AWS has a feature called *spot instances* in which you bid on instances rather than pay a fixed price. If someone bids a higher price than you, you'll lose the instance. Because spot instances can disappear at any moment, they tend to be significantly cheaper than normal instances. For distributed computation systems like MapReduce, they're a great option because fault tolerance is handled at the software layer.

1.8.3 *Vibrant open source ecosystem for Big Data*

The open source community has created a plethora of Big Data technologies over the past few years. All the technologies taught in this book are open source and free to use.

There are five categories of open source projects you'll learn about. Remember, this is not a survey book—the intent is not to just teach a bunch of technologies. The goal is to learn the fundamental principles so that you'll be able to evaluate and choose the right tools for your needs:

- *Batch computation systems*—Batch computation systems are high throughput, high latency systems. Batch computation systems can do nearly arbitrary computations, but they may take hours or days to do so. The only batch computation system we'll use is Hadoop. The Hadoop project has two subprojects: the Hadoop Distributed File System (HDFS) and Hadoop MapReduce. HDFS is a distributed, fault-tolerant storage system that can scale to petabytes of data. MapReduce is a horizontally scalable computation framework that integrates with HDFS.
- *Serialization frameworks*—Serialization frameworks provide tools and libraries for using objects between languages. They can serialize an object into a byte array from any language, and then deserialize that byte array into an object in any language. Serialization frameworks provide a Schema Definition Language for defining objects and their fields, and they provide mechanisms to safely version objects so that a schema can be evolved without invalidating existing objects. The three notable serialization frameworks are Thrift, Protocol Buffers, and Avro.

- *Random-access NoSQL databases*—There has been a plethora of NoSQL databases created in the past few years. Between Cassandra, HBase, MongoDB, Voldemort, Riak, CouchDB, and others, it's hard to keep track of them all. These databases all share one thing in common: they sacrifice the full expressiveness of SQL and instead specialize in certain kinds of operations. They all have different semantics and are meant to be used for specific purposes. They're *not* meant to be used for arbitrary data warehousing. In many ways, choosing a NoSQL database to use is like choosing between a hash map, sorted map, linked list, or vector when choosing a data structure to use in a program. You know beforehand exactly what you're going to do, and you choose appropriately. Cassandra will be used as part of the example application we'll build.

- *Messaging/queuing systems*—A messaging/queuing system provides a way to send and consume messages between processes in a fault-tolerant and asynchronous manner. A message queue is a key component for doing realtime processing. We'll use Apache Kafka in this book.

- *Realtime computation system*—Realtime computation systems are high throughput, low latency, stream-processing systems. They can't do the range of computations a batch-processing system can, but they process messages extremely quickly. We'll use Storm in this book. Storm topologies are easy to write and scale.

As these open source projects have matured, companies have formed around some of them to provide enterprise support. For example, Cloudera provides Hadoop support, and DataStax provides Cassandra support. Other projects are company products. For example, Riak is a product of Basho technologies, MongoDB is a product of 10gen, and RabbitMQ is a product of SpringSource, a division of VMWare.

1.9   *Example application: SuperWebAnalytics.com*

We'll build an example Big Data application throughout this book to illustrate the concepts. We'll build the data management layer for a Google Analytics–like service. The service will be able to track billions of pageviews per day.

The service will support a variety of different metrics. Each metric will be supported in real time. The metrics range from simple counting metrics to complex analyses of how visitors are navigating a website.

These are the metrics we'll support:

- *Pageview counts by URL sliced by time*—Example queries are "What are the pageviews for each day over the past year?" and "How many pageviews have there been in the past 12 hours?"

- *Unique visitors by URL sliced by time*—Example queries are "How many unique people visited this domain in 2010?" and "How many unique people visited this domain each hour for the past three days?"

- *Bounce-rate analysis*—"What percentage of people visit the page without visiting any other pages on this website?"

We'll build out the layers that store, process, and serve queries to the application.

1.10 *Summary*

You saw what can go wrong when scaling a relational system with traditional techniques like sharding. The problems faced go beyond scaling as the system becomes more complex to manage, extend, and even understand. As you learn how to build Big Data systems in the upcoming chapters, we'll focus as much on robustness as we do on scalability. As you'll see, when you build things the right way, both robustness and scalability are achievable in the same system.

The benefits of data systems built using the Lambda Architecture go beyond just scaling. Because your system will be able to handle much larger amounts of data, you'll be able to collect even more data and get more value out of it. Increasing the amount and types of data you store will lead to more opportunities to mine your data, produce analytics, and build new applications.

Another benefit of using the Lambda Architecture is how robust your applications will be. There are many reasons for this; for example, you'll have the ability to run computations on your whole dataset to do migrations or fix things that go wrong. You'll never have to deal with situations where there are multiple versions of a schema active at the same time. When you change your schema, you'll have the capability to update all data to the new schema. Likewise, if an incorrect algorithm is accidentally deployed to production and corrupts the data you're serving, you can easily fix things by recomputing the corrupted values. As you'll see, there are many other reasons why your Big Data applications will be more robust.

Finally, performance will be more predictable. Although the Lambda Architecture as a whole is generic and flexible, the individual components comprising the system are specialized. There is very little "magic" happening behind the scenes, as compared to something like a SQL query planner. This leads to more predictable performance.

Don't worry if a lot of this material still seems uncertain. We have a lot of ground yet to cover and we'll revisit every topic introduced in this chapter in depth throughout the course of the book. In the next chapter you'll start learning how to build the Lambda Architecture. You'll start at the very core of the stack with how you model and schematize the master copy of your dataset.

Part 1

Batch layer

Part 1 focuses on the batch layer of the Lambda Architecture. Chapters alternate between theory and illustration.

Chapter 2 discusses how you model and schematize the data in your master dataset. Chapter 3 illustrates these concepts using the tool Apache Thrift.

Chapter 4 discusses the requirements for storage of your master dataset. You'll see that many features typically provided by database solutions are not needed for the master dataset, and in fact get in the way of optimizing master dataset storage. A simpler and less feature-full storage solution meets the requirements better. Chapter 5 illustrates practical storage of a master dataset using the Hadoop Distributed Filesystem.

Chapter 6 discusses computing arbitrary functions on your master dataset using the MapReduce paradigm. MapReduce is general enough to compute any scalable function. Although MapReduce is powerful, you'll see that higher-level abstractions make it far easier to use. Chapter 7 shows a powerful high-level abstraction to MapReduce called JCascalog.

To connect all the concepts together, chapters 8 and 9 implement the complete batch layer for the running example SuperWebAnalytics.com. Chapter 8 shows the overall architecture and algorithms, while chapter 9 shows the working code in all its details.

Data model for Big Data

2

This chapter covers

- Properties of data
- The fact-based data model
- Benefits of a fact-based model for Big Data
- Graph schemas

In the last chapter you saw what can go wrong when using traditional tools for building data systems, and we went back to first principles to derive a better design. You saw that every data system can be formulated as computing functions on data, and you learned the basics of the Lambda Architecture, which provides a practical way to implement an arbitrary function on arbitrary data in real time.

At the core of the Lambda Architecture is the master dataset, which is highlighted in figure 2.1. The master dataset is the source of truth in the Lambda Architecture. Even if you were to lose all your serving layer datasets and speed layer datasets, you could reconstruct your application from the master dataset. This is because the batch views served by the serving layer are produced via functions on the master dataset, and since the speed layer is based only on recent data, it can construct itself within a few hours.

The master dataset is the only part of the Lambda Architecture that absolutely must be safeguarded from corruption. Overloaded machines, failing disks, and

27

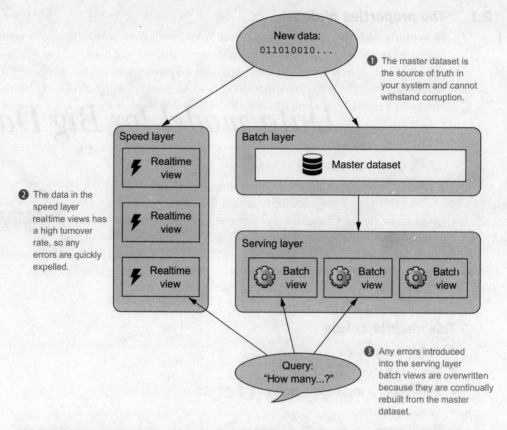

Figure 2.1   The master dataset in the Lambda Architecture serves as the source of truth for your Big Data system. Errors at the serving and speed layers can be corrected, but corruption of the master dataset is irreparable.

power outages all could cause errors, and human error with dynamic data systems is an intrinsic risk and inevitable eventuality. You must carefully engineer the master dataset to prevent corruption in all these cases, as fault tolerance is essential to the health of a long-running data system.

There are two components to the master dataset: the data model you use and how you physically store the master dataset. This chapter is about designing a data model for the master dataset and the properties such a data model should have. You'll learn about physically storing a master dataset in the next chapter.

In this chapter you'll do the following:

- Learn the key properties of data
- See how these properties are maintained in the fact-based model
- Examine the advantages of the fact-based model for the master dataset
- Express a fact-based model using graph schemas

Let's begin with a discussion of the rather general term *data*.

2.1 *The properties of data*

In keeping with the applied focus of the book, we'll center our discussion around an example application. Suppose you're designing the next big social network—Face-Space. When a new user—let's call him Tom—joins your site, he starts to invite his friends and family. What information should you store regarding Tom's connections? You have a number of choices, including the following:

- The sequence of Tom's friend and unfriend events
- Tom's current list of friends
- Tom's current number of friends

Figure 2.2 exhibits these options and their relationships.

This example illustrates information dependency. Note that each layer of information can be derived from the previous one (the one to its left), but it's a one-way process. From the sequence of friend and unfriend events, you can determine the other quantities. But if you only have the number of friends, it's impossible to determine exactly who they are. Similarly, from the list of current friends, it's impossible to determine if Tom was previously a friend with Jerry, or whether Tom's network has been growing as of late.

The notion of dependency shapes the definitions of the terms we'll use:

- *Information* is the general collection of knowledge relevant to your Big Data system. It's synonymous with the colloquial usage of the word *data*.
- *Data* refers to the information that can't be derived from anything else. Data serves as the axioms from which everything else derives.
- *Queries* are questions you ask of your data. For example, you query your financial transaction history to determine your current bank account balance.
- *Views* are information that has been derived from your base data. They are built to assist with answering specific types of queries.

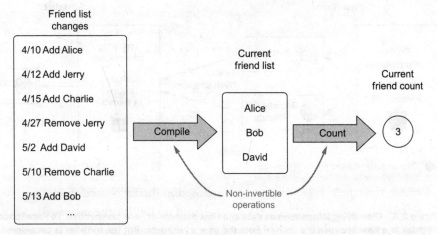

Figure 2.2 Three possible options for storing friendship information for FaceSpace. Each option can be derived from the one to its left, but it's a one-way process.

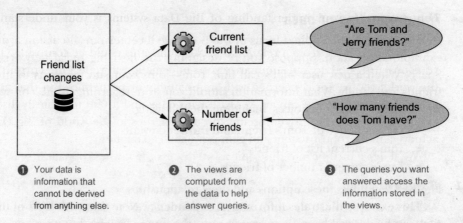

Figure 2.3   The relationships between data, views, and queries

Figure 2.3 illustrates the FaceSpace information dependency in terms of data, views, and queries.

It's important to observe that one person's data can be another's view. Suppose Face-Space becomes a monstrous hit, and an advertising firm creates a crawler that scrapes demographic information from user profiles. FaceSpace has complete access to all the information Tom provided—for example, his complete birthdate of March 13, 1984. But Tom is sensitive about his age, and he only makes his birthday (March 13) available on his public profile. His birthday is a view from FaceSpace's perspective because it's derived from his birthdate, but it's data to the advertiser because they have limited information about Tom. This relationship is shown in figure 2.4.

Having established a shared vocabulary, we can now introduce the key properties of data: *rawness*, *immutability*, and *perpetuity* (or the "eternal trueness of data").

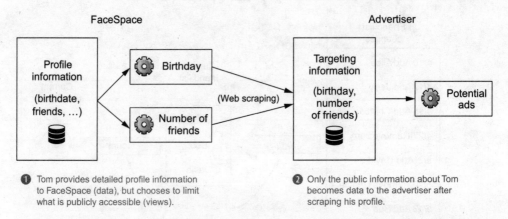

Figure 2.4   Classifying information as data or a view depends on your perspective. To FaceSpace, Tom's birthday is a view because it's derived from the user's birthdate. But the birthday is considered data to a third-party advertiser.

Foundational to your understanding of Big Data systems is your understanding of these three key concepts.

If you're coming from a relational background, this could be confusing. Typically you constantly update and summarize your information to reflect the current state of the world; you're not concerned with immutability or perpetuity. But that approach limits the questions you can answer with your data, and it fails to robustly discourage errors and corruption. By enforcing these properties in the world of Big Data, you achieve a more robust system and gain powerful capabilities.

We'll delve further into this topic as we discuss the rawness of data.

2.1.1 Data is raw

A data system answers questions about information you've acquired in the past. When designing your Big Data system, you want to be able to answer as many questions as possible. In the FaceSpace example, your FaceSpace data is more valuable than the advertiser's because you can deduce more information about Tom. We'll colloquially call this property *rawness*. If you can, you want to store the rawest data you can get your hands on. The rawer your data, the more questions you can ask of it.

The FaceSpace example helps illustrate the value of rawness, but let's consider another example to help drive the point home. Stock market trading is a fountain of information, with millions of shares and billions of dollars changing hands on a daily basis. With so many trades taking place, stock prices are historically recorded daily as an opening price, high price, low price, and closing price. But those bits of data often don't provide the big picture and can potentially skew your perception of what happened. For instance, look at figure 2.5. It records the price data for Google, Apple, and Amazon stocks on a day when Google announced new products targeted at their competitors.

This data suggests that Amazon may not have been affected by Google's announcement, as its stock price moved only slightly. It also suggests that the announcement had either no effect on Apple, or a positive effect.

But if you have access to data stored at a finer time granularity, you can get a clearer picture of the events on that day and probe further into potential cause and

Company	Symbol	Previous	Open	High	Low	Close	Net
Google	GOOG	564.68	567.70	573.99	566.02	569.30	+4.62
Apple	AAPL	572.02	575.00	576.74	571.92	574.50	+2.48
Amazon	AMZN	225.61	225.01	227.50	223.30	225.62	+0.01

Financial reporting promotes daily net change in closing prices.
What conclusions would you draw about the impact of
Google's announcements?

Figure 2.5   A summary of one day of trading for Google, Apple, and Amazon stocks: previous close, opening, high, low, close, and net change.

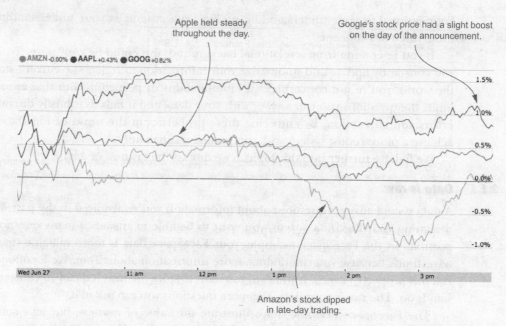

Figure 2.6   Relative stock price changes of Google, Apple, and Amazon on June 27, 2012, compared to closing prices on June 26 (www.google.com/finance). Short-term analysis isn't supported by daily records but can be performed by storing data at finer time resolutions.

effect relationships. Figure 2.6 depicts the minute-by-minute relative changes in the stock prices of all three companies, which suggests that both Amazon and Apple were indeed affected by the announcement, Amazon more so than Apple.

Also note that the additional data can suggest new ideas you may not have considered when examining the original daily stock price summary. For instance, the more granular data makes you wonder if Amazon was more greatly affected because the new Google products compete with Amazon in both the tablet and cloud-computing markets.

Storing raw data is hugely valuable because you rarely know in advance all the questions you want answered. By keeping the rawest data possible, you maximize your ability to obtain new insights, whereas summarizing, overwriting, or deleting information limits what your data can tell you. The trade-off is that rawer data typically entails more of it—sometimes much more. But Big Data technologies are designed to manage petabytes and exabytes of data. Specifically, they manage the storage of your data in a distributed, scalable manner while supporting the ability to directly query the data.

Although the concept is straightforward, it's not always clear what information you should store as your raw data. We'll provide a couple of examples to help guide you in making this decision.

UNSTRUCTURED DATA IS RAWER THAN NORMALIZED DATA

When deciding what raw data to store, a common hazy area is the line between *parsing* and *semantic normalization*. Semantic normalization is the process of reshaping free-form information into a structured form of data.

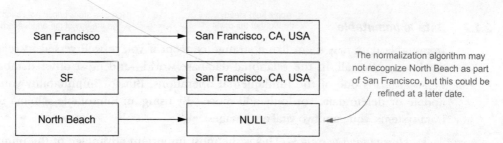

The normalization algorithm may not recognize North Beach as part of San Francisco, but this could be refined at a later date.

Figure 2.7   Semantic normalization of unstructured location responses to city, state, and country. A simple algorithm will normalize "North Beach" to NULL if it doesn't recognize it as a San Francisco neighborhood.

For example, FaceSpace may request Tom's location. He may input anything for that field, such as *San Francisco, CA, SF, North Beach,* and so forth. A semantic normalization algorithm would try to match the input with a known place—see figure 2.7.

If you come across a form of data such as an unstructured location string, should you store the unstructured string or the semantically normalized form? We argue that it's better to store the unstructured string, because your semantic normalization algorithm may improve over time. If you store the unstructured string, you can renormalize that data at a later time when you have improved your algorithms. In the preceding example, you may later adapt the algorithm to recognize North Beach as a neighborhood in San Francisco, or you may want to use the neighborhood information for another purpose.

> **STORE UNSTRUCTURED DATA WHEN…**   As a rule of thumb, if your algorithm for extracting the data is simple and accurate, like extracting an age from an HTML page, you should store the results of that algorithm. If the algorithm is subject to change, due to improvements or broadening the requirements, store the unstructured form of the data.

MORE INFORMATION DOESN'T NECESSARILY MEAN RAWER DATA

It's easy to presume that more data equates to rawer data, but that's not always the case. Let's say that Tom is a blogger, and he wants to add his posts to his FaceSpace profile. What exactly should you store once Tom provides the URL of his blog?

Storing the pure text of the blog entries is certainly a possibility. But any phrases in italics, boldface, or large font were deliberately emphasized by Tom and could prove useful in text analysis. For example, you could use this additional information for an index to make FaceSpace searchable. We'd thus argue that the annotated text entries are a rawer form of data than ASCII text strings.

At the other end of the spectrum, you could also store the full HTML of Tom's blog as your data. While it's considerably more information in terms of total bytes, the color scheme, stylesheets, and JavaScript code of the site can't be used to derive any additional information about Tom. They serve only as the container for the contents of the site and shouldn't be part of your raw data.

2.1.2   *Data is immutable*

Immutable data may seem like a strange concept if you're well versed in relational databases. After all, in the relational database world—and most other databases as well—*update* is one of the fundamental operations. But for immutability you don't update or delete data, you only add more.[1] By using an immutable schema for Big Data systems, you gain two vital advantages:

- *Human-fault tolerance*—This is the most important advantage of the immutable model. As we discussed in chapter 1, human-fault tolerance is an essential property of data systems. People will make mistakes, and you must limit the impact of such mistakes and have mechanisms for recovering from them. With a mutable data model, a mistake can cause data to be lost, because values are actually overridden in the database. With an immutable data model, *no data can be lost*. If bad data is written, earlier (good) data units still exist. Fixing the data system is just a matter of deleting the bad data units and recomputing the views built from the master dataset.

- *Simplicity*—Mutable data models imply that the data must be indexed in some way so that specific data objects can be retrieved and updated. In contrast, with an immutable data model you only need the ability to append new data units to the master dataset. This doesn't require an index for your data, which is a huge simplification. As you'll see in the next chapter, storing a master dataset is as simple as using flat files.

The advantages of keeping your data immutable become evident when comparing with a mutable schema. Consider the basic mutable schema shown in figure 2.8, which you could use for FaceSpace.

User information					
id	name	age	gender	employer	location
1	Alice	25	female	Apple	Atlanta, GA
2	Bob	36	male	SAS	Chicago, IL
3	Tom	28	male	Google	San Francisco, CA
4	Charlie	25	male	Microsoft	Washington, DC
...	...	...	...	...	...

Should Tom move to a different city, this value would be owerwritten.

Figure 2.8   A mutable schema for FaceSpace user information. When details change—say, Tom moves to Los Angeles—previous values are overwritten and lost.

---

[1] There are a few scenarios in which you can delete data, but these are special cases and not part of the day-to-day workflow of your system. We'll discuss these scenarios in section 2.1.3.

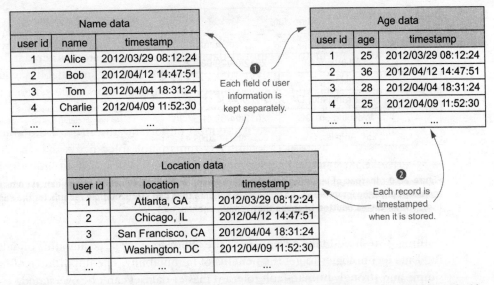

Figure 2.9 An equivalent immutable schema for FaceSpace user information. Each field is tracked in a separate table, and each row has a timestamp for when it's known to be true. (Gender and employer data are omitted for space, but are stored similarly.)

Should Tom move to Los Angeles, you'd update the highlighted entry to reflect his current location—but in the process, you'd also lose all knowledge that Tom ever lived in San Francisco.

With an immutable schema, things look different. Rather than storing a current snapshot of the world, as done by the mutable schema, you create a separate record every time a user's information evolves. Accomplishing this requires two changes. First, you track each field of user information in a separate table. Second, you tie each unit of data to a moment in time when the information is known to be true. Figure 2.9 shows a corresponding immutable schema for storing FaceSpace information.

Tom first joined FaceSpace on April 4, 2012, and provided his profile information. The time you first learn this data is reflected in the record's timestamp. When he subsequently moves to Los Angeles on June 17, 2012, you add a new record to the location table, timestamped by when he changed his profile—see figure 2.10.

You now have two location records for Tom (user ID #3), and because the data units are tied to particular times, they can both be true. Tom's *current location* involves a simple query on the data: look at all the locations, and pick the one with the most recent timestamp. By keeping each field in a separate table, you only record the information that changed. This requires less space for storage and guarantees that each record is new information and is not simply carried over from the last record.

One of the trade-offs of the immutable approach is that it uses more storage than a mutable schema. First, the user ID is specified for every property, rather than just once per row, as with a mutable approach. Additionally, the entire history of events is stored rather than just the current view of the world. But Big Data isn't called "Big Data" for

Location data		
user id	location	timestamp
1	Atlanta, GA	2012/03/29 08:12:24
2	Chicago, IL	2012/04/12 14:47:51
3	San Francisco, CA	2012/04/04 18:31:24
4	Washington, DC	2012/04/09 11:52:30
3	Los Angeles, CA	2012/06/17 20:09:48
...	...	...

1 The initial information provided by Tom (user id 3), timestamped when he first joined FaceSpace.

2 When Tom later moves to a new location, you add an additional record timestamped by when you received the new data.

Figure 2.10   Instead of updating preexisting records, an immutable schema uses new records to represent changed information. An immutable schema thus can store multiple records for the same user. (Other tables omitted because they remain unchanged.)

nothing. You should take advantage of the ability to store large amounts of data using Big Data technologies to get the benefits of immutability. The importance of having a simple and strongly human-fault tolerant master dataset can't be overstated.

2.1.3   Data is eternally true

The key consequence of immutability is that each piece of data is true in perpetuity. That is, a piece of data, once true, must always be true. Immutability wouldn't make sense without this property, and you saw how tagging each piece of data with a time-stamp is a practical way to make data eternally true.

This mentality is the same as when you learned history in school. The fact *The United States consisted of thirteen states on July 4, 1776,* is always true due to the specific date; the fact that the number of states has increased since then is captured in additional (also perpetual) data.

In general, your master dataset consistently grows by adding new immutable and eternally true pieces of data. There are some special cases, though, in which you do delete data, and these cases are not incompatible with data being eternally true. Let's consider the cases:

- *Garbage collection*—When you perform garbage collection, you delete all data units that have low value. You can use garbage collection to implement data-retention policies that control the growth of the master dataset. For example, you may decide to implement a policy that keeps only one location per person per year instead of the full history of each time a user changes locations.
- *Regulations*—Government regulations may require you to purge data from your databases under certain conditions.

In both of these cases, deleting the data is not a statement about the truthfulness of the data. Instead, it's a statement about the value of the data. Although the data is eternally true, you may prefer to "forget" the information either because you must or because it doesn't provide enough value for the storage cost.

We'll proceed by introducing a data model that uses these key properties of data.

> ## Deleting immutable data?
> You may be wondering how it is possible to delete immutable data. On the face of it, this seems like a contradiction. It is important to distinguish that the deleting we are referring to is a special and rare case. In normal usage, data is immutable, and you enforce that property by taking actions such as setting the appropriate permissions. Since deleting data is rare, the utmost care can be taken to ensure that it is done safely. We believe deleting data is most safely accomplished by producing a second copy of the master dataset with the offending data filtered out, running analytic jobs to verify that the correct data was filtered, and then and only then replacing the old version of the master dataset.

2.2 The fact-based model for representing data

Data is the set of information that can't be derived from anything else, but there are many ways you could choose to represent it within the master dataset. Besides traditional relational tables, structured XML and semistructured JSON documents are other possibilities for storing data. We, however, recommend the fact-based model for this purpose. In the fact-based model, you deconstruct the data into fundamental units called (unsurprisingly) *facts*.

In the discussion of immutability, you got a glimpse of the fact-based model, in that the master dataset continually grows with the addition of immutable, timestamped data. We'll now expand on what we already discussed to explain the fact-based model in full. We'll first introduce the model in the context of the FaceSpace example and discuss its basic properties. We'll then continue with discussing how and why you should make your facts identifiable. To wrap up, we'll explain the benefits of using the fact-based model and why it's an excellent choice for your master dataset.

2.2.1 Example facts and their properties

Figure 2.11 depicts examples of facts about Tom from the FaceSpace data, as well as two core properties of facts—they are *atomic* and *timestamped*.

Facts are atomic because they can't be subdivided further into meaningful components. Collective data, such as Tom's friend list in the figure, are represented as multiple, independent facts. As a consequence of being atomic, there's no redundancy of information across distinct facts. Facts having timestamps should come as no surprise, given our earlier discussion about data—the timestamps make each fact immutable and eternally true.

These properties make the fact-based model a simple and expressive model for your dataset, yet there is an additional property we recommend imposing on your facts: *identifiability*.

MAKING FACTS IDENTIFIABLE

Besides being atomic and timestamped, facts should be associated with a uniquely identifiable piece of data. This is most easily explained by example.

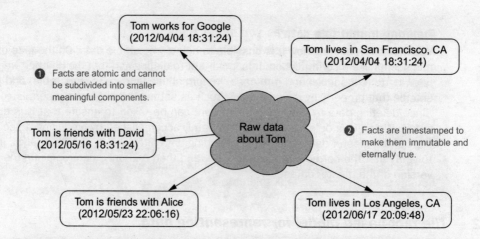

Figure 2.11   All of the raw data concerning Tom is deconstructed into timestamped, atomic units we call facts.

Suppose you want to store data about pageviews on FaceSpace. Your first approach might look something like this (in pseudo-code):

```
struct PageView:
  DateTime timestamp
  String url
  String ip_address
```

Facts using this structure don't uniquely identify a particular pageview event. If multiple pageviews come in at the same time for the same URL from the same IP address, each pageview will have the exact same data record. Consequently, if you encounter two identical pageview records, there's no way to tell whether they refer to two distinct events or if a duplicate entry was accidentally introduced into your dataset.

To distinguish different pageviews, you can add a *nonce* to your schema—a 64-bit number randomly generated for each pageview:

```
struct PageView:
  Datetime timestamp
  String url
  String ip_address
  Long nonce
```

The nonce, combined with the other fields, uniquely identifies a particular pageview.

The addition of the nonce makes it possible to distinguish pageview events from each other, and if two pageview data units are identical (all fields, including the nonce), you know they refer to the exact same event.

Making facts identifiable means that you can write the same fact to the master dataset multiple times without changing the semantics of the master dataset. Your queries can filter out the duplicate facts when doing their computations. As it turns out, and as you'll see later, having distinguishable facts makes implementing the rest of the Lambda Architecture much easier.

Duplicates aren't as rare as you might think

At a first look, it may not be obvious why we care so much about identity and duplicates. After all, to avoid duplicates, the first inclination would be to ensure that an event is recorded just once. Unfortunately life isn't always so simple when dealing with Big Data.

Once FaceSpace becomes a hit, it will require hundreds, then thousands, of web servers. Building the master dataset will require aggregating the data from each of these servers to a central system—no trivial task. There are data collection tools suitable for this situation—Facebook's Scribe, Apache Flume, syslog-ng, and many others—but any solution must be fault tolerant.

One common "fault" these systems must anticipate is a network partition where the destination datastore becomes unavailable. For these situations, fault-tolerant systems commonly handle failed operations by retrying until they succeed. Because the sender will not know which data was last received, a standard approach is to resend all data yet to be acknowledged by the recipient. But if part of the original attempt did make it to the metastore, you'd end up with duplicates in your dataset.

There are ways to make these kinds of operations transactional, but it can be fairly tricky and entail performance costs. An important part of ensuring correctness in your systems is avoiding tricky solutions. By embracing distinguishable facts, you remove the need for transactional appends to the master dataset and make it easier to reason about the correctness of the full system. After all, why place difficult burdens on yourself when a small tweak to your data model can avoid those challenges altogether?

To quickly recap, the fact-based model

- Stores your raw data as atomic facts
- Keeps the facts immutable and eternally true by using timestamps
- Ensures each fact is identifiable so that query processing can identify duplicates

Next we'll discuss the benefits of choosing the fact-based model for your master dataset.

2.2.2 Benefits of the fact-based model

With a fact-based model, the master dataset will be an ever-growing list of immutable, atomic facts. This isn't a pattern that relational databases were built to support—if you come from a relational background, your head may be spinning. The good news is that by changing your data model paradigm, you gain numerous advantages. Specifically, your data

- Is queryable at any time in its history
- Tolerates human errors
- Handles partial information
- Has the advantages of both normalized and denormalized forms

Let's look at each of these advantages in turn.

THE DATASET IS QUERYABLE AT ANY TIME IN ITS HISTORY

Instead of storing only the current state of the world, as you would using a mutable, relational schema, you have the ability to query your data for any time covered by your dataset. This is a direct consequence of facts being timestamped and immutable. "Updates" and "deletes" are performed by adding new facts with more recent time-stamps, but because no data is actually removed, you can reconstruct the state of the world at the time specified by your query.

THE DATA IS HUMAN-FAULT TOLERANT

Human-fault tolerance is achieved by simply deleting any erroneous facts. Suppose you mistakenly stored that Tom moved from San Francisco to Los Angeles—see figure 2.12.

By removing the Los Angeles fact, Tom's location is automatically "reset" because the San Francisco fact becomes the most recent information.

THE DATASET EASILY HANDLES PARTIAL INFORMATION

Storing one fact per record makes it easy to handle partial information about an entity without introducing NULL values into your dataset. Suppose Tom provided his age and gender but not his location or profession. Your dataset would only have facts for the known information—any "absent" fact would be logically equivalent to NULL. Additional information that Tom provides at a later time would naturally be intro-duced via new facts.

THE DATA STORAGE AND QUERY PROCESSING LAYERS ARE SEPARATE

There is another key advantage of the fact-based model that is in part due to the struc-ture of the Lambda Architecture itself. By storing the information at both the batch and serving layers, you have the benefit of keeping your data in both normalized and denormalized forms and reaping the benefits of both.

> **NORMALIZATION IS AN OVERLOADED TERM**   Data normalization is completely unrelated to the *semantic normalization* term that we used earlier. In this case, data normalization refers to storing data in a structured manner to minimize redundancy and promote consistency.

Location data		
user id	location	timestamp
1	Atlanta, GA	2012/03/29 08:12:24
2	Chicago, IL	2012/04/12 14:47:51
3	San Francisco, CA	2012/04/04 18:31:24
4	Washington, DC	2012/04/09 11:52:30
~~3~~	~~Los Angeles, CA~~	~~2012/06/17 20:09:48~~
...	...	...

Human faults can easily be corrected by simply deleting erroneous facts. The record is automatically reset by using earlier timestamps.

Figure 2.12   To correct for human errors, simply remove the incorrect facts. This process automatically resets to an earlier state by "uncovering" any relevant previous facts.

Employment		
row id	name	company
1	Bill	Microsoft
2	Larry	BackRub
3	Sergey	BackRub
4	Steve	Apple
...	...	...

Data in this table is denormalized because the same information is stored redundantly—in this case, the company name can be repeated.

With this table, you can quickly determine the number of employees at each company, but many rows must be updated when change occurs—in this case, when BackRub changed to Google.

Figure 2.13 A simple denormalized schema for storing employment information

Let's set the stage with an example involving relational tables—the context where data normalization is most frequently encountered. Relational tables require you to choose between normalized and denormalized schemas based on what's most important to you: query efficiency or data consistency. Suppose you wanted to store the employment information for various people of interest. Figure 2.13 offers a simple denormalized schema suitable for this purpose.

In this denormalized schema, the same company name could potentially be stored in multiple rows. This would allow you to quickly determine the number of employees for each company, but you would need to update many rows should a company change its name. Having information stored in multiple locations increases the risk of it becoming inconsistent.

In comparison, consider the normalized schema in figure 2.14.

Data in a normalized schema is stored in only one location. If BackRub should change its name to Google, there's a single row in the Company table that needs to be altered. This removes the risk of inconsistency, but you must join the tables to answer queries—a potentially expensive computation.

User		
user id	name	company id
1	Bill	3
2	Larry	2
3	Sergey	2
4	Steve	1
...	...	...

Company	
company id	name
1	Apple
2	BackRub
3	Microsoft
4	IBM
...	...

For normalized data, each fact is stored in only one location and relationships between datasets are used to answer queries. This simplifies the consistency of data, but joining tables could be expensive.

Figure 2.14 Two normalized tables for storing the same employment information

The mutually exclusive choice between normalized and denormalized schemas is necessary because, for relational databases, queries are performed directly on the data at the storage level. You must therefore weigh the importance of query efficiency versus data consistency and choose between the two schema types.

In contrast, the objectives of query processing and data storage are cleanly separated in the Lambda Architecture. Take a look at the batch and server layers in figure 2.15.

In the Lambda Architecture, the master dataset is fully normalized. As you saw in the discussion of the fact-based model, no data is stored redundantly. Updates are easily handled because adding a new fact with a current timestamp "overrides" any previous related facts.

Similarly, the batch views are like denormalized tables in that one piece of data from the master dataset may get indexed into many batch views. The key difference is that the batch views are defined as functions on the master dataset. Accordingly, there is no need to update a batch view because it will be continually rebuilt from the master dataset. This has the additional benefit that the batch views and master dataset will never be out of sync. The Lambda Architecture gives you the conceptual benefits of full normalization with the performance benefits of indexing data in different ways to optimize queries.

In summary, all of these benefits make the fact-based model an excellent choice for your master dataset. But that's enough discussion at the theoretical level—let's dive into the details of practically implementing a fact-based data model.

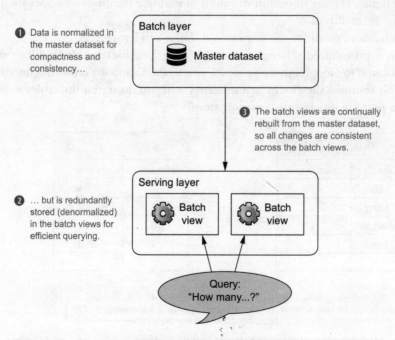

Figure 2.15   The Lambda Architecture has the benefits of both normalization and denormalization by separating objectives at different layers.

2.3 Graph schemas

Each fact within a fact-based model captures a single piece of information. But the facts alone don't convey the structure behind the data. That is, there's no description of the types of facts contained in the dataset, nor any explanation of the relationships between them. In this section we'll introduce *graph schemas*—graphs that capture the structure of a dataset stored using the fact-based model. We'll discuss the elements of a graph schema and the need to make a schema enforceable.

Let's begin by first structuring our FaceSpace facts as a graph.

2.3.1 Elements of a graph schema

In the last section we discussed FaceSpace facts in great detail. Each fact represents either a piece of information about a user or a relationship between two users. Figure 2.16 depicts a *graph schema* representing the relationships between the FaceSpace facts. It provides a useful visualization of your users, their individual information, and the friendships between them.

The figure highlights the three core components of a graph schema—*nodes, edges,* and *properties*:

- *Nodes are the entities in the system.* In this example, the nodes are the FaceSpace users, represented by a user ID. As another example, if FaceSpace allows users to identify themselves as part of a group, then the groups would also be represented by nodes.
- *Edges are relationships between nodes.* The connotation in FaceSpace is straightforward—an edge between users represents a FaceSpace friendship. You could

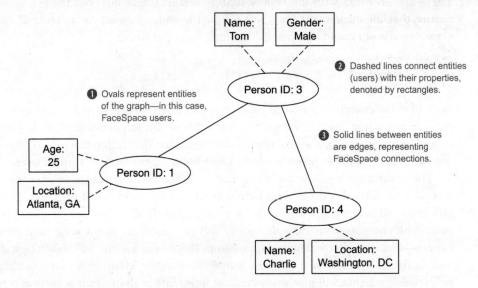

Figure 2.16   Visualizing the relationship between FaceSpace facts

later add additional edge types between users to identify coworkers, family members, or classmates.

- *Properties are information about entities.* In this example, age, gender, location, and all other pieces of individual information are properties.

EDGES ARE STRICTLY BETWEEN NODES   Even though properties and nodes are visually connected in the figure, these lines are not edges. They are present only to help illustrate the association between users and their personal information. We denote the difference by using solid lines for edges and dashed lines for property connections.

The graph schema provides a complete description of all the data contained within a dataset. Next we'll discuss the need to ensure that all facts within a dataset rigidly adhere to the schema.

2.3.2   *The need for an enforceable schema*

At this point, information is stored as facts, and a graph schema describes the types of facts contained in the dataset. You're all set, right? Well, not quite. You still need to decide in what format you'll store your facts.

A first idea might be to use a semistructured text format like JSON. This would provide simplicity and flexibility, allowing essentially anything to be written to the master dataset. But in this case it's too flexible for our needs.

To illustrate this problem, suppose you chose to represent Tom's age using JSON:

```
{"id": 3, "field":"age", "value":28, "timestamp": 1333589484}
```

There are no issues with the representation of this single fact, but there's no way to ensure that all subsequent facts will follow the same format. As a result of human error, the dataset could also possibly include facts like these:

```
{"name":"Alice", "field":"age", "value":25,
   "timestamp":"2012/03/29 08:12:24"}
{"id":2, "field":"age", "value":36}
```

Both of these examples are valid JSON, but they have inconsistent formats or missing data. In particular, in the last section we stressed the importance of having a timestamp for each fact, but a text format can't enforce this requirement. To effectively use your data, you must provide guarantees about the contents of your dataset.

The alternative is to use an enforceable schema that rigorously defines the structure of your facts. Enforceable schemas require a bit more work up front, but they guarantee all required fields are present and ensure all values are of the expected type. With these assurances, a developer will be confident about what data they can expect—that each fact will have a timestamp, that a user's name will always be a string, and so forth. The key is that when a mistake is made creating a piece of data, an enforceable schema will give errors at that time, rather than when someone is trying to use the data later in a different system. The closer the error appears to the bug, the easier it is to catch and fix.

In the next chapter you'll see how to implement an enforceable schema using a *serialization framework*. A serialization framework provides a language-neutral way to define the nodes, edges, and properties of your schema. It then generates code (potentially in many different languages) that serializes and deserializes the objects in your schema so they can be stored in and retrieved from your master dataset.

We're aware that at this point you may be hungry for details. Not to worry—we believe the best way to learn is by doing. In the next section we'll design the fact-based model for SuperWebAnalytics.com in its entirety, and in the following chapter we'll implement it using a serialization framework.

2.4   A complete data model for SuperWebAnalytics.com

In this section we aim to tie together all the material from the chapter using the SuperWebAnalytics.com example. We'll begin with figure 2.17, which contains a graph schema suitable for our purpose.

In this schema there are two types of nodes: *people* and *pages*. As you can see, there are two distinct categories of people nodes to distinguish people with a known identity from people you can only identify using a web browser cookie.

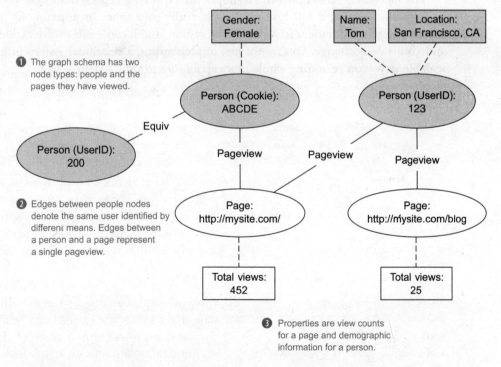

Figure 2.17   The graph schema for SuperWebAnalytics.com. There are two node types: people and pages. People nodes and their properties are slightly shaded to distinguish the two.

Edges in the schema are rather simple. A *pageview* edge occurs between a person and a page for each distinct view, whereas an *equiv* edge occurs between two person nodes when they represent the same individual. The latter would occur when a person initially identified by only a cookie is fully identified at a later time.

Properties are also self-explanatory. Pages have total pageview counts, and people have basic demographic information: name, gender, and location.

One of the beauties of the fact-based model and graph schemas is that they can evolve as different types of data become available. A graph schema provides a consistent interface to arbitrarily diverse data, so it's easy to incorporate new types of information. Schema additions are done by defining new node, edge, and property types. Due to the atomicity of facts, these additions do not affect previously existing fact types.

2.5   Summary

How you model your master dataset creates the foundation for your Big Data system. The decisions made about the master dataset determine the kind of analytics you can perform on your data and how you'll consume that data. The structure of the master dataset must support evolution of the kinds of data stored, because your company's data types may change considerably over the years.

The fact-based model provides a simple yet expressive representation of your data by naturally keeping a full history of each entity over time. Its append-only nature makes it easy to implement in a distributed system, and it can easily evolve as your data and your needs change. You're not just implementing a relational system in a more scalable way—you're adding whole new capabilities to your system as well.

Data model for
Big Data: Illustration

This chapter covers

- Apache Thrift
- Implementing a graph schema using Apache Thrift
- Limitations of serialization frameworks

In the last chapter you saw the principles of forming a data model—the value of raw data, dealing with semantic normalization, and the critical importance of immutability. You saw how a graph schema can satisfy all these properties and saw what the graph schema looks like for SuperWebAnalytics.com.

This is the first of the *illustration chapters,* in which we demonstrate the concepts of the previous chapter using real-world tools. You can read just the theory chapters of the book and learn the whole Lambda Architecture, but the illustration chapters show you the nuances of mapping the theory to real code. In this chapter we'll implement the SuperWebAnalytics.com data model using Apache Thrift, a serialization framework. You'll see that even in a task as straightforward as writing a schema, there is friction between the idealized theory and what you can achieve in practice.

3.1   Why a serialization framework?

Many developers go down the path of writing their raw data in a schemaless format like JSON. This is appealing because of how easy it is to get started, but this approach quickly leads to problems. Whether due to bugs or misunderstandings between different developers, data corruption inevitably occurs. It's our experience that data corruption errors are some of the most time-consuming to debug.

Data corruption issues are hard to debug because you have very little context on how the corruption occurred. Typically you'll only notice there's a problem when there's an error downstream in the processing—long after the corrupt data was written. For example, you might get a null pointer exception due to a mandatory field being missing. You'll quickly realize that the problem is a missing field, but you'll have absolutely no information about how that data got there in the first place.

When you create an enforceable schema, you get errors at the time of writing the data—giving you full context as to how and why the data became invalid (like a stack trace). In addition, the error prevents the program from corrupting the master dataset by writing that data.

Serialization frameworks are an easy approach to making an enforceable schema. If you've ever used an object-oriented, statically typed language, using a serialization framework will be immediately familiar. Serialization frameworks generate code for whatever languages you wish to use for reading, writing, and validating objects that match your schema.

However, serialization frameworks are limited when it comes to achieving a fully rigorous schema. After discussing how to apply a serialization framework to the SuperWebAnalytics.com data model, we'll discuss these limitations and how to work around them.

3.2   Apache Thrift

Apache Thrift (http://thrift.apache.org/) is a tool that can be used to define statically typed, enforceable schemas. It provides an interface definition language to describe the schema in terms of generic data types, and this description can later be used to automatically generate the actual implementation in multiple programming languages.

OUR USE OF APACHE THRIFT   Thrift was initially developed at Facebook for building cross-language services. It can be used for many purposes, but we'll limit our discussion to its usage as a serialization framework.

Other serialization frameworks

There are other tools similar to Apache Thrift, such as Protocol Buffers and Avro. Remember, the purpose of this book is not to provide a survey of all possible tools for every situation, but to use an appropriate tool to illustrate the fundamental concepts. As a serialization framework, Thrift is practical, thoroughly tested, and widely used.

The workhorses of Thrift are the *struct* and *union* type definitions. They're composed of other fields, such as

- Primitive data types (strings, integers, longs, and doubles)
- Collections of other types (lists, maps, and sets)
- Other structs and unions

In general, unions are useful for representing nodes, structs are natural representations of edges, and properties use a combination of both. This will become evident from the type definitions needed to represent the SuperWebAnalytics.com schema components.

3.2.1 Nodes

For our SuperWebAnalytics.com user nodes, an individual is identified either by a user ID or a browser cookie, but not both. This pattern is common for nodes, and it matches exactly with a union data type—a single value that may have any of several representations.

In Thrift, unions are defined by listing all possible representations. The following code defines the SuperWebAnalytics.com nodes using Thrift unions:

```
union PersonID {
  1: string cookie;
  2: i64 user_id;
}

union PageID {
  1: string url;
}
```

Note that unions can also be used for nodes with a single representation. Unions allow the schema to evolve as the data evolves—we'll discuss this further later in this section.

3.2.2 Edges

Each edge can be represented as a struct containing two nodes. The name of an edge struct indicates the relationship it represents, and the fields in the edge struct contain the entities involved in the relationship.

The schema definition is very simple:

```
struct EquivEdge {
  1: required PersonID id1;
  2: required PersonID id2;
}

struct PageViewEdge {
  1: required PersonID person;
  2: required PageID page;
  3: required i64 nonce;
}
```

The fields of a Thrift struct can be denoted as required or optional. If a field is defined as required, then a value for that field must be provided, or else Thrift will give an error upon serialization or deserialization. Because each edge in a graph schema must have two nodes, they are required fields in this example.

3.2.3   Properties

Last, let's define the properties. A property contains a node and a value for the property. The value can be one of many types, so it's best represented using a union structure.

Let's start by defining the schema for page properties. There's only one property for pages, so it's really simple:

```
union PagePropertyValue {
  1: i32 page_views;
}

struct PageProperty {
  1: required PageID id;
  2: required PagePropertyValue property;
}
```

Next let's define the properties for people. As you can see, the location property is more complex and requires another struct to be defined:

```
struct Location {
  1: optional string city;
  2: optional string state;
  3: optional string country;
}

enum GenderType {
  MALE = 1,
  FEMALE = 2
}

union PersonPropertyValue {
  1: string full_name;
  2: GenderType gender;
  3: Location location;
}

struct PersonProperty {
  1: required PersonID id;
  2: required PersonPropertyValue property;
}
```

The location struct is interesting because the city, state, and country fields could have been stored as separate pieces of data. In this case, they're so closely related it makes sense to put them all into one struct as optional fields. When consuming location information, you'll almost always want all of those fields.

3.2.4 *Tying everything together into data objects*

At this point, the edges and properties are defined as separate types. Ideally you'd want to store all of the data together to provide a single interface to access your information. Furthermore, it also makes your data easier to manage if it's stored in a single dataset. This is accomplished by wrapping every property and edge type into a `DataUnit` union—see the following code listing.

Listing 3.1 Completing the SuperWebAnalytics.com schema

```
union DataUnit {
  1: PersonProperty person_property;
  2: PageProperty page_property;
  3: EquivEdge equiv;
  4: PageViewEdge page_view;
}

struct Pedigree {
  1: required i32 true_as_of_secs;
}

struct Data {
  1: required Pedigree pedigree;
  2: required DataUnit dataunit;
}
```

Each `DataUnit` is paired with its metadata, which is kept in a `Pedigree` struct. The pedigree contains the timestamp for the information, but could also potentially contain debugging information or the source of the data. The final `Data` struct corresponds to a fact from the fact-based model.

3.2.5 *Evolving your schema*

Thrift is designed so that schemas can evolve over time. This is a crucial property, because as your business requirements change you'll need to add new kinds of data, and you'll want to do so as effortlessly as possible.

The key to evolving Thrift schemas is the numeric identifiers associated with each field. Those IDs are used to identify fields in their serialized form. When you want to change the schema but still be backward compatible with existing data, you must obey the following rules:

- *Fields may be renamed.* This is because the serialized form of an object uses the field IDs, not the names, to identify fields.
- *A field may be removed, but you must never reuse that field ID.* When deserializing existing data, Thrift will ignore all fields with field IDs not included in the schema. If you were to reuse a previously removed field ID, Thrift would try to deserialize that old data into the new field, which will lead to either invalid or incorrect data.

- *Only optional fields can be added to existing structs.* You can't add required fields because existing data won't have those fields and thus won't be deserializable. (Note that this doesn't apply to unions, because unions have no notion of required and optional fields.)

As an example, should you want to change the SuperWebAnalytics.com schema to store a person's age and the links between web pages, you'd make the following changes to your Thrift definition file (changes in bold font).

Listing 3.2   Extending the SuperWebAnalytics.com schema

```
union PersonPropertyValue {
  1: string full_name;
  2: GenderType gender;
  3: Location location;
  4: i16 age;
}
struct LinkedEdge {
  1: required PageID source;
  2: required PageID target;
}

union DataUnit {
  1: PersonProperty person_property;
  2: PageProperty page_property;
  3: EquivEdge equiv;
  4: PageViewEdge page_view;
  5: LinkedEdge page_link;
}
```

Notice that adding a new age property is done by adding it to the corresponding union structure, and a new edge is incorporated by adding it into the `DataUnit` union.

3.3   *Limitations of serialization frameworks*

Serialization frameworks only check that all required fields are present and are of the expected type. They're unable to check richer properties like "Ages should be non-negative" or "true-as-of timestamps should not be in the future." Data not matching these properties would indicate a problem in your system, and you wouldn't want them written to your master dataset.

This may not seem like a limitation because serialization frameworks seem somewhat similar to how schemas work in relational databases. In fact, you may have found relational database schemas a pain to work with and worry that making schemas even stricter would be even more painful. But we urge you not to confuse the incidental complexities of working with relational database schemas with the value of schemas themselves. The difficulties of representing nested objects and doing schema migrations with relational databases are non-existent when applying serialization frameworks to represent immutable objects using graph schemas.

The right way to think about a schema is as a function that takes in a piece of data and returns whether it's valid or not. The schema language for Apache Thrift lets you represent a subset of these functions where only field existence and field types are checked. The ideal tool would let you implement any possible schema function.

Such an ideal tool—particularly one that is language neutral—doesn't exist, but there are two approaches you can take to work around these limitations with a serialization framework like Apache Thrift:

- *Wrap your generated code in additional code that checks the additional properties you care about, like ages being non-negative.* This approach works well as long as you're only reading/writing data from/to a single language—if you use multiple languages, you have to duplicate the logic in many languages.
- *Check the extra properties at the very beginning of your batch-processing workflow.* This step would split your dataset into "valid data" and "invalid data" and send a notification if any invalid data was found. This approach makes it easier to implement the rest of your workflow, because anything getting past the validity check can be assumed to have the stricter properties you care about. But this approach doesn't prevent the invalid data from being written to the master dataset and doesn't help with determining the context in which the corruption happened.

Neither approach is ideal, but it's hard to see how you can do better if your organization reads/writes data in multiple languages. You have to decide whether you'd rather maintain the same logic in multiple languages or lose the context in which corruption was introduced. The only approach that would be perfect would be a serialization framework that is also a general-purpose programming language that translates itself into whatever languages it's targeting. Such a tool doesn't exist, though it's theoretically possible.

3.4 Summary

For the most part, implementing the enforceable graph schema for SuperWebAnalytics.com was straightforward. You saw the friction that appears when using a serialization framework for this purpose—namely, the inability to enforce every property you care about. The tooling will rarely capture your requirements perfectly, but it's important to know what would be possible with ideal tools. That way you're cognizant of the trade-offs you're making and can keep an eye out for better tools (or make your own). This will be a common theme as we go through the theory and illustration chapters.

In the next chapter you'll learn how to physically store a master dataset in the batch layer so that it can be processed easily and efficiently.

4

Data storage
on the batch layer

This chapter covers

- Storage requirements for the master dataset
- Distributed filesystems
- Improving efficiency with vertical partitioning

In the last two chapters you learned about a data model for the master dataset and how you can translate that data model into a graph schema. You saw the importance of making data immutable and eternal. The next step is to learn how to physically store that data in the batch layer. Figure 4.1 recaps where we are in the Lambda Architecture.

Like the last two chapters, this chapter is dedicated to the master dataset. The master dataset is typically too large to exist on a single server, so you must choose how you'll distribute your data across multiple machines. The way you store your master dataset will impact how you consume it, so it's vital to devise your storage strategy with your usage patterns in mind.

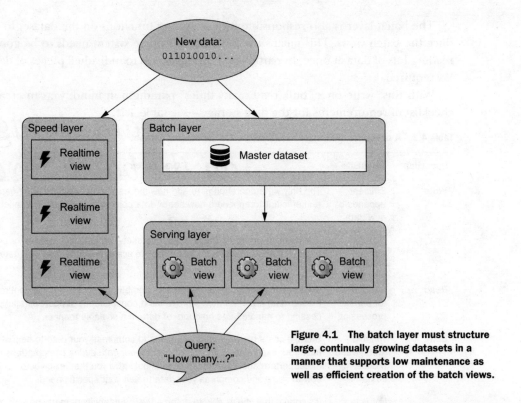

Figure 4.1 The batch layer must structure large, continually growing datasets in a manner that supports low maintenance as well as efficient creation of the batch views.

In this chapter you'll do the following:

- Determine the requirements for storing the master dataset
- See why distributed filesystems are a natural fit for storing a master dataset
- See how the batch layer storage for the SuperWebAnalytics.com project maps to distributed filesystems

We'll begin by examining how the role of the batch layer within the Lambda Architecture affects how you should store your data.

4.1 Storage requirements for the master dataset

To determine the requirements for data storage, you must consider how your data will be written and how it will be read. The role of the batch layer within the Lambda Architecture affects both areas—we'll discuss each at a high level before providing a full list of requirements.

In chapter 2 we emphasized two key properties of data: data is immutable and eternally true. Consequently, each piece of your data will be written once and only once. There is no need to ever alter your data—the only write operation will be to add a new data unit to your dataset. The storage solution must therefore be optimized to handle a large, constantly growing set of data.

The batch layer is also responsible for computing functions on the dataset to produce the batch views. This means the batch layer storage system needs to be good at reading lots of data at once. In particular, random access to individual pieces of data is *not* required.

With this "write once, bulk read many times" paradigm in mind, we can create a checklist of requirements for the data storage—see table 4.1.

Table 4.1   **A checklist of storage requirements for the master dataset**

Operation	Requisite	Discussion
Write	Efficient appends of new data	The only write operation is to add new pieces of data, so it must be easy and efficient to append a new set of data objects to the master dataset.
	Scalable storage	The batch layer stores the complete dataset—potentially terabytes or petabytes of data. It must therefore be easy to scale the storage as your dataset grows.
Read	Support for parallel processing	Constructing the batch views requires computing functions on the entire master dataset. The batch storage must consequently support parallel processing to handle large amounts of data in a scalable manner.
Both	Tunable storage and processing costs	Storage costs money. You may choose to compress your data to help minimize your expenses, but decompressing your data during computations can affect performance. The batch layer should give you the flexibility to decide how to store and compress your data to suit your specific needs.
	Enforceable immutability	It's critical that you're able to enforce the immutability property on your master dataset. Of course, computers by their very nature are mutable, so there will always be a way to mutate the data you're storing. The best you can do is put checks in place to disallow mutable operations. These checks should prevent bugs or other random errors from trampling over existing data.

Let's now take a look at a class of technologies that meets these requirements.

4.2   *Choosing a storage solution for the batch layer*

With the requirements checklist in hand, you can now consider options for batch layer storage. With such loose requirements—not even needing random access to the data—it seems like you could use pretty much any distributed database for the master dataset. So let's first consider the viability of using a key/value store, the most common type of distributed database, for the master dataset.

4.2.1   *Using a key/value store for the master dataset*

We haven't discussed distributed key/value stores yet, but you can essentially think of them as giant persistent hashmaps that are distributed among many machines. If you're storing a master dataset on a key/value store, the first thing you have to figure out is what the keys should be and what the values should be.

What a value should be is obvious—it's a piece of data you want to store—but what should a key be? There's no natural key in the data model, nor is one necessary because the data is meant to be consumed in bulk. So you immediately hit an impedance mismatch between the data model and how key/value stores work. The only really viable idea is to generate a UUID to use as a key.

But this is only the start of the problems with using key/value stores for a master dataset. Because key/value stores need fine-grained access to key/value pairs to do random reads and writes, you can't compress multiple key/value pairs together. So you're severely limited in tuning the trade-off between storage costs and processing costs.

Key/value stores are meant to be used as mutable stores, which is a problem if enforcing immutability is so crucial for the master dataset. Unless you modify the code of the key/value store you're using, you typically can't disable the ability to modify existing key/value pairs.

The biggest problem, though, is that a key/value store has a lot of things you don't need: random reads, random writes, and all the machinery behind making those work. In fact, most of the implementation of a key/value store is dedicated to these features you don't need at all. This means the tool is enormously more complex than it needs to be to meet your requirements, making it much more likely you'll have a problem with it. Additionally, the key/value store indexes your data and provides unneeded services, which will increase your storage costs and lower your performance when reading and writing data.

4.2.2 Distributed filesystems

It turns out there's a type of technology that you're already intimately familiar with that's a perfect fit for batch layer storage: filesystems.

Files are sequences of bytes, and the most efficient way to consume them is by scanning through them. They're stored sequentially on disk (sometimes they're split into blocks, but reading and writing is still essentially sequential). You have full control over the bytes of a file, and you have the full freedom to compress them however you want. Unlike a key/value store, a filesystem gives you exactly what you need and no more, while also not limiting your ability to tune storage cost versus processing cost. On top of that, filesystems implement fine-grained permissions systems, which are perfect for enforcing immutability.

The problem with a regular filesystem is that it exists on just a single machine, so you can only scale to the storage limits and processing power of that one machine. But it turns out that there's a class of technologies called *distributed filesystems* that is quite similar to the filesystems you're familiar with, except they spread their storage across a cluster of computers. They scale by adding more machines to the cluster. Distributed filesystems are designed so that you have fault tolerance when a machine goes down, meaning that if you lose one machine, all your files and data will still be accessible.

There are some differences between distributed filesystems and regular filesystems. The operations you can do with a distributed filesystem are often more limited than you can do with a regular filesystem. For instance, you may not be able to write to the middle of a file or even modify a file at all after creation. Oftentimes having small files can be inefficient, so you want to make sure you keep your file sizes relatively large to make use of the distributed filesystem properly (the details depend on the tool, but 64 MB is a good rule of thumb).

4.3   *How distributed filesystems work*

It's tough to talk in the abstract about how any distributed filesystem works, so we'll ground our explanation with a specific tool: the Hadoop Distributed File System (HDFS). We feel the design of HDFS is sufficiently representative of how distributed file-systems work to demonstrate how such a tool can be used for the batch layer.

HDFS and Hadoop MapReduce are the two prongs of the Hadoop project: a Java framework for distributed storage and distributed processing of large amounts of data. Hadoop is deployed across multiple servers, typically called a *cluster*, and HDFS is a distributed and scalable filesystem that manages how data is stored across the cluster. Hadoop is a project of significant size and depth, so we'll only provide a high-level description.

In an HDFS cluster, there are two types of nodes: a single namenode and multiple datanodes. When you upload a file to HDFS, the file is first chunked into blocks of a fixed size, typically between 64 MB and 256 MB. Each block is then replicated across multiple datanodes (typically three) that are chosen at random. The namenode keeps track of the file-to-block mapping and where each block is located. This design is shown in figure 4.2.

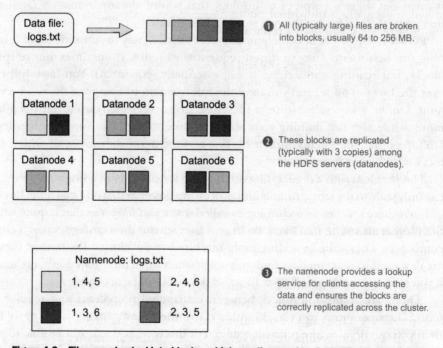

❶ All (typically large) files are broken into blocks, usually 64 to 256 MB.

❷ These blocks are replicated (typically with 3 copies) among the HDFS servers (datanodes).

❸ The namenode provides a lookup service for clients accessing the data and ensures the blocks are correctly replicated across the cluster.

Figure 4.2   Files are chunked into blocks, which are dispersed to datanodes in the cluster.

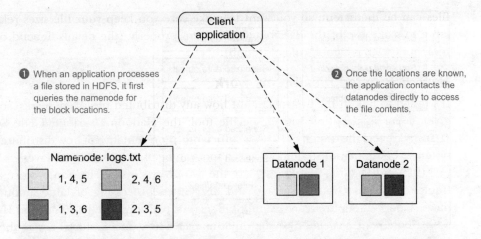

Figure 4.3 Clients communicate with the namenode to determine which datanodes hold the blocks for the desired file.

Distributing a file in this way across many nodes allows it to be easily processed in parallel. When a program needs to access a file stored in HDFS, it contacts the namenode to determine which datanodes host the file contents. This process is illustrated in figure 4.3.

Additionally, with each block replicated across multiple nodes, your data remains available even when individual nodes are offline. Of course, there are limits to this fault tolerance: if you have a replication factor of three, three nodes go down at once, and you're storing millions of blocks, chances are that some blocks happened to exist on exactly those three nodes and will be unavailable.

Implementing a distributed filesystem is a difficult task, but you've now learned what's important from a user perspective. To summarize, these are the important things to know:

- Files are spread across multiple machines for scalability and also to enable parallel processing.
- File blocks are replicated across multiple nodes for fault tolerance.

Let's now explore how to store a master dataset using a distributed filesystem.

4.4 Storing a master dataset with a distributed filesystem

Distributed filesystems vary in the kinds of operations they permit. Some distributed filesystems let you modify existing files, and others don't. Some allow you to append to existing files, and some don't have that feature. In this section we'll look at how you can store a master dataset on a distributed filesystem with only the most bare-boned of features, where a file can't be modified at all after being created.

Clearly, with unmodifiable files you can't store the entire master dataset in a single file. What you can do instead is spread the master dataset among many files, and store

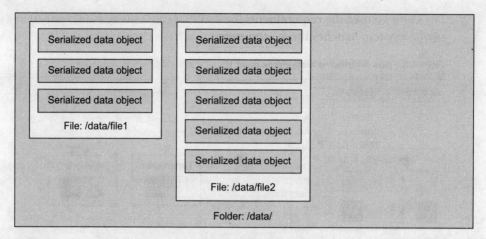

Figure 4.4   Spreading the master dataset throughout many files

all those files in the same folder. Each file would contain many serialized data objects, as illustrated in figure 4.4.

To append to the master dataset, you simply add a new file containing the new data objects to the master dataset folder, as is shown in figure 4.5.

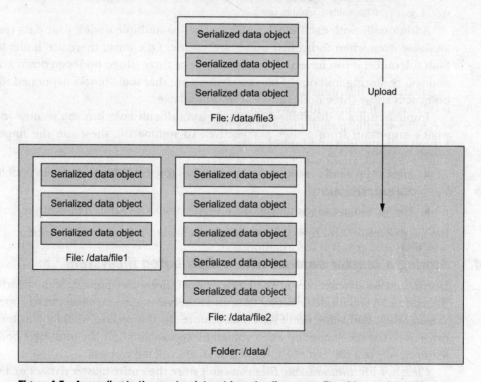

Figure 4.5   Appending to the master dataset by uploading a new file with new data records

Let's now go over the requirements for master dataset storage and verify that a distributed filesystem matches those requirements. This is shown in table 4.2.

Table 4.2 How distributed filesystems meet the storage requirement checklist

Operation	Requisite	Discussion
Write	Efficient appends of new data	Appending new data is as simple as adding a new file to the folder containing the master dataset.
	Scalable storage	Distributed filesystems evenly distribute the storage across a cluster of machines. You increase storage space and I/O throughput by adding more machines.
Read	Support for parallel processing	Distributed filesystems spread all data across many machines, making it possible to parallelize the processing across many machines. Distributed filesystems typically integrate with computation frameworks like MapReduce to make that processing easy to do (discussed in chapter 6).
Both	Tunable storage and processing costs	Just like regular filesystems, you have full control over how you store your data units within the files. You choose the file format for your data as well as the level of compression. You're free to do individual record compression, block-level compression, or neither.
	Enforceable immutability	Distributed filesystems typically have the same permissions systems you're used to using in regular filesystems. To enforce immutability, you can disable the ability to modify or delete files in the master dataset folder for the user with which your application runs. This redundant check will protect your previously existing data against bugs or other human mistakes.

At a high level, distributed filesystems are straightforward and a natural fit for the master dataset. Of course, like any tool they have their quirks, and these are discussed in the following illustration chapter. But it turns out that there's a little more you can exploit with the files and folders abstraction to improve storage of the master dataset, so let's now talk about using folders to enable vertical partitioning.

4.5   Vertical partitioning

Although the batch layer is built to run functions on the entire dataset, many computations don't require looking at all the data. For example, you may have a computation that only requires information collected during the past two weeks. The batch storage should allow you to partition your data so that a function only accesses data relevant to its computation. This process is called *vertical partitioning*, and it can greatly contribute to making the batch layer more efficient. While it's not strictly necessary for the batch layer, as the batch layer is capable of looking at all the data at once and filtering out what it doesn't need, vertical partitioning enables large performance gains, so it's important to know how to use the technique.

Vertically partitioning data on a distributed filesystem can be done by sorting your data into separate folders. For example, suppose you're storing login information on a

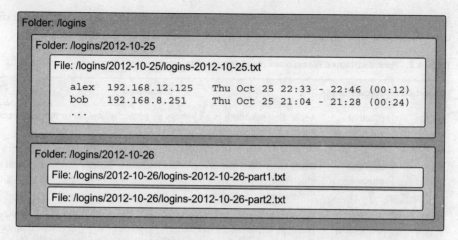

Figure 4.6   A vertical partitioning scheme for login data. By sorting information for each date in separate folders, a function can select only the folders containing data relevant to its computation.

distributed filesystem. Each login contains a username, IP address, and timestamp. To vertically partition by day, you can create a separate folder for each day of data. Each day folder would have many files containing the logins for that day. This is illustrated in figure 4.6.

Now if you only want to look at a particular subset of your dataset, you can just look at the files in those particular folders and ignore the other files.

4.6   *Low-level nature of distributed filesystems*

While distributed filesystems provide the storage and fault-tolerance properties you need for storing a master dataset, you'll find using their APIs directly too low-level for the tasks you need to run. We'll illustrate this using regular Unix filesystem operations and show the difficulties you can get into when doing tasks like appending to a master dataset or vertically partitioning a master dataset.

Let's start with appending to a master dataset. Suppose your master dataset is in the folder /master and you have a folder of data in /new-data that you want to put inside your master dataset. Suppose the data in the folders is contained in files, as shown in figure 4.7.

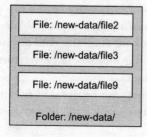

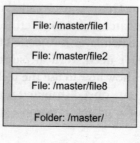

Figure 4.7   An example of a folder of data you may want to append to a master dataset. It's possible for filenames to overlap.

The most obvious thing to try is something like the following pseudo-code:

```
foreach file : "/new-data"
  mv file "/master/"
```

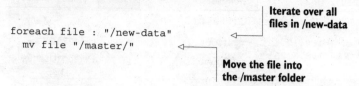

**Iterate over all
files in /new-data**

**Move the file into
the /master folder**

Unfortunately, this code has serious problems. If the master dataset folder contains any files of the same name, then the mv operation will fail. To do it correctly, you have to be sure you rename the file to a random filename and so avoid conflicts.

There's another problem. One of the core requirements of storage for the master dataset is the ability to tune the trade-offs between storage costs and processing costs. When storing a master dataset on a distributed filesystem, you choose a file format and compression format that makes the trade-off you desire. What if the files in /new-data are of a different format than in /master? Then the mv operation won't work at all—you instead need to copy the records out of /new-data and into a brand new file with the file format used in /master.

Let's now take a look at doing the same operation but with a vertically partitioned master dataset. Suppose now /new-data and /master look like figure 4.8.

Just putting the files from /new-data into the root of /master is wrong because it wouldn't respect the vertical partitioning of /master. Either the append operation should be disallowed—because /new-data isn't correctly vertically partitioned—or /new-data should be vertically partitioned as part of the append operation. But when you're just using a files-and-folders API directly, it's very easy to make a mistake and break the vertical partitioning constraints of a dataset.

All the operations and checks that need to happen to get these operations working correctly strongly indicate that files and folders are too low-level of an abstraction for manipulating datasets. In the following illustration chapter, you'll see an example of a library that automates these operations.

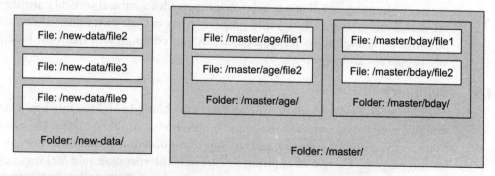

Figure 4.8   If the target dataset is vertically partitioned, appending data to it is not as simple as just adding files to the dataset folder.

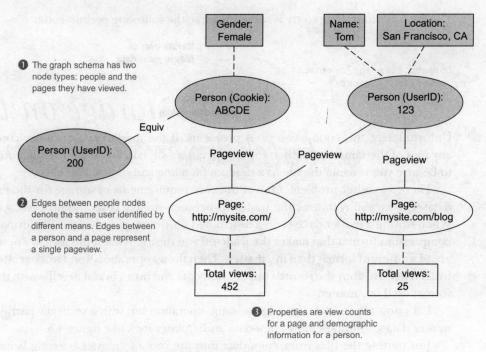

❶ The graph schema has two node types: people and the pages they have viewed.

❷ Edges between people nodes denote the same user identified by different means. Edges between a person and a page represent a single pageview.

❸ Properties are view counts for a page and demographic information for a person.

Figure 4.9   The graph schema for SuperWebAnalytics.com

4.7   *Storing the SuperWebAnalytics.com master dataset on a distributed filesystem*

Let's now look at how you can make use of a distributed filesystem to store the master dataset for SuperWebAnalytics.com.

When you last left this project, you had created a graph schema to represent the dataset. Every edge and property is represented via its own independent `DataUnit`. Figure 4.9 recaps what the graph schema looks like.

A key observation is that a graph schema provides a natural vertical partitioning of the data. You can store all edge and property types in their own folders. Vertically partitioning the data this way lets you efficiently run computations that only look at certain properties and edges.

4.8   Summary

The high-level requirements for storing data in the Lambda Architecture batch layer are straightforward. You observed that these requirements could be mapped to a required checklist for a storage solution, and you saw that a distributed filesystem is a natural fit for this purpose. Using and applying a distributed filesystem should feel very familiar.

In the next chapter you'll see how to handle the nitty-gritty details of using a distributed filesystem in practice, and how to deal with the low-level nature of files and folders with a higher-level abstraction.

Data storage on the batch layer: Illustration

This chapter covers

- Using the Hadoop Distributed File System (HDFS)
- Pail, a higher-level abstraction for manipulating datasets

In the last chapter you saw the requirements for storing a master dataset and how a distributed filesystem is a great fit for those requirements. But you also saw how using a filesystem API directly felt way too low-level for the kinds of operations you need to do on the master dataset. In this chapter we'll show you how to use a specific distributed filesystem—HDFS—and then show how to automate the tasks you need to do with a higher-level API.

Like all illustration chapters, we'll focus on specific tools to show the nitty-gritty of applying the higher-level concepts of the previous chapter. As always, our goal is not to compare and contrast all the possible tools but to reinforce the higher-level concepts.

5.1   *Using the Hadoop Distributed File System*

You've already learned the basics of how HDFS works. Let's quickly review those:

- Files are split into blocks that are spread among many nodes in the cluster.
- Blocks are replicated among many nodes so the data is still available even when machines go down.
- The namenode keeps track of the blocks for each file and where those blocks are stored.

Getting started with Hadoop

Setting up Hadoop can be an arduous task. Hadoop has numerous configuration parameters that should be tuned for your hardware to perform optimally. To avoid getting bogged down in details, we recommend downloading a preconfigured virtual machine for your first encounter with Hadoop. A virtual machine will accelerate your learning of HDFS and MapReduce, and you'll have a better understanding when setting up your own cluster.

At the time of this writing, Hadoop vendors Cloudera, Hortonworks, and MapR all have images publicly available. We recommend having access to Hadoop so you can follow along with the examples in this and later chapters.

Let's take a look at using HDFS's API to manipulate files and folders. Suppose you wanted to store all logins on a server. Following are some example logins:

```
$ cat logins-2012-10-25.txt
alex      192.168.12.125   Thu Oct 25 22:33 - 22:46 (00:12)
bob       192.168.8.251    Thu Oct 25 21:04 - 21:28 (00:24)
charlie   192.168.12.82    Thu Oct 25 21:02 - 23:14 (02:12)
doug      192.168.8.13     Thu Oct 25 20:30 - 21:03 (00:33)
...
```

To store this data on HDFS, you can create a directory for the dataset and upload the file:

```
$ hadoop fs -mkdir /logins
$ hadoop fs -put logins-2012-10-25.txt /logins
```

> The "hadoop fs" commands are Hadoop shell commands that interact directly with HDFS. A full list is available at http://hadoop.apache.org/.

> Uploading a file automatically chunks and distributes the blocks across the datanodes.

You can list the directory contents:

```
$ hadoop fs -ls -R /logins
-rw-r--r--   3 hdfs hadoop  175802352 2012-10-26 01:38
    /logins/logins-2012-10-25.txt
```

> The ls command is based on the Unix command of the same name.

And you can verify the contents of the file:

```
$ hadoop fs -cat /logins/logins-2012-10-25.txt
alex      192.168.12.125    Thu Oct 25 22:33 - 22:46 (00:12)
bob       192.168.8.251     Thu Oct 25 21:04 - 21:28 (00:24)
...
```

As we mentioned earlier, the file was automatically chunked into blocks and distributed among the datanodes when it was uploaded. You can identify the blocks and their locations through the following command:

```
$ hadoop fsck /logins/logins-2012-10-25.txt  -files -blocks -locations

/logins/logins-2012-10-25.txt 175802352 bytes, 2 block(s):    ◄──┐ The file is stored
OK                                                                │ in two blocks.
0. blk_-1821909382043065392_1523 len=134217728
   repl=3 [10.100.0.249:50010, 10.100.1.4:50010, 10.100.0.252:50010]
1. blk_2733341693279525583_1524 len=41584624
   repl=3 [10.100.0.255:50010, 10.100.1.2:50010, 10.100.1.5:50010]
```
The IP addresses and port numbers
of the datanodes hosting each block

5.1.1 The small-files problem

Hadoop HDFS and MapReduce are tightly integrated to form a framework for storing and processing large amounts of data. We'll discuss MapReduce in detail in the following chapters, but a characteristic of Hadoop is that computing performance is significantly degraded when data is stored in many small files in HDFS. There can be an order of magnitude difference in performance between a MapReduce job that consumes 10 GB stored in many small files versus a job processing that same data stored in a few large files.

The reason is that a MapReduce job launches multiple tasks, one for each block in the input dataset. Each task requires some overhead to plan and coordinate its execution, and because each small file requires a separate task, the cost is repeatedly incurred. This property of MapReduce means you'll want to consolidate your data should small files become abundant within your dataset. You can achieve this either by writing code that uses the HDFS API or by using a custom MapReduce job, but both approaches require considerable work and knowledge of Hadoop internals.

5.1.2 Towards a higher-level abstraction

It's an important emphasis of this book that solutions be not only scalable, fault-tolerant, and performant, but *elegant* as well. One part of a solution being elegant is that it must be able to express the computations you care about in a concise manner.

When it comes to manipulating a master dataset, you saw in the last chapter the following two important operations:

- Appending to a dataset
- Vertically partitioning a dataset and not allowing an existing partitioning to be violated

In addition to these requirements, we'll add an HDFS-specific requirement: efficiently consolidating small files together into larger files.

As you saw in the last chapter, accomplishing these tasks with files and folders directly is tedious and error-prone. So we'll present a library for accomplishing these tasks in an elegant manner.

In contrast to the code that used the HDFS API, consider the following listing, which uses the Pail library.

Listing 5.1   Abstractions of HDFS maintenance tasks

```java
import java.io.IOException;
import backtype.hadoop.pail.Pail;

public class PailMove {

  public static void mergeData(String masterDir, String updateDir)
    throws IOException
  {
    Pail target = new Pail(masterDir);
    Pail source = new Pail(updateDir);
    target.absorb(source);
    target.consolidate();
  }
}
```

Pails are wrappers around HDFS folders.

With the Pail library, appends are one-line operations.

Small data files within the pail can also be consolidated with a single function call.

With Pail, you can append folders in one line of code and consolidate small files in another. When appending, if the data of the target folder is of a different file format, Pail will automatically coerce the new data to the correct file format. If the target folder has a different vertical partitioning scheme, Pail will throw an exception. Most importantly, a higher-level abstraction like Pail allows you to work with your data directly rather than using low-level containers like files and directories.

A QUICK RECAP

Before you learn more about Pail, now is a good time to step back and regain the bigger perspective. Recall that the master dataset is the source of truth within the Lambda Architecture, and as such the batch layer must handle a large, growing dataset without fail. Furthermore, there must be an easy and effective means of transforming the data into batch views to answer actual queries.

This chapter is more technical than the previous ones, but always keep in mind how everything integrates within the Lambda Architecture.

5.2   *Data storage in the batch layer with Pail*

Pail is a thin abstraction over files and folders from the dfs-datastores library (http://github.com/nathanmarz/dfs-datastores). This abstraction makes it significantly easier to manage a collection of records for batch processing. As the name suggests, Pail uses *pails*, folders that keep metadata about the dataset. By using this metadata, Pail allows you to safely act on the batch layer without worrying about violating its integrity. The goal of Pail is simply to make the operations you care about—appending to a dataset, vertical partitioning, and consolidation—safe, easy, and performant.

Under the hood, Pail is just a Java library that uses the standard Hadoop APIs. It handles the low-level filesystem interaction, providing an API that isolates you from the complexity of Hadoop's internals. The intent is to allow you to focus on the data itself instead of concerning yourself with how it's stored and maintained.

Why the focus on Pail?

Pail, along with many other packages covered in this book, was written by Nathan while developing the Lambda Architecture. We introduce these technologies not to promote them, but to discuss the context of their origins and the problems they solve. Because Pail was developed by Nathan, it perfectly matches the requirements of the master dataset as laid out so far, and those requirements naturally emerge from the first principles of queries as a function of all data. Feel free to use other libraries or to develop your own—our emphasis is to show a specific way to bridge the concepts of building Big Data systems with the available tooling.

You've already seen the characteristics of HDFS that make it a viable choice for storing the master dataset in the batch layer. As you explore Pail, keep in mind how it preserves the advantages of HDFS while streamlining operations on the data. After we've covered the basic operations of Pail, we'll summarize the overall value provided by the library.

Now let's dive right in and see how Pail works by creating and writing data to a pail.

5.2.1 Basic Pail operations

The best way to understand how Pail works is to follow along and run the presented code on your computer. To do this, you'll need to download the source from GitHub and build the dfs-datastores library. If you don't have a Hadoop cluster or virtual machine available, your local filesystem will be treated as HDFS in the examples. You'll then be able to see the results of these commands by inspecting the relevant directories on your filesystem.

Let's start off by creating a new pail and storing some data:

```
public static void simpleIO() throws IOException {
    Pail pail = Pail.create("/tmp/mypail");
    TypedRecordOutputStream os = pail.openWrite();
    os.writeObject(new byte[] {1, 2, 3});
    os.writeObject(new byte[] {1, 2, 3, 4});
    os.writeObject(new byte[] {1, 2, 3, 4, 5});
    os.close();
}
```

Provides an output stream to a new file in the Pail

Creates a default pail in the specified directory

A pail without metadata is limited to storing byte arrays.

Closes the current file

When you check your filesystem, you'll see that a folder for /tmp/mypail was created and contains two files:

```
root:/ $ ls /tmp/mypail
f2fa3af0-5592-43e0-a29c-fb6b056af8a0.pailfile
pail.meta
```

> **The records are stored within pailfiles.**

> **The metadata describes the contents and structure of the pail.**

The pailfile contains the records you just stored. The file is created atomically, so all the records you created will appear at once—that is, an application that reads from the pail won't see the file until the writer closes it. Furthermore, pailfiles use globally unique names (so it'll be named differently on your filesystem). These unique names allow multiple sources to write concurrently to the same pail without conflict.

The other file in the directory contains the pail's metadata. This metadata describes the type of the data as well as how it's stored within the pail. The example didn't specify any metadata when constructing the pail, so this file contains the default settings:

```
root:/ $ cat /tmp/mypail/pail.meta
---
format: SequenceFile
args: {}
```

> **The format of files in the pail; a default pail stores data in key/value pairs within Hadoop SequenceFiles.**

> **The arguments describe the contents of the pail; an empty map directs Pail to treat the data as uncompressed byte arrays.**

Later in the chapter you'll see another pail.meta file containing more-substantial metadata, but the overall structure will remain the same. We'll next cover how to store real objects in Pail, not just binary records.

5.2.2   Serializing objects into pails

To store objects within a pail, you must provide Pail with instructions for serializing and deserializing your objects to and from binary data. Let's return to the server log-ins example to demonstrate how this is done.

The following listing has a simplified class to represent a login.

Listing 5.2   A no-frills class for logins

```
public class Login {
  public String userName;
  public long loginUnixTime;

  public Login(String _user, long _login) {
    userName = _user;
    loginUnixTime = _login;
  }
}
```

To store these Login objects in a pail, you need to create a class that implements the PailStructure interface. The next listing defines a LoginPailStructure that describes how serialization should be performed.

Listing 5.3 Implementing the PailStructure interface

```
public class LoginPailStructure implements PailStructure<Login>{

  public Class getType() {
    return Login.class;
  }

  public byte[] serialize(Login login) {
    ByteArrayOutputStream byteOut = new ByteArrayOutputStream();
    DataOutputStream dataOut = new DataOutputStream(byteOut);
    byte[] userBytes = login.userName.getBytes();
    try {
      dataOut.writeInt(userBytes.length);
      dataOut.write(userBytes);
      dataOut.writeLong(login.loginUnixTime);
      dataOut.close();
    } catch(IOException e) {
      throw new RuntimeException(e);
    }
    return byteOut.toByteArray();
  }

  public Login deserialize(byte[] serialized) {
    DataInputStream dataIn =
        new DataInputStream(new ByteArrayInputStream(serialized));
    try {
      byte[] userBytes = new byte[dataIn.readInt()];
      dataIn.read(userBytes);
      return new Login(new String(userBytes), dataIn.readLong());
    } catch(IOException e) {
      throw new RuntimeException(e);
    }
  }

  public List<String> getTarget(Login object) {
    return Collections.EMPTY_LIST;
  }

  public boolean isValidTarget(String... dirs) {
    return true;
  }
}
```

A pail with this structure will only store Login objects.

Login objects must be serialized when stored in pailfiles.

Logins are later reconstructed when read from pailfiles.

The getTarget method defines the vertical partitioning scheme, but it's not used in this example.

isValidTarget determines whether the given path matches the vertical partitioning scheme, but it's also not used in this example.

By passing this LoginPailStructure to the Pail create function, the resulting pail will use these serialization instructions. You can then give it Login objects directly, and Pail will handle the serialization automatically.

```
public static void writeLogins() throws IOException {
    Pail<Login> loginPail = Pail.create("/tmp/logins",
                                   new LoginPailStructure());
    TypedRecordOutputStream out = loginPail.openWrite();
    out.writeObject(new Login("alex", 1352679231));
    out.writeObject(new Login("bob", 1352674216));
    out.close();
}
```

Creates a pail with the new pail structure

Likewise, when you read the data, Pail will deserialize the records for you. Here's how you can iterate through all the objects you just wrote:

A pail supports the Iterable interface for its object type.

```
public static void readLogins() throws IOException {
    Pail<Login> loginPail = new Pail<Login>("/tmp/logins");
    for(Login l : loginPail) {
        System.out.println(l.userName + " " + l.loginUnixTime);
    }
}
```

Once your data is stored within a pail, you can use Pail's built-in operations to safely act on it.

5.2.3   *Batch operations using Pail*

Pail has built-in support for a number of common operations. These operations are where you'll see the benefits of managing your records with Pail rather than doing it manually. The operations are all implemented using MapReduce, so they scale regardless of the amount of data in your pail, whether gigabytes or terabytes. We'll talk about MapReduce a lot more in later chapters, but the key takeaway is that the operations are automatically parallelized and executed across a cluster of worker machines.

In the previous section we discussed the importance of append and consolidate operations. As you'd expect, Pail has support for both. The append operation is particularly smart. It checks the pails to verify that it's valid to append the pails together. For example, it won't allow you to append a pail containing strings to a pail containing integers. If the pails store the same type of records but in different file formats, it coerces the data to match the format of the target pail. This means the trade-off you decided on between storage costs and processing performance will be enforced for that pail.

By default, the consolidate operation merges small files to create new files that are as close to 128 MB as possible—a standard HDFS block size. This operation also parallelizes itself via MapReduce.

For our logins example, suppose you had additional logins in a separate pail and wanted to merge the data into the original pail. The following code performs both the append and consolidate operations:

```
public static void appendData() throws IOException {
    Pail<Login> loginPail = new Pail<Login>("/tmp/logins");
    Pail<Login> updatePail = new Pail<Login>("/tmp/updates");
```

```
    loginPail.absorb(updatePail);
    loginPail.consolidate();
}
```

The major upstroke is that these built-in functions let you focus on what you want to do with your data rather than worry about how to manipulate files correctly.

5.2.4 *Vertical partitioning with Pail*

We mentioned earlier that you can vertically partition your data in HDFS by using multiple folders. Imagine trying to manage the vertical partitioning manually. It's all too easy to forget that two datasets are partitioned differently and mistakenly append them. Similarly, it wouldn't be hard to accidentally violate the partitioning structure when consolidating your data. Thankfully, Pail is smart about enforcing the structure of a pail and protects you from making these kinds of mistakes.

To create a partitioned directory structure for a pail, you must implement two additional methods of the `PailStructure` interface:

- `getTarget`—Given a record, `getTarget` determines the directory structure where the record should be stored and returns the path as a list of `Strings`.
- `isValidTarget`—Given an array of `Strings`, `isValidTarget` builds a directory path and determines if it's consistent with the vertical partitioning scheme.

Pail uses these methods to enforce its structure and automatically map records to their correct subdirectories.

The following code demonstrates how to partition `Login` objects so that records are grouped by the login date.

Listing 5.4 A vertical partitioning scheme for `Login` records

```
public class PartitionedLoginPailStructure extends LoginPailStructure {
    SimpleDateFormat formatter = new SimpleDateFormat("yyyy-MM-dd");

    public List<String> getTarget(Login object) {
        ArrayList<String> directoryPath = new ArrayList<String>();
        Date date = new Date(object.loginUnixTime * 1000L);
        directoryPath.add(formatter.format(date));
        return directoryPath;
    }

    public boolean isValidTarget(String... strings) {
        if(strings.length != 1) return false;
        try {
            return (formatter.parse(strings[0]) != null);
        }
        catch(ParseException e) {
            return false;
        }
    }
}
```

Logins are vertically partitioned in folders corresponding to the login date.

The timestamp of the Login object is converted to an understandable form.

isValidTarget verifies that the directory structure has a depth of one and that the folder name is a date.

With this new pail structure, Pail determines the correct subfolder whenever it writes a new Login object:

```
public static void partitionData() throws IOException {
  Pail<Login> pail = Pail.create("/tmp/partitioned_logins",
                       new PartitionedLoginPailStructure());
  TypedRecordOutputStream os = pail.openWrite();
  os.writeObject(new Login("chris", 1352702020));
  os.writeObject(new Login("david", 1352788472));
  os.close();
}
```

1352702020 is the timestamp for 2012-11-11, 22:33:40 PST.

1352788472 is the timestamp for 2012-11-12, 22:34:32 PST.

Examining this new pail directory confirms the data was partitioned correctly:

```
root:/ $ ls -R /tmp/partitioned_logins
2012-11-11   2012-11-12   pail.meta

/tmp/partitioned_logins/2012-11-11:
d8c0822b-6caf-4516-9c74-24bf805d565c.pailfile

/tmp/partitioned_logins/2012-11-12:
d8c0822b-6caf-4516-9c74-24bf805d565c.pailfile
```

Folders for the different login dates are created within the pail.

5.2.5 *Pail file formats and compression*

Pail stores data in multiple files within its directory structure. You can control how Pail stores records in those files by specifying the file format Pail should be using. This lets you control the trade-off between the amount of storage space Pail uses and the performance of reading records from Pail. As discussed earlier in the chapter, this is a fundamental control you need to dial up or down to match your application needs.

You can implement your own custom file format, but by default Pail uses Hadoop SequenceFiles. This format is very widely used, allows an individual file to be processed in parallel via MapReduce, and has native support for compressing the records in the file.

To demonstrate these options, here's how to create a pail that uses the Sequence-File format with gzip block compression:

Contents of the pail will be gzip compressed.

```
public static void createCompressedPail() throws IOException {
  Map<String, Object> options = new HashMap<String, Object>();
  options.put(SequenceFileFormat.CODEC_ARG,
              SequenceFileFormat.CODEC_ARG_GZIP);
  options.put(SequenceFileFormat.TYPE_ARG,
              SequenceFileFormat.TYPE_ARG_BLOCK);
  LoginPailStructure struct = new LoginPailStructure();
  Pail compressed = Pail.create("/tmp/compressed",
                      new PailSpec("SequenceFile", options, struct));
}
```

Blocks of records will be compressed together (as compared to compressing rows individually).

Creates a new pail to store Login options with the desired format

You can then observe these properties in the pail's metadata.

```
root:/ $ cat /tmp/compressed/pail.meta
---
format: SequenceFile
structure: manning.LoginPailStructure   ◄──── The full class name of
args:                                          the LoginPailStructure
  compressionCodec: gzip      ◄────
  compressionType: block         The compression
                                 options for the pailfiles
```

Whenever records are added to this pail, they'll be automatically compressed. This pail will use significantly less space but will have a higher CPU cost for reading and writing records.

5.2.6 Summarizing the benefits of Pail

Having invested the time probing the inner workings of Pail, it's important to understand the benefits it provides over raw HDFS. Table 5.1 summarizes the impact of Pail in regard to our earlier checklist of batch layer storage requirements.

Table 5.1 The advantages of Pail for storing the master dataset

Operation	Criteria	Discussion
Write	Efficient appends of new data	Pail has a first-class interface for appending data and prevents you from performing invalid operations—something the raw HDFS API won't do for you.
	Scalable storage	The namenode holds the entire HDFS namespace in memory and can be taxed if the filesystem contains a vast number of small files. Pail's consolidate operator decreases the total number of HDFS blocks and eases the demand on the namenode.
Read	Support for parallel processing	The number of tasks in a MapReduce job is determined by the number of blocks in the dataset. Consolidating the contents of a pail lowers the number of required tasks and increases the efficiency of processing the data.
	Ability to vertically partition data	Output written into a pail is automatically partitioned with each fact stored in its appropriate directory. This directory structure is strictly enforced for all Pail operations.
Both	Tunable storage/ processing costs	Pail has built-in support to coerce data into the format specified by the pail structure. This coercion occurs automatically while performing operations on the pail.
	Enforceable immutability	Because Pail is just a thin wrapper around files and folders, you can enforce immutability, just as you can with HDFS directly, by setting the appropriate permissions.

That concludes our whirlwind tour of Pail. It's a useful and powerful abstraction for interacting with your data in the batch layer, while isolating you from the details of the underlying filesystem.

5.3   *Storing the master dataset for SuperWebAnalytics.com*

You saw in the last chapter how straightforward the high-level concepts are for storing the SuperWebAnalytics.com data: use a distributed filesystem and vertically partition by storing different properties and edges in different subfolders. Let's now make use of the tools you've learned about to make this a reality.

Recall the Thrift schema we developed for SuperWebAnalytics.com. Here's an excerpt of the schema:

All facts in the dataset are represented as a timestamp and a base unit of data.

```
struct Data {
    1: required Pedigree pedigree;
    2: required DataUnit dataunit;
}
```

The fundamental data unit describes the edges and properties of the dataset.

```
union DataUnit {
    1: PersonProperty person_property;
    2: PageProperty page_property;
    3: EquivEdge equiv;
    4: PageViewEdge page_view;
}
```

Property value can be of multiple types.

```
union PersonPropertyValue {
    1: string full_name;
    2: GenderType gender;
    3: Location location;
}
```

How we want to map this schema to folders is shown in figure 5.1.

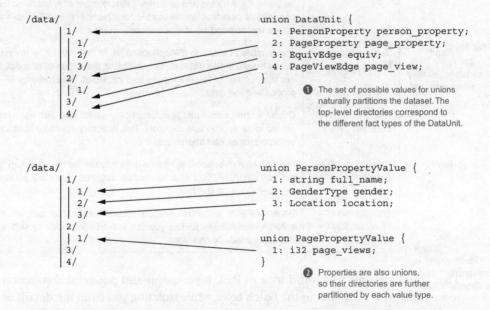

Figure 5.1   **The unions within a graph schema provide a natural vertical partitioning scheme for a dataset.**

To use HDFS and Pail for SuperWebAnalytics.com, you must define a structured pail to store `Data` objects that also enforces this vertical partitioning scheme. This code is a bit involved, so we'll present it in steps:

1 First, you'll create an abstract pail structure for storing Thrift objects. Thrift serialization is independent of the type of data being stored, and the code is cleaner by separating this logic.

2 Next, you'll derive a pail structure from the abstract class for storing SuperWeb-Analytics.com `Data` objects.

3 Finally, you'll define a further subclass that will implement the desired vertical partitioning scheme.

Throughout this section, don't worry about the details of the code. What matters is that this code works for any graph schema, and it continues to work even as the schema evolves over time.

5.3.1 A structured pail for Thrift objects

Creating a pail structure for Thrift objects is surprisingly easy because Thrift does the heavy lifting for you. The following listing demonstrates how to use Thrift utilities to serialize and deserialize your data.

> **Listing 5.5 A generic abstract pail structure for serializing `Thrift` objects**

Java generics allow the pail structure to be used for any Thrift object.

```
public abstract class ThriftPailStructure<T extends Comparable>
    implements PailStructure<T>
{
    private transient TSerializer ser;
    private transient TDeserializer des;
```

TSerializer and TDeserializer are Thrift utilities for serializing objects to and from binary arrays.

The Thrift utilities are lazily built, constructed only when required.

```
    private TSerializer getSerializer() {
        if(ser==null) ser = new TSerializer();
        return ser;
    }

    private TDeserializer getDeserializer() {
        if(des==null) des = new TDeserializer();
        return des;
    }
```

The object is cast to a basic Thrift object for serialization.

```
    public byte[] serialize(T obj) {
        try {
            return getSerializer().serialize((TBase)obj);
        } catch (TException e) {
            throw new RuntimeException(e);
        }
    }
```

A new Thrift object is constructed prior to deserialization.

```
    public T deserialize(byte[] record) {
        T ret = createThriftObject();
        try {
```

```
                   getDeserializer().deserialize((TBase)ret, record);
               } catch (TException e) {
                   throw new RuntimeException(e);
               }
               return ret;
           }

           protected abstract T createThriftObject();       ◄───┐
       }
```

> The constructor of the Thrift object must be implemented in the child class.

5.3.2   A basic pail for SuperWebAnalytics.com

Next, you can define a basic class for storing SuperWebAnalytics.com `Data` objects by creating a concrete subclass of `ThriftPailStructure`, shown next.

Listing 5.6   A concrete implementation for `Data` objects

```
       public class DataPailStructure extends ThriftPailStructure<Data> {
           public Class getType() {
               return Data.class;
           }

           protected Data createThriftObject() {    ◄───
               return new Data();
           }

           public List<String> getTarget(Data object) {    ◄───
               return Collections.EMPTY_LIST;
           }

           public boolean isValidTarget(String... dirs) {
               return true;
           }
       }
```

> Specifies that the pail stores Data objects

> Needed by ThriftPailStructure to create an object for deserialization

> This pail structure doesn't use vertical partitioning.

5.3.3   A split pail to vertically partition the dataset

The last step is to create a pail structure that implements the vertical partitioning strategy for a graph schema. It's also the most involved step. All of the following snippets are extracted from the `SplitDataPailStructure` class that accomplishes this task.

At a high level, the `SplitDataPailStructure` code inspects the `DataUnit` class to create a map between Thrift IDs and classes to process the corresponding type. Figure 5.2 demonstrates this map for SuperWebAnalytics.com.

```
union DataUnit {
  1: PersonProperty person_property;          Map<Short, FieldStructure>
  2: PageProperty page_property;               {{1: PropertyStructure},
  3: EquivEdge equiv;                           {2: PropertyStructure},
  4: PageViewEdge page_view;                    {3: EdgeStructure},
}                                               {4: EdgeStructure}}
```

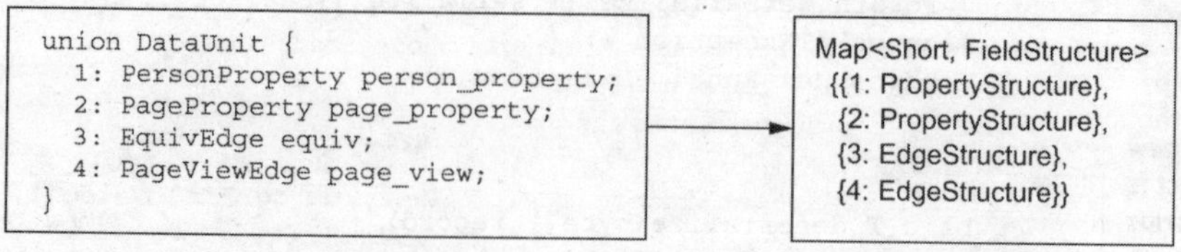

Figure 5.2   The `SplitDataPailStructure` field map for the `DataUnit` class of SuperWebAnalytics.com

The next listing contains the code that generates the field map. It works for any graph schema, not just this example.

Listing 5.7 Code to generate the field map for a graph schema

```java
public class SplitDataPailStructure extends DataPailStructure {

    public static HashMap<Short, FieldStructure> validFieldMap =
        new HashMap<Short, FieldStructure>();

    static {
        for(DataUnit._Fields k: DataUnit.metaDataMap.keySet()) {
            FieldValueMetaData md = DataUnit.metaDataMap.get(k).valueMetaData;
            FieldStructure fieldStruct;
            if(md instanceof StructMetaData &&
               ((StructMetaData) md).structClass
                 .getName().endsWith("Property"))
            {
                fieldStruct = new PropertyStructure(
                    ((StructMetaData) md).structClass);
            } else {
                fieldStruct = new EdgeStructure();
            }
            validFieldMap.put(k.getThriftFieldId(), fieldStruct);
        }
    }

    // remainder of class elided
```

FieldStructure is an interface for both edges and properties.

Thrift code to inspect and iterate over the DataUnit object

Properties are identified by the class name of the inspected object.

If class name doesn't end with "Property", it must be an edge.

As mentioned in the code annotation, `FieldStructure` is an interface shared by both `PropertyStructure` and `EdgeStructure`. The definition of the interface is as follows:

```java
protected static interface FieldStructure {
    public boolean isValidTarget(String[] dirs);
    public void fillTarget(List<String> ret, Object val);
}
```

Later we'll provide the details for the `EdgeStructure` and `PropertyStructure` classes. For now, we're just looking at how this interface is used to accomplish the vertical partitioning of the table:

```java
// methods are from SplitDataPailStructure

public List<String> getTarget(Data object) {
    List<String> ret = new ArrayList<String>();
    DataUnit du = object.get_dataunit();
    short id = du.getSetField().getThriftFieldId();
    ret.add("" + id);
    validFieldMap.get(id).fillTarget(ret, du.getFieldValue());
    return ret;
}
```

The top-level directory is determined by inspecting the DataUnit.

Any further partitioning is passed to the FieldStructure.

The validity
check first
verifies the
DataUnit field
ID is in the
field map.

```
public boolean isValidTarget(String[] dirs) {
  if(dirs.length==0) return false;
  try {
    short id = Short.parseShort(dirs[0]);
    FieldStructure s = validFieldMap.get(id);
    if(s==null)
      return false;
    else
      return s.isValidTarget(dirs);
  } catch(NumberFormatException e) {
    return false;
  }
}
```

Any additional checks
are passed to the
FieldStructure.

The `SplitDataPailStructure` is responsible for the top-level directory of the vertical partitioning, and it passes the responsibility of any additional subdirectories to the `FieldStructure` classes. Therefore, once you define the `EdgeStructure` and `PropertyStructure` classes, your work will be done.

Edges are structs and hence cannot be further partitioned. This makes the `EdgeStructure` class trivial:

```
protected static class EdgeStructure implements FieldStructure {
  public boolean isValidTarget(String[] dirs) { return true; }
  public void fillTarget(List<String> ret, Object val) { }
}
```

But properties are unions, like the `DataUnit` class. The code similarly uses inspection to create a set of valid Thrift field IDs for the given property class. For completeness we provide the full listing of the class here, but the key points are the construction of the set and the use of this set in fulfilling the `FieldStructure` contract.

Listing 5.8 The `PropertyStructure` class

The set of
Thrift IDs of
the property
value types

Parses the Thrift
metadata to get
the field ID of the
property value

```
protected static class PropertyStructure implements FieldStructure {
  private TFieldIdEnum valueId;
  private HashSet<Short> validIds;

  public PropertyStructure(Class prop) {
    try {
      Map<TFieldIdEnum, FieldMetaData> propMeta = getMetadataMap(prop);
      Class valClass = Class.forName(prop.getName() + "Value");
      valueId = getIdForClass(propMeta, valClass);

      validIds = new HashSet<Short>();
      Map<TFieldIdEnum, FieldMetaData> valMeta
        = getMetadataMap(valClass);
      for(TFieldIdEnum valId: valMeta.keySet()) {
        validIds.add(valId.getThriftFieldId());
      }
    } catch(Exception e) {
      throw new RuntimeException(e);
    }
  }
```

A Property is a Thrift struct
containing a property value
field; this is the ID for that field.

Parses the
metadata to get
all valid field IDs
of the property
value

```
public boolean isValidTarget(String[] dirs) {
  if(dirs.length < 2) return false;        ⟵  The vertical
  try { 1((check))                              partitioning of a
    short s = Short.parseShort(dirs[1]);        property value has a
    return validIds.contains(s);                depth of at least two.
  } catch(NumberFormatException e) {
    return false;
  }
}

public void fillTarget(List<String> ret, Object val) {
  ret.add("" + ((TUnion) ((TBase)val)
    .getFieldValue(valueId))
    .getSetField()                          Uses the Thrift IDs to
    .getThriftFieldId());        ⟵          create the directory
  }                                         path for the current
}                                           fact

private static Map<TFieldIdEnum, FieldMetaData>
  getMetadataMap(Class c)                ⟵     getMetadataMap
{                                              and getIdForClass
  try {                                        are helper functions
    Object o = c.newInstance();                for inspecting Thrift
    return (Map) c.getField("metaDataMap").get(o);  objects.
  } catch (Exception e) {
    throw new RuntimeException(e);
  }
}

private static TFieldIdEnum getIdForClass(
  Map<TFieldIdEnum, FieldMetaData> meta, Class toFind)
{
  for(TFieldIdEnum k: meta.keySet()) {
    FieldValueMetaData md = meta.get(k).valueMetaData;
    if(md instanceof StructMetaData) {
      if(toFind.equals(((StructMetaData) md).structClass)) {
        return k;
      }
    }
  }

  throw new RuntimeException("Could not find " + toFind.toString() +
    " in " + meta.toString());
}
```

After that last bit of code, take a break—you've earned it. The good news is that this was a one-time cost. Once you've defined a pail structure for your master dataset, future interaction with the batch layer will be straightforward. Moreover, this code can be applied to any project where you've created a Thrift graph schema.

5.4   Summary

You learned that maintaining a dataset within HDFS involves the common tasks of appending new data to the master dataset, vertically partitioning data into many folders, and consolidating small files. You witnessed that accomplishing these tasks using the HDFS API directly is tedious and prone to human error.

You then were introduced to the Pail abstraction. Pail isolates you from the file formats and directory structure of HDFS, making it easy to do robust, enforced vertical partitioning and perform common operations on your dataset. Using the Pail abstraction ultimately takes very few lines of code. Vertical partitioning happens automatically, and tasks like appends and consolidation are simple one-liners. This means you can focus on how you want to process your records rather than on the details of how to store those records.

With HDFS and Pail, we've presented a way of storing the master dataset that meets all the requirements and is elegant to use. Whether you choose to use these tools or not, we hope we've set a bar for how elegant this piece of an architecture can be, and that you'll aim to achieve at least the same level of elegance.

In the next chapter you'll learn how to leverage the record storage to accomplish the next key step of the Lambda Architecture: computing batch views.

Batch layer

6

This chapter covers

- Computing functions on the batch layer
- Splitting a query into precomputed and on-the-fly components
- Recomputation versus incremental algorithms
- The meaning of scalability
- The MapReduce paradigm
- A higher-level way of thinking about MapReduce

The goal of a data system is to answer arbitrary questions about your data. Any question you could ask of your dataset can be implemented as a function that takes all of your data as input. Ideally, you could run these functions on the fly whenever you query your dataset. Unfortunately, a function that uses your entire dataset as input will take a very long time to run. You need a different strategy if you want your queries answered quickly.

In the Lambda Architecture, the batch layer precomputes the master dataset into batch views so that queries can be resolved with low latency. This requires striking a balance between what will be precomputed and what will be computed at execution time to complete the query. By doing a little bit of computation on the fly to complete queries, you save yourself from needing to precompute absurdly large batch views. The key is to precompute just enough information so that the query can be completed quickly.

In the last two chapters, you learned how to form a data model for your dataset and how to store your data in the batch layer in a scalable way. In this chapter you'll take the next step of learning how to compute arbitrary functions on that data. We'll start by introducing some motivating examples that we'll use to illustrate the concepts of computation on the batch layer. Then you'll learn in detail how to compute indexes of the master dataset that the application layer will use to complete queries. You'll examine the trade-offs between *recomputation algorithms*, the style of algorithm emphasized in the batch layer, and *incremental algorithms*, the kind of algorithms typically used with relational databases. You'll see what it means for the batch layer to be scalable, and then you'll learn about MapReduce, a paradigm for scalable and nearly arbitrary batch computation. You'll see that although MapReduce is a great primitive, it's quite a low-level abstraction. We'll finish things off by showing you a higher-level paradigm that can be executed via MapReduce.

6.1   *Motivating examples*

Let's consider some example queries to motivate the theoretical discussions in this chapter. These queries illustrate the concepts of batch computation—each example shows how you would compute the query as a function that takes the entire master dataset as input. Later you'll modify these implementations to use precomputation rather than execute them completely on the fly.

6.1.1   *Number of pageviews over time*

The first example query operates over a dataset of pageviews, where each pageview record contains a URL and timestamp. The goal of the query is to determine the total number of pageviews of a URL for a range given in hours.

This query can be written in pseudo-code like so:

```
function pageviewsOverTime(masterDataset, url, startHour, endHour) {
    pageviews = 0
    for(record in masterDataset) {
        if(record.url == url &&
           record.time >= startHour &&
           record.time <= endHour) {
           pageviews += 1
           }
    }
    return pageviews
}
```

To compute this query using a function of the entire dataset, you simply iterate through every record, and keep a counter of all the pageviews for that URL that fall within the specified range. After exhausting all the records, you then return the final value of the counter.

6.1.2 Gender inference

The next example query operates over a dataset of name records and predicts the likely gender for a person. The algorithm first performs semantic normalization on the names for the person, doing conversions like *Bob* to *Robert* and *Bill* to *William*. The algorithm then makes use of a model that provides the probability of a gender for each name.

The resulting inference algorithm looks like this:

Normalizes all names associated with the person ⟶

```
function genderInference(masterDataset, personId) {
    names = new Set()
    for(record in masterDataset) {
        if(record.personId == personId) {
            names.add(normalizeName(record.name))
        }
    }
    maleProbSum = 0.0                        ⟵  Averages each name's
    for(name in names) {                         probability of being male
        maleProbSum += maleProbabilityOfName(name)
    }
    malePrcb = maleProbSum / names.size()
    if(maleProb > 0.5) {        ⟵
        return "male"                Returns the gender with
    } else {                         the highest likelihood
        return "female"
    }
}
```

An interesting aspect of this query is that the results can change as the name normalization algorithm and name-to-gender model improve over time, and not just when new data is received.

6.1.3 Influence score

The final example operates over a Twitter-inspired dataset containing *reaction* records. Each reaction record contains `sourceId` and `responderId` fields, indicating that `responderId` retweeted or replied to `sourceId`'s post.

The query determines an *influencer* score for each person in the social network. The score is computed in two steps. First, the top influencer for each person is selected based on the number of reactions the influencer caused in that person. Then, someone's influence score is set to the number of people for which he or she was the top influencer.

The algorithm to determine a user's influence score is as follows:

```
function influence_score(masterDataset, personId) {    Computes amount of influence
    influence = new Map()                                between all pairs of people
    for(record in masterDataset) {      ⟵
        curr = influence.get(record.responderId) || new Map(default=0)
        curr[record.sourceId] += 1
```

```
        influence.set(record.sourceId, curr)
    }

    score = 0
    for(entry in influence) {
        if(topKey(entry.value) == personId) {
            score += 1
        }
    }
    return score
}
```

Counts the number of people for whom personId is the top influencer

In this code, the `topKey` function is mocked because it's straightforward to implement. Otherwise, the algorithm simply counts the number of reactions between each pair of people and then counts the number of people for whom the queried user is the top influencer.

6.2   *Computing on the batch layer*

Let's take a step back and review how the Lambda Architecture works at a high level. When processing queries, each layer in the Lambda Architecture has a key, complementary role, as shown in figure 6.1.

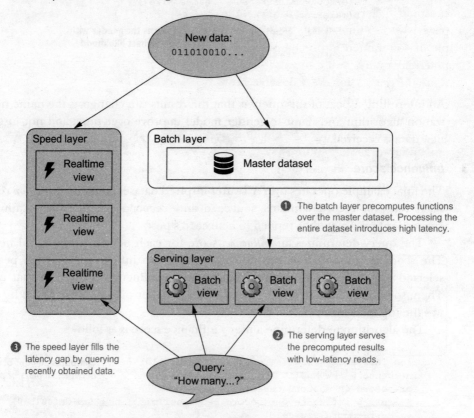

Figure 6.1   The roles of the Lambda Architecture layers in servicing queries on the dataset

The batch layer runs functions over the master dataset to precompute intermediate data called *batch views*. The batch views are loaded by the serving layer, which indexes them to allow rapid access to that data. The speed layer compensates for the high latency of the batch layer by providing low-latency updates using data that has yet to be precomputed into a batch view. Queries are then satisfied by processing data from the serving layer views and the speed layer views, and merging the results.

A linchpin of the architecture is that for *any* query, it's possible to precompute the data in the batch layer to expedite its processing by the serving layer. These precomputations over the master dataset take time, but you should view the high latency of the batch layer as an opportunity to do deep analyses of the data and connect diverse pieces of data together. Remember, low-latency query serving is achieved through other parts of the Lambda Architecture.

A naive strategy for computing on the batch layer would be to precompute all possible queries and cache the results in the serving layer. Such an approach is illustrated in figure 6.2.

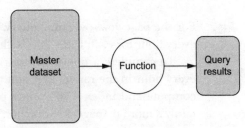

Unfortunately you can't always precompute *everything*. Consider the pageviews-over-time query as an example. If you wanted to precompute every potential query, you'd need to determine

Figure 6.2 Precomputing a query by running a function on the master dataset directly

mine the answer for every possible range of hours for every URL. But the number of ranges of hours within a given time frame can be huge. In a one-year period, there are approximately 380 million distinct hour ranges. To precompute the query, you'd need to precompute and index 380 million values *for every URL*. This is obviously infeasible and an unworkable solution.

Instead, you can precompute intermediate results and then use these results to complete queries on the fly, as shown in figure 6.3.

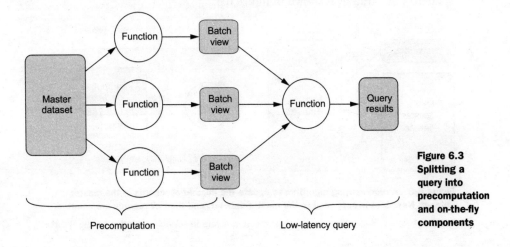

Figure 6.3 Splitting a query into precomputation and on-the-fly components

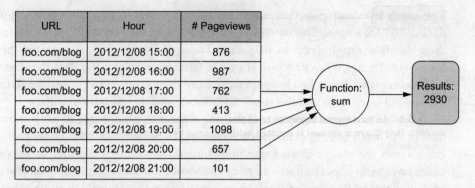

Figure 6.4   Computing the number of pageviews by querying an indexed batch view

For the pageviews-over-time query, you can precompute the number of pageviews for every hour for each URL. This is illustrated in figure 6.4.

To complete a query, you retrieve from the index the number of pageviews for every hour in the range, and sum the results. For a single year, you only need to precompute and index 8,760 values per URL (365 days, 24 hours per day). This is certainly a more manageable number.

6.3   *Recomputation algorithms vs. incremental algorithms*

Because your master dataset is continually growing, you must have a strategy for updating your batch views when new data becomes available. You could choose a *recomputation* algorithm, throwing away the old batch views and recomputing functions over the entire master dataset. Alternatively, an *incremental* algorithm will update the views directly when new data arrives.

As a basic example, consider a batch view containing the total number of records in your master dataset. A recomputation algorithm would update the count by first appending the new data to the master dataset and then counting all the records from scratch. This strategy is shown in figure 6.5.

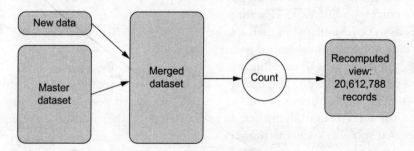

Figure 6.5   A recomputing algorithm to update the number of records in the master dataset. New data is appended to the master dataset, and then all records are counted.

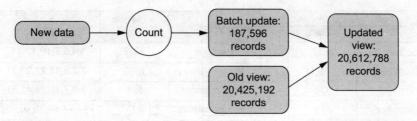

Figure 6.6 An incremental algorithm to update the number of records in the master dataset. Only the new dataset is counted, with the total used to update the batch view directly.

An incremental algorithm, on the other hand, would count the number of new data records and add it to the existing count, as demonstrated in figure 6.6.

You might be wondering why you would ever use a recomputation algorithm when you can use a vastly more efficient incremental algorithm instead. But efficiency is not the only factor to be considered. The key trade-offs between the two approaches are performance, human-fault tolerance, and the generality of the algorithm. We'll discuss both types of algorithms in regard to each of these issues. You'll discover that although incremental approaches can provide additional efficiency, you *must* also have recomputation versions of your algorithms.

6.3.1 *Performance*

There are two aspects to the performance of a batch-layer algorithm: the amount of resources required to update a batch view with new data, and the size of the batch views produced.

An incremental algorithm almost always uses significantly less resources to update a view because it uses new data and the current state of the batch view to perform an update. For a task such as computing pageviews over time, the view will be significantly smaller than the master dataset because of the aggregation. A recomputation algorithm looks at the entire master dataset, so the amount of resources needed for an update can be multiple orders of magnitude higher than an incremental algorithm. But the size of the batch view for an incremental algorithm can be significantly larger than the corresponding batch view for a recomputation algorithm. This is because the view needs to be formulated in such a way that it can be incrementally updated.

We'll demonstrate through two separate examples.

First, suppose you need to compute the average number of pageviews for each URL within a particular domain. The batch view generated by a recomputation algorithm would contain a map from each URL to its corresponding average. But this isn't suitable for an incremental algorithm, because updating the average incrementally requires that you also know the number of records used for computing the previous average. An incremental view would therefore store both the average and the total

URL	# Unique visitors
foo.com	2217
foo.com/blog	1899
foo.com/about	524
foo.com/careers	413
foo.com/faq	1212
...	...

Recomputation batch view

URL	# Unique visitors	Visitor IDs
foo.com	2217	1,4,5,7,10,12,14,....
foo.com/blog	1899	2,3,5,17,22,23,27,...
foo.com/about	524	3,6,7,19,24,42,51,...
foo.com/careers	413	12,17,19,29,40,42,...
foo.com/faq	1212	8,10,21,37,39,46,55,...
...	...	...

Incremental batch view

Figure 6.7   A comparison between a recomputation view and an incremental view for determining the number of unique visitors per URL

count for each URL, increasing the size of the incremental view over the recomputation-based view by a constant factor.

In other scenarios, the increase in the batch view size for an incremental algorithm is much more severe. Consider a query that computes the number of unique visitors for each URL. Figure 6.7 demonstrates the differences between batch views using recomputation and incremental algorithms.

A recomputation view only requires a map from the URL to the unique count. In contrast, an incremental algorithm only examines the new pageviews, so its view must contain the full set of visitors for each URL so it can determine which records in the new data correspond to return visits. As such, the incremental view could potentially be as large as the master dataset!

The batch view generated by an incremental algorithm isn't always this large, but it can be far larger than the corresponding recomputation-based view.

6.3.2   *Human-fault tolerance*

The lifetime of a data system is extremely long, and bugs can and will be deployed to production during that time period. You therefore must consider how your batch update algorithm will tolerate such mistakes. In this regard, recomputation algorithms are inherently human-fault tolerant, whereas with an incremental algorithm, human mistakes can cause serious problems.

Consider as an example a batch-layer algorithm that computes a global count of the number of records in the master dataset. Now suppose you make a mistake and deploy an algorithm that increments the global count for each record by two instead of by one. If your algorithm is recomputation-based, all that's required is to fix the algorithm and redeploy the code—your batch view will be correct the next time the batch layer runs. This is because the recomputation-based algorithm recomputes the batch view from scratch.

But if your algorithm is incremental, then correcting your view isn't so simple. The only option is to identify the records that were overcounted, determine how many times each one was overcounted, and then correct the count for each affected record. Accomplishing this with a high degree of confidence is not always possible. You may have detailed logging that helps you with these tasks, but your logs may not always have the required information, because you can't anticipate every type of mistake that will be made in the future. Many times you'll have to do an ad hoc, best-guess modification of your view—and you have to make certain you don't mess that up as well.

Hoping you have the right logs to fix mistakes is not sound engineering practice. It bears repeating: human mistakes are inevitable. As you've seen, recomputation-based algorithms have much stronger human-fault tolerance than incremental algorithms.

6.3.3   *Generality of the algorithms*

Although incremental algorithms can be faster to run, they must often be tailored to address the problem at hand. For example, you've seen that an incremental algorithm for computing the number of unique visitors can generate prohibitively large batch views. This cost can be offset by probabilistic counting algorithms, such as HyperLog-Log, that store intermediate statistics to estimate the overall unique count.[1] This reduces the storage cost of the batch view, but at the price of making the algorithm approximate instead of exact.

The gender-inference query introduced in the beginning of this chapter illustrates another issue: incremental algorithms shift complexity to on-the-fly computations. As you improve your semantic normalization algorithm, you'll want to see those improvements reflected in the results of your queries. Yet, if you do the normalization as part of the precomputation, your batch view will be out of date whenever you improve the normalization. The normalization must occur during the on-the-fly portion of the query when using an incremental algorithm. Your view will have to contain every name seen for each person, and your on-the-fly code will have to renormalize each name every time a query is performed. This increases the latency of the on-the-fly component and could very well take too long for your application's requirements.

Because a recomputation algorithm continually rebuilds the entire batch view, the structure of the batch view and the complexity of the on-the-fly component are both simpler, leading to a more general algorithm.

6.3.4   *Choosing a style of algorithm*

Table 6.1 summarizes this section in terms of recomputation and incremental algorithms.

The key takeaway is that you must *always* have recomputation versions of your algorithms. This is the only way to ensure human-fault tolerance for your system, and human-fault tolerance is a non-negotiable requirement for a robust system.

---

[1]   We'll discuss HyperLogLog further in subsequent chapters.

Table 6.1 Comparing recomputation and incremental algorithms

	Recomputation algorithms	Incremental algorithms
Performance	Requires computational effort to process the entire master dataset	Requires less computational resources but may generate much larger batch views
Human-fault tolerance	Extremely tolerant of human errors because the batch views are continually rebuilt	Doesn't facilitate repairing errors in the batch views; repairs are ad hoc and may require estimates
Generality	Complexity of the algorithm is addressed during precomputation, resulting in simple batch views and low-latency, on-the-fly processing	Requires special tailoring; may shift complexity to on-the-fly query processing
Conclusion	Essential to supporting a robust data-processing system	Can increase the efficiency of your system, but only as a supplement to recomputation algorithms

Additionally, you have the option to add incremental versions of your algorithms to make them more resource-efficient.

For the remainder of this chapter, we'll focus solely on recomputation algorithms, though in chapter 18 we'll come back to the topic of incrementalizing the batch layer.

6.4 *Scalability in the batch layer*

The word *scalability* gets thrown around a lot, so let's carefully define what it means in a data systems context. Scalability is the ability of a system to maintain performance under increased load by adding more resources. *Load* in a Big Data context is a combination of the total amount of data you have, how much new data you receive every day, how many requests per second your application serves, and so forth.

More important than a system being scalable is a system being *linearly scalable*. A linearly scalable system can maintain performance under increased load by adding resources in proportion to the increased load. A nonlinearly scalable system, despite being "scalable," isn't particular useful. Suppose the number of machines you need in relation to the load on your system has a quadratic relationship, like in figure 6.8. The costs of running your system would rise dramatically over time. Increasing your load ten-fold would increase your costs by a hundred. Such a system isn't feasible from a cost perspective.

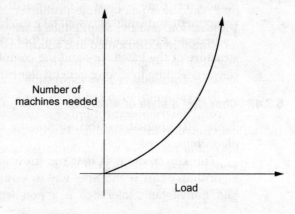

Number of machines needed

Load

Figure 6.8   Nonlinear scalability

When a system is linearly scalable, costs rise in proportion to the load. This is a critically important property of a data system.

> **What scalability doesn't mean...**
>
> Counterintuitively, a scalable system doesn't necessarily have the ability to *increase* performance by adding more machines. For an example of this, suppose you have a website that serves a static HTML page. Let's say that every web server you have can serve 1,000 requests/sec within a latency requirement of 100 milliseconds. You won't be able to lower the latency of serving the web page by adding more machines—an individual request is not parallelizable and must be satisfied by a single machine. But you can scale your website to increased requests per second by adding more web servers to spread the load of serving the HTML.
>
> More practically, with algorithms that are parallelizable, you might be able to increase performance by adding more machines, but the improvements will diminish the more machines you add. This is because of the increased overhead and communication costs associated with having more machines.

We delved into this discussion about scalability to set the scene for introducing MapReduce, a distributed computing paradigm that can be used to implement a batch layer. As we cover the details of its workings, keep in mind that it's linearly scalable: should the size of your master dataset double, then twice the number of servers will be able to build the batch views with the same latency.

6.5 *MapReduce: a paradigm for Big Data computing*

MapReduce is a distributed computing paradigm originally pioneered by Google that provides primitives for scalable and fault-tolerant batch computation. With MapReduce, you write your computations in terms of *map* and *reduce* functions that manipulate key/value pairs. These primitives are expressive enough to implement nearly any function, and the MapReduce framework executes those functions over the master dataset in a distributed and robust manner. Such properties make MapReduce an excellent paradigm for the precomputation needed in the batch layer, but it's also a low-level abstraction where expressing computations can be a large amount of work.

The canonical MapReduce example is *word count*. Word count takes a dataset of text and determines the number of times each word appears throughout the text. The map function in MapReduce executes once per line of text and emits any number of key/value pairs. For word count, the map function emits a key/value pair for every word in the text, setting the key to the word and the value to 1:

```
function word_count_map(sentence) {
  for(word in sentence.split(" ")) {
     emit(word, 1)
  }
}
```

MapReduce then arranges the output from the map functions so that all values from the same key are grouped together.

The reduce function then takes the full list of values sharing the same key and emits new key/value pairs as the final output. In word count, the input is a list of 1 values for each word, and the reducer simply sums the values to compute the count for that word:

```
function word_count_reduce(word, values) {
    sum = 0
    for(val in values) {
        sum += val
    }
    emit(word, sum)
}
```

There's a lot happening under the hood to run a program like word count across a cluster of machines, but the MapReduce framework handles most of the details for you. The intent is for you to focus on *what* needs to be computed without worrying about the details of *how* it's computed.

6.5.1 *Scalability*

The reason why MapReduce is such a powerful paradigm is because programs written in terms of MapReduce are inherently scalable. A program that runs on 10 gigabytes of data will also run on 10 petabytes of data. MapReduce automatically parallelizes the computation across a cluster of machines regardless of input size. All the details of concurrency, transferring data between machines, and execution planning are abstracted for you by the framework.

Let's walk through how a program like word count executes on a MapReduce cluster. The input to your MapReduce program is stored within a distributed filesystem such as the Hadoop Distributed File System (HDFS) you encountered in the last chapter. Before processing the data, the program first determines which machines in your cluster host the blocks containing the input—see figure 6.9.

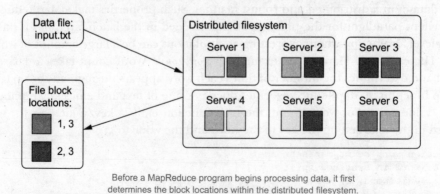

Before a MapReduce program begins processing data, it first
determines the block locations within the distributed filesystem.

Figure 6.9   Locating the servers hosting the input files for a MapReduce program

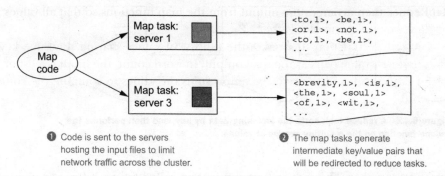

❶ Code is sent to the servers hosting the input files to limit network traffic across the cluster.

❷ The map tasks generate intermediate key/value pairs that will be redirected to reduce tasks.

Figure 6.10　MapReduce promotes data locality, running tasks on the servers that host the input data.

After determining the locations of the input, MapReduce launches a number of map tasks proportional to the input data size. Each of these tasks is assigned a subset of the input and executes your map function on that data. Because the amount of the code is typically far less than the amount of the data, MapReduce attempts to assign tasks to servers that host the data to be processed. As shown in figure 6.10, moving the code to the data avoids the need to transfer all that data across the network.

Like map tasks, there are also reduce tasks spread across the cluster. Each of these tasks is responsible for computing the reduce function for a subset of keys generated by the map tasks. Because the reduce function requires all values associated with a given key, a reduce task can't begin until all map tasks are complete.

Once the map tasks finish executing, each emitted key/value pair is sent to the reduce task responsible for processing that key. Therefore, each map task distributes its output among all the reducer tasks. This transfer of the intermediate key/value pairs is called *shuffling* and is illustrated in figure 6.11.

Once a reduce task receives all of the key/value pairs from every map task, it sorts the key/value pairs by key. This has the effect of organizing all the values for any given

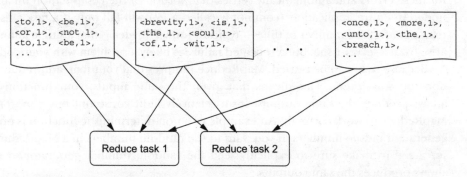

During the shuffle phase, all of the key/value pairs generated by the map tasks are distributed among the reduce tasks. In this process, all of the pairs with the same key are sent to the same reducer.

Figure 6.11　The shuffle phase distributes the output of the map tasks to the reduce tasks.

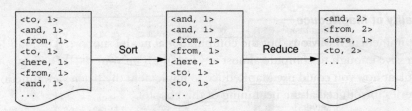

Figure 6.12   A reduce task sorts the incoming data by key, and then performs the reduce function on the resulting groups of values.

key to be together. The reduce function is then called for each key and its group of values, as demonstrated in figure 6.12.

As you can see, there are many moving parts to a MapReduce program. The important takeaways from this overview are the following:

- MapReduce programs execute in a fully distributed fashion with no central point of contention.
- MapReduce is scalable: the map and reduce functions you provide are executed in parallel across the cluster.
- The challenges of concurrency and assigning tasks to machines is handled for you.

6.5.2   *Fault-tolerance*

Distributed systems are notoriously testy. Network partitions, server crashes, and disk failures are relatively rare for a single server, but the likelihood of something going wrong greatly increases when coordinating computation over a large cluster of machines. Thankfully, in addition to being easily parallelizable and inherently scalable, MapReduce computations are also fault tolerant.

A program can fail for a variety of reasons: a hard disk can reach capacity, the process can exceed available memory, or the hardware can break down. MapReduce watches for these errors and automatically retries that portion of the computation on another node. An entire application (commonly called a *job*) will fail only if a task fails more than a configured number of times—typically four. The idea is that a single failure may arise from a server issue, but a repeated failure is likely a problem with your code.

Because tasks can be retried, MapReduce requires that your map and reduce functions be *deterministic*. This means that given the same inputs, your functions must always produce the same outputs. It's a relatively light constraint but important for MapReduce to work correctly. An example of a non-deterministic function is one that generates random numbers. If you want to use random numbers in a MapReduce job, you need to make sure to explicitly seed the random number generator so that it always produces the same outputs.

6.5.3   *Generality of MapReduce*

It's not immediately obvious, but the computational model supported by MapReduce is expressive enough to compute almost any functions on your data. To illustrate this, let's look at how you could use MapReduce to implement the batch view functions for the queries introduced at the beginning of this chapter.

IMPLEMENTING NUMBER OF PAGEVIEWS OVER TIME

The following MapReduce code produces a batch view for pageviews over time:

```
function map(record) {
    key = [record.url, toHour(record.timestamp)]
    emit(key, 1)
}

function reduce(key, vals) {
    emit(new HourPageviews(key[0], key[1], sum(vals)))
}
```

This code is very similar to the word count code, but the key emitted from the mapper is a struct containing the URL and the hour of the pageview. The output of the reducer is the desired batch view containing a mapping from [url, hour] to the number of pageviews for that hour.

IMPLEMENTING GENDER INFERENCE

The following MapReduce code infers the gender of supplied names:

```
function map(record) {
    emit(record.userid, normalizeName(record.name))    ◁── Semantic normalization
}                                                            occurs during the
                                                             mapping stage.
function reduce(userid, vals) {
    allNames = new Set()
    for(normalizedName in vals) {                      ┐ A set is used
        allNames.add(normalizedName)          ◁───     ┤ to remove any
    }                                                  ┘ potential duplicates.
    maleProbSum = 0.0
    for(name in allNames) {
        maleProbSum += maleProbabilityOfName(name)  ◁── ┐ Averages the
    }                                                   ┤ probabilities
    maleProb = maleProbSum / allNames.size()            ┘ of being male.
    if(maleProb > 0.5) {          ◁──────
        gender = "male"                   Returns the most
    } else {                              likely gender.
        gender = "female"
    }
    emit(new InferredGender(userid, gender))
}
```

Gender inference is similarly straightforward. The map function performs the name semantic normalization, and the reduce function computes the predicted gender for each user.

IMPLEMENTING INFLUENCE SCORE

The influence-score precomputation is more complex than the previous two examples and requires two MapReduce jobs to be chained together to implement the logic. The idea is that the output of the first MapReduce job is fed as the input to the second MapReduce job. The code is as follows:

```
function map1(record) {
    emit(record.responderId, record.sourceId)
}

function reduce1(userid, sourceIds) {
    influence = new Map(default=0)
    for(sourceId in sourceIds) {
        influence[sourceId] += 1
    }
    emit(topKey(influence))
}

function map2(record) {
    emit(record, 1)
}

function reduce2(influencer, vals) {
    emit(new InfluenceScore(influencer, sum(vals)))
}
```

> **The first job determines the top influencer for each user.**

> **The top influencer data is then used to determine the number of people each user influences.**

It's typical for computations to require multiple MapReduce jobs—that just means multiple levels of grouping were required. Here the first job requires grouping all reactions for each user to determine that user's top influencer. The second job then groups the records by top influencer to determine the influence scores.

Take a step back and look at what MapReduce is doing at a fundamental level:

- It arbitrarily partitions your data through the key you emit in the map phase. Arbitrary partitioning lets you connect your data together for later processing while still processing everything in parallel.
- It arbitrarily transforms your data through the code you provide in the map and reduce phases.

It's hard to envision anything more general that could still be a scalable, distributed system.

> ### MapReduce vs. Spark
> Spark is a relatively new computation system that has gained a lot of attention. Spark's computation model is "resilient distributed datasets." Spark isn't any more general or scalable than MapReduce, but its model allows it to have much higher performance for algorithms that have to repeatedly iterate over the same dataset (because Spark is able to cache that data in memory rather than read it from disk every time). Many machine-learning algorithms iterate over the same data repeatedly, making Spark particularly well suited for that use case.

6.6   *Low-level nature of MapReduce*

Unfortunately, although MapReduce is a great primitive for batch computation—providing you a generic, scalable, and fault-tolerant way to compute functions of large datasets—it doesn't lend itself to particularly elegant code. You'll find that Map-Reduce programs written manually tend to be long, unwieldy, and difficult to understand. Let's explore some of the reasons why this is the case.

6.6.1   *Multistep computations are unnatural*

The influence-score example showed a computation that required two MapReduce jobs. What's missing from that code is what connects the two jobs together. Running a MapReduce job requires more than just a mapper and a reducer—it also needs to know where to read its input and where to write its output. And that's the catch—to get that code to work, you'd need a place to put the intermediate output between step 1 and step 2. Then you'd need to clean up the intermediate output to prevent it from using up valuable disk space for longer than necessary.

This should immediately set off alarm bells, as it's a clear indication that you're working at a low level of abstraction. You want an abstraction where the whole computation can be represented as a single conceptual unit and details like temporary path management are automatically handled for you.

6.6.2   *Joins are very complicated to implement manually*

Let's look at a more complicated example: implementing a join via MapReduce. Suppose you have two separate datasets: one containing records with the fields id and age, and another containing records with the fields user_id, gender, and location. You wish to compute, for every id that exists in both datasets, the age, gender, and location. This operation is called an *inner join* and is illustrated in figure 6.13. Joins are extremely common operations, and you're likely familiar with them from tools like SQL.

id	age
3	25
1	71
7	37
8	21

user_id	gender	location
1	m	USA
9	f	Brazil
3	m	Japan

Inner join

id	age	gender	location
1	71	m	USA
3	25	m	Japan

Figure 6.13   Example of a two-sided inner join

To do a join via MapReduce, you need to read two independent datasets in a single MapReduce job, so the job needs to be able to distinguish between records from the two datasets. Although we haven't shown it in our pseudo-code so far, MapReduce frameworks typically provide context as to where a record comes from, so we'll extend our pseudo-code to include this context. This is the code to implement an inner join:

Use the source directory the record came from to determine if the record is on the left or right side of the join.

Set the MapReduce key to be the id or user_id, respectively. This will cause all records of those ids on either side of the join to get to the same reduce invocation. If you were joining on multiple keys at once, you'd put a collection as the MapReduce key.

The values you care to put in the output record are put into a list here. Later they'll be concatenated with records from the other side of the join to produce the output.

```
function join_map(sourcedir, record) {
  if(sourcedir=="/data/age") {
    emit(record.id, {"side" = "l"
, "values" = [record.age]})
  } else {
    emit(record.user_id,
        {"side" = "r",
            "values" = [record.gender, record.location])
  }
}

function join_reduce(id, records) {
  side_l = []
  side_r = []

  for(record : records) {
    values = record.get("values")
    if(record.get("side") == "l") {
      side_l.add(values)
    } else {
      side_r.add(values)
    }
  }

  for(l : side_l) {
    for(r : side_r) {
      emit(concat([id], l, r), null)
    }
  }
}
```

When reducing, first split records from either side of the join into "left" and "right" lists.

The id is added to the concatenated values to produce the final result. Note that because MapReduce always operates in terms of key/value pairs, in this case you emit the result as the key and set the value to null. You could also do it the other way around.

To achieve the semantics of joining, concatenate every record on each side of the join with every record on the other side of the join.

Although this is not a terrible amount of code, it's still quite a bit of grunt work to get the mechanics working correctly. There's complexity here: determining which side of the join a record belongs to is tied to specific directories, so you have to tweak the code to do a join on different directories. Additionally, MapReduce forcing everything to be in terms of key/value pairs feels inappropriate for the output of this job, which is just a list of values.

And this is only a simple two-sided inner join joining on a single field. Imagine joining on multiple fields, with five sides to the join, with some sides as outer joins and some as inner joins. You obviously don't want to manually write out the join code every time, so you should be able to specify the join at a higher level of abstraction.

6.6.3 *Logical and physical execution tightly coupled*

Let's look at one more example to really nail down why MapReduce is a low level of abstraction. Let's extend the word-count example to filter out the words *the* and *a*, and have it emit the doubled count rather than the count. Here's the code to accomplish this:

```
EXCLUDE_WORDS = Set("a", "the")

function map(sentence) {
  for(word : sentence) {
    if(not EXCLUDE_WORDS.contains(word)) {
      emit(word, 1)
    }
  }
}

function reduce(word, amounts) {
  result = 0
  for(amt : amounts) {
    result += amt
  }

  emit(result * 2)
}
```

This code works, but it seems to be mixing together multiple tasks into the same function. Good programming practice involves separating independent functionality into their own functions. The way you really think about this computation is illustrated in figure 6.14.

You could split this code so that each MapReduce job is doing just a single one of those functions. But a MapReduce job implies a specific physical execution: first a set of mapper processes runs to execute the map portion, then disk and network I/O happens to get the intermediate records to the reducer, and then a set of reducer processes runs to produce the output. Modularizing the code would create more MapReduce jobs than necessary, making the computation hugely inefficient.

And so you have a tough trade-off to make—either weave all the functionality together, engaging in bad software-engineering practices, or modularize the code, leading to poor resource usage. In reality, you shouldn't have to make this trade-off at all and should instead get the best of both worlds: full modularity with the code compiling to the optimal physical execution. Let's now see how you can accomplish this.

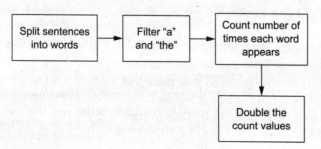

Figure 6.14 Decomposing modified word-count problem

6.7 *Pipe diagrams: a higher-level way of thinking about batch computation*

In this section we'll introduce a much more natural way of thinking about batch computation called *pipe diagrams*. Pipe diagrams can be compiled to execute as an efficient series of MapReduce jobs. As you'll see, every example we show—including all of SuperWebAnalytics.com—can be concisely represented via pipe diagrams.

The motivation for pipe diagrams is simply to enable us to talk about batch computation within the Lambda Architecture without getting lost in the details of MapReduce pseudo-code. Conciseness and intuitiveness are key here—both of which MapReduce lacks, and both of which pipe diagrams excel at. Additionally, pipe diagrams let us talk about the specific algorithms and data-processing transformations for solving example problems without getting mired in the details of specific tooling.

> ### Pipe diagrams in practice
>
> Pipe diagrams aren't a hypothetical concept; all of the higher-level MapReduce tools are a fairly direct mapping of pipe diagrams, including Cascading, Pig, Hive, and Cascalog. Spark is too, to some extent, though its data model doesn't natively include the concept of tuples with an arbitrary number of named fields.

6.7.1 *Concepts of pipe diagrams*

The idea behind pipe diagrams is to think of processing in terms of tuples, functions, filters, aggregators, joins, and merges—concepts you're likely already familiar with from SQL. For example, figure 6.15 shows the pipe diagram for the modified word-count example from section 6.6.3 with filtering and doubling added.

The computation starts with tuples with a single field named sentence. The split function transforms a single sentence tuple into many tuples with the additional field word. split takes as input the sentence field and creates the word field as output.

Figure 6.16 shows an example of what happens to a set of sentence tuples after applying split to them. As you can see, the sentence field gets duplicated among all the new tuples.

Of course, functions in pipe diagrams aren't limited to a set of prespecified functions. They can be any function you can implement in any general-purpose programming language. The same applies to filters and aggregators.

Next, the filter to remove *a* and *the* is applied, having the effect shown in figure 6.17.

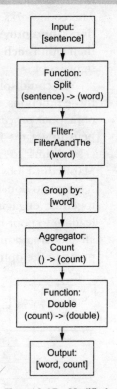

Figure 6.15 Modified word-count pipe diagram

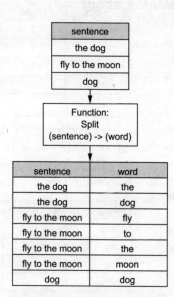

Figure 6.16   Illustration of a pipe diagram function

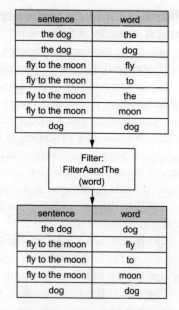

Figure 6.17   Illustration of a pipe diagram filter

Next, the entire set of tuples is grouped by the word field, and the count aggregator is applied to each group. This transformation is illustrated in figure 6.18.

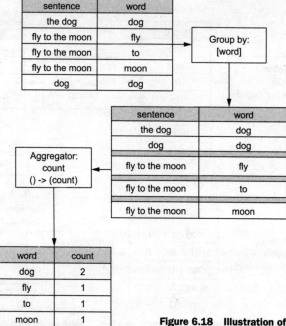

Figure 6.18   Illustration of pipe diagram group by and aggregation

Next, the count is doubled to create the new field
double, as shown in figure 6.19.

Finally, at the end the desired fields for output
are chosen and the rest of the fields are discarded.

As you can see, one of the keys to pipe diagrams
is that fields are immutable once created. One obvious optimization that you can make is to discard
fields as soon as they're no longer needed (preventing unnecessary serialization and network I/O).
For the most part, tools that implement pipe diagrams do this optimization for you automatically.
So in reality, the preceding example would execute
as shown in figure 6.20.

There are two other important operations in
pipe diagrams, and both these operations are used
for combining independent tuple sets.

The first is the join operator, which allows you
to do inner and outer joins among any number of
tuple sets. Tools vary in how you specify the join
fields for each side, but we find the simplest nota-

word	count
dog	2
fly	1
to	1
moon	1

Function:
double
(count) -> (double)

word	count	double
dog	2	4
fly	1	2
to	1	2
moon	1	2

**Figure 6.19   Illustration of
running function double**

tion is to choose as join fields whatever fields are common on all sides of the join. This
requires you to make sure the fields you want to join on are all named exactly the
same. Then, each side of the join is marked as *inner* or *outer*. Figure 6.21 shows some
example joins.

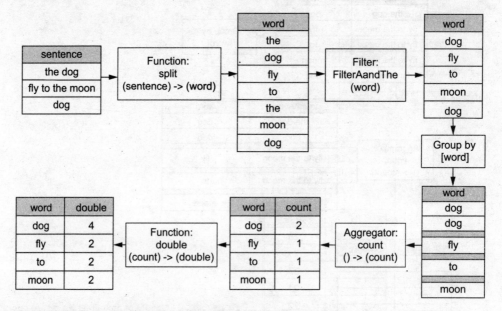

Figure 6.20   Fields are automatically discarded when no longer needed.

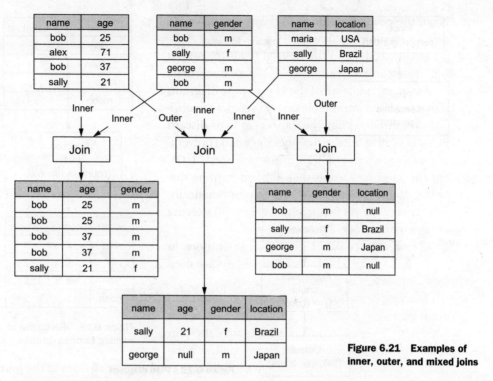

Figure 6.21 Examples of inner, outer, and mixed joins

The second operation is the merge operation, which combines independent tuple sets into a single tuple set. The merge operation requires all tuple sets to have the same number of fields and specifies new names for the tuples. Figure 6.22 shows an example merge.

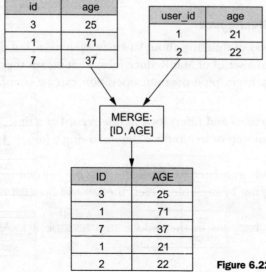

Figure 6.22 Example of pipe diagram merge operation

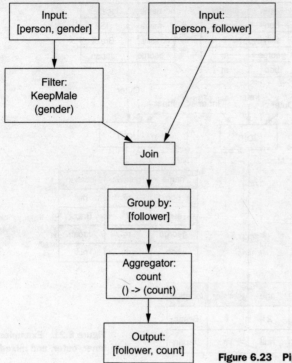

Figure 6.23   Pipe diagram

Let's now look at a more interesting example. Suppose you have one dataset with fields [person, gender], and another dataset of [person, follower]. Now suppose you want to compute the number of males each person follows. The pipe diagram for this computation looks like figure 6.23.

6.7.2   *Executing pipe diagrams via MapReduce*

Pipe diagrams are a high-level way of thinking about batch computation, but they can be straightforwardly compiled to a series of MapReduce jobs. That means they can be executed in a scalable manner. Every pipe diagram operation can be translated to MapReduce:

- *Functions and filters*—Functions and filters look at one record at a time, so they can be run either in a map step or in a reduce step following a join or aggregation.
- *Group by*—Group by is easily translated to MapReduce via the key emitted in the map step. If you're grouping by multiple values, the key will be a list of those values.
- *Aggregators*—Aggregation happens in the reduce step because it looks at all tuples for a group.

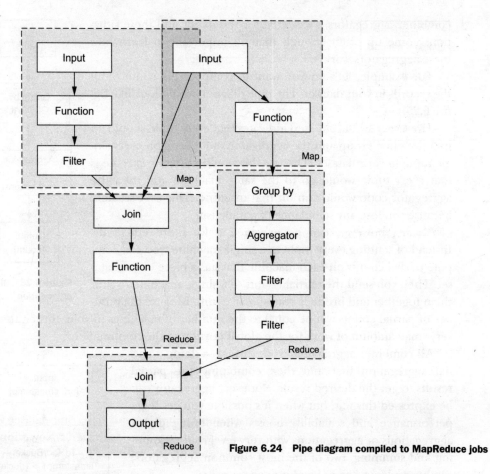

Figure 6.24   Pipe diagram compiled to MapReduce jobs

- *Join*—You've already seen the basics of implementing joins, and you've seen they require some code in the map step and some code in the reduce step. The code you saw in section 6.6.2 for a two-sided inner join can be extended to handle any number of sides and any mixture of inner and outer joins.

- *Merge*—A merge operation just means the same code will run on multiple sets of data.

Most importantly, a smart compiler will pack as many operations into the same map or reduce step as possible to minimize MapReduce steps and maximize efficiency. This lets you decompose your computation into independent steps without sacrificing performance in the process. Figure 6.24 shows an abbreviated pipe diagram and uses boxes to show how it would compile to MapReduce jobs. The reduce step following other reduce steps implies a map step in between to set up the join.

6.7.3   *Combiner aggregators*

There's a specialized kind of aggregator that can execute a lot more efficiently than normal aggregators: combiner aggregators. There are a few situations in which using combiner aggregators is essential for scalability, and these situations come up often enough that it's important to learn how these aggregators work.

For example, let's say you want to compute the count of all the records in your dataset. The pipe diagram would look like figure 6.25.

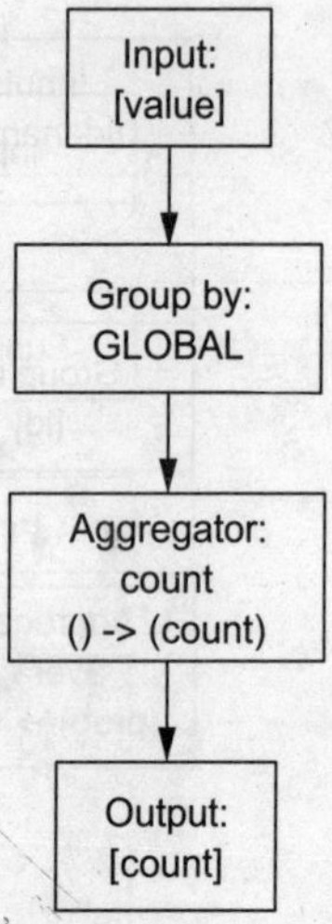

The GroupBy GLOBAL step indicates that every tuple should go into the same group and the aggregator should run on every single tuple in your dataset. The way this would normally execute is that every tuple would go to the same machine and then the aggregator code would run on that machine. This isn't scalable because you lose any semblance of parallelism.

Count, however, can be executed a lot more efficiently. Instead of sending every tuple to a single machine, you can compute partial counts on each machine that has a piece of the dataset. Then you send the partial counts to a single machine to sum them together and produce your global count. Because the number of partial counts will be equal to the number of machines in your cluster, this is a very small amount of work for the global portion of the computation.

All combiner aggregators work this way—doing a partial aggregation first and then combining the partial results to get the desired result. Not every aggregator can be expressed this way, but when it's possible you get huge performance and scalability boosts when doing global aggregations or aggregations with very few groups. Counting and summing, two of the most common aggregators, can be implemented as combiner aggregators.

6.7.4   Pipe diagram examples

In the beginning of the chapter, we introduced three example problems for batch computation. Now let's take a look at how you can solve these problems in a practical and scalable manner with pipe diagrams.

Pageviews over time is straightforward, as shown in figure 6.26. Simply convert each timestamp to a time bucket, and then count the number of pageviews per URL/ bucket.

Gender inference is also easy, as shown in figure 6.27. Simply normalize each name, use the maleProbabilityOf-Name function to get the probability of each name, and then compute the average male probability per person. Finally,

Figure 6.25   Global aggregation

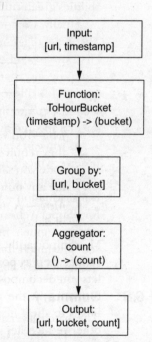

Figure 6.26   Pipe diagram for pageviews over time

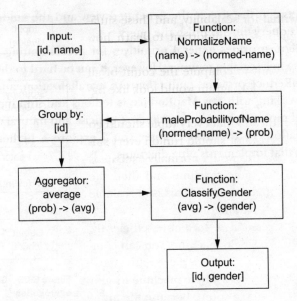

**Figure 6.27   Pipe diagram
for gender inference**

run a function that classifies people with average prob-
abilities greater than 0.5 as male, and lower as female.

Finally, we come to the influence-score problem.
The pipe diagram for this is shown in figure 6.28.
First, the top influencer is chosen for each person by
grouping by `responder-id` and selecting the influencer who that person responded to the most. The
second step simply counts how many times each influencer appeared as someone else's top influencer.

As you can see, these example problems all decompose very nicely into pipe diagrams, and the pipe diagrams map nicely to how you think about the data
transformations. When we build out the batch layer
for SuperWebAnalytics.com in chapter 8—which
requires much more involved computations—you'll
see how much time and effort are saved by using this
higher level of abstraction.

6.8   Summary

The batch layer is the core of the Lambda Architecture. The batch layer is high latency by its nature, and
you should use the high latency as an opportunity to
do deep analysis and expensive calculations you can't
do in real time. You saw that when designing batch

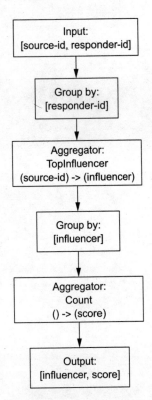

**Figure 6.28   Pipe diagram for
influence score**

views, there's a trade-off between the size of the generated view and the amount of work that will be required at query time to finish the query.

The MapReduce paradigm provides general primitives for precomputing query functions across all your data in a scalable manner. However, it can be hard to think in MapReduce. Although MapReduce provides fault tolerance, parallelization, and task scheduling, it's clear that working with raw MapReduce is tedious and limiting. You saw that thinking in terms of pipe diagrams is a much more concise and natural way to think about batch computation. In the next chapter you'll explore a higher-level abstraction called JCascalog that implements pipe diagrams.

Batch layer: Illustration

This chapter covers

- Sources of complexity in data-processing code
- JCascalog as a practical implementation of pipe diagrams
- Applying abstraction and composition techniques to data processing

In the last chapter you saw how pipe diagrams are a natural and concise way to specify computations that operate over large amounts of data. You saw that pipe diagrams can be executed as a series of MapReduce jobs for parallelism and scalability.

In this illustration chapter, we'll look at a tool that's a fairly direct mapping of pipe diagrams: JCascalog. There's a lot to cover in JCascalog, so this chapter is a lot more involved than the previous illustration chapters. Like always, you can still learn the full theory of the Lambda Architecture without reading the illustration chapters. But with JCascalog, in particular, we aim to open your minds as to what is possible with data-processing tools. A key point is that your data-processing code is no different than any other code you write. As such, it requires good abstractions that are reusable and composable. Abstraction and composition are the cornerstones of good software engineering.

Rather than just focus on how JCascalog lets you implement pipe diagrams, we'll go beyond that and show how JCascalog enables a whole range of abstraction and composition techniques that just aren't possible with other tools. We've found that most developers think in terms of SQL being the gold standard of data manipulation tools, and we find that mindset to be severely limiting. Many data-processing tools suffer from incidental complexities that arise, not from the nature of the problem, but from the design of the tool itself. We'll discuss some of these complexities, and then show how JCascalog gets around these classic pitfalls. You'll see that JCascalog enables programming techniques that allow you to write very concise, very elegant code.

7.1   An illustrative example

Word count is the canonical MapReduce example, so let's take a look at how it's implemented using JCascalog.

For introductory purposes, we'll explicitly store the input dataset—the Gettysburg address—in an in-memory list where each phrase is stored separately:

```
List SENTENCE = Arrays.asList(
    Arrays.asList("Four score and seven years ago our fathers"),
    Arrays.asList("brought forth on this continent a new nation"),
    Arrays.asList("conceived in Liberty and dedicated to"),
    Arrays.asList("the proposition that all men are created equal"),
    ...
```

Truncated for brevity →

The following snippet is a complete JCascalog implementation of word count for this dataset.

Queries output to be written to the console →

Specifies the output types returned by the query

Reads each sentence from the input

```
Api.execute(new StdoutTap(),
    new Subquery("?word", "?count")
        .predicate(SENTENCE, "?sentence")
        .predicate(new Split(), "?sentence").out("?word")
        .predicate(new Count(), "?count"));
```

Tokenizes each sentence into separate words

Determines the count for each word

The first thing to note is that this code is really concise! JCascalog's high-level nature may make it difficult to believe it's a MapReduce interface, but when this code is executed, it runs as a MapReduce job.

Upon running this code, it would print the output to your console, returning results similar to the following partial listing (for brevity):

```
RESULTS
----------
But    1
Four   1
God    1
It     3
```

```
Liberty 1
Now     1
The     2
We      2
```

Let's go through this word-count code line by line to understand what it's doing. If every detail isn't completely clear, don't worry. We'll look at JCascalog in much greater depth later in the chapter.

In JCascalog, inputs and outputs are defined via an abstraction called a *tap*. The tap abstraction allows results to be displayed on the console, stored in HDFS, or written to a database. The first line reads "execute the following computation and direct the results to the console."

```
Api.execute(new StdoutTap(), ...
```

The second line begins the definition of the computation. Computations are represented via instances of the Subquery class. This subquery will emit a set of tuples containing two fields named ?word and ?count:

```
new Subquery("?word", "?count")
```

The next line sources the input data for the query. It reads from the SENTENCE dataset and emits tuples containing one field named ?sentence. As with outputs, the tap abstraction allows inputs from different sources, such as in-memory values, HDFS files, or the results from other queries:

```
.predicate(SENTENCE, "?sentence")
```

The fourth line splits each sentence into a set of words, giving the Split function the ?sentence field as input and storing the output in a new field called ?word:

```
.predicate(new Split(), "?sentence").out("?word")
```

The Split function is not part of the JCascalog API but demonstrates how new user-defined functions can be integrated into queries. Its operation is defined via the following class. Its definition should be fairly intuitive; it takes in input sentences and emits a new tuple for each word in the sentence:

```
public static class Split extends CascalogFunction {
  public void operate(FlowProcess process, FunctionCall call) {      Partitions
    String sentence = call.getArguments().getString(0);              a sentence
    for (String word: sentence.split(" ")) {      ◄─────             into words
      call.getOutputCollector().add(new Tuple(word));  ◄─┐
    }                                                     │
  }                                               Emits each word
}                                                 in its own tuple
```

Finally, the last line counts the number of times each word appears and stores the result in the ?count variable:

```
.predicate(new Count(), "?count"));
```

Now that you've had a taste of JCascalog, let's take a look at some of the common pitfalls of data-processing tools that can lead to unnecessary complexity.

7.2   *Common pitfalls of data-processing tools*

As with any code, keeping your data-processing code simple is essential so that you can reason about your system and ensure correctness. Complexity in code arises in two forms: *essential complexity* that is inherent in the problem to be solved, and *accidental complexity* that arises solely from the approach to the solution. By minimizing accidental complexity, your code will be easier to maintain and you'll have greater confidence in its correctness.

In this section we'll look at two sources of accidental complexity in data-processing code: custom languages and poorly composable abstractions.

7.2.1   *Custom languages*

A common source of complexity in data-processing tools is the use of custom languages. Examples of this include SQL for relational databases or Pig and Hive for Hadoop. Using a custom language for data processing, while tempting, introduces a number of serious complexity problems.

The use of custom languages introduces a language barrier that requires an interface to interact with other parts of your code. This interface is a common source of errors and an unavoidable source of complexity. As an example, SQL injection attacks take advantage of an improperly defined interface between user-facing code and the generated SQL statements for querying a relational database. Because of this interface, you have to be constantly on your guard to ensure you don't make any mistakes.

The language barrier also causes all kinds of other complexity issues. Modularization can become painful—the custom language may support namespaces and functions, but ultimately these are not going to be as good as their general-purpose language counterparts. Furthermore, if you want to incorporate your own business logic into queries, you must create your own user-defined functions (UDFs) and register them with the language.

Lastly, you have to coordinate switching between your general-purpose language and your data-processing language. For instance, you may write a query using a custom language and then want to use the Pail class from chapter 5 to append the resulting data to an existing store. The Pail invocation is just standard Java code, so you'll need to write shell scripts that perform tasks in the correct order. Because you're working in multiple languages stitched together via scripts, mechanisms like exceptions and exception handling break down—you have to check return codes to make sure you don't continue to the next step when the prior step failed.

These are all examples of accidental complexity that can be avoided completely when your data-processing tool is a library for your general-purpose language. You can then freely intermix regular code with data-processing code, use your normal mechanisms for modularization, and have exceptions work properly. As you'll see, it's possible for a regular library to be concise and just as pleasant to work with as a custom language.

7.2.2 *Poorly composable abstractions*

Another common source of accidental complexity can occur when using multiple abstractions in conjunction. It's important that your abstractions can be composed together to create new and greater abstractions—otherwise you're unable to reuse code and you keep reinventing the wheel in slightly different ways.

A good example of this is the Average aggregator in Apache Pig (another abstraction for MapReduce). At the time of this writing, the implementation has over 300 lines of code and 15 separate method definitions. Its intricacy is due to code optimizations for improved performance that coordinate work in both map and reduce phases.

The problem with Pig's implementation is that it re-implements the functionality of the Count and Sum aggregators without being able to reuse the code written for those aggregators. This is unfortunate because it's more code to maintain, and every time an improvement is made to Count and Sum, those changes need to be incorporated into Average as well. It's much better to define Average as the *composition* of a count aggregation, a sum aggregation, and the division function.

Unfortunately, Pig's abstractions don't allow you to define Average in that way. In JCascalog though, that is exactly how Average is defined:

```
PredicateMacroTemplate Average =
  PredicateMacroTemplate.build("?val")
    .out("?avg")
    .predicate(new Count(), "?count")
    .predicate(new Sum(), "?val").out("?sum")
    .predicate(new Div(), "?sum", "?count").out("?avg");
```

In addition to its simplicity, this definition of Average is as efficient as the Pig implementation because it reuses the previously optimized Count and Sum aggregators. The reason JCascalog allows this sort of composition but Pig doesn't is entirely due to fundamental differences in how computations are expressed in JCascalog versus Pig. We'll cover this functionality of JCascalog in depth later—the takeaway here is the importance of abstractions being composable. There are many other examples of composition that we'll explore throughout this chapter.

Now that you've seen some common sources of complexity in data-processing tools, let's begin our exploration of JCascalog.

7.3 *An introduction to JCascalog*

JCascalog is a Java library that provides composable abstractions for expressing MapReduce computations. Recall that the goal of this book is to illustrate the concepts of Big Data, using specific tools to ground those concepts. There are other tools that provide higher-level interfaces to MapReduce—Hive, Pig, and Cascading among the most popular—but many of them still have limitations in their ability to abstract and compose data-processing code. We've chosen JCascalog because it was specifically written to enable new abstraction and composition techniques to reduce the complexity of batch processing.

JCascalog is a declarative abstraction where computations are expressed via logical constraints. Rather than providing explicit instructions on how to derive the desired output, you instead describe the output in terms of the input. From that description, JCascalog determines the most efficient way to perform the calculation via a series of MapReduce jobs.

If you're experienced with relational databases, JCascalog will seem both strange and familiar at the same time. You'll recognize familiar concepts like declarative programming, joins, and aggregations, albeit in different packaging. But it may seem different because rather than SQL, it's an API based on logic programming.

7.3.1   The JCascalog data model

JCascalog's data model is the same as that of the pipe diagrams in the last chapter. JCascalog manipulates and transforms *tuples*—named lists of values where each value can be any type of object. A set of tuples shares a *schema* that specifies how many fields are in each tuple and the name of each field. Figure 7.1 illustrates an example set of tuples with a shared schema.

When executing a query, JCascalog represents the initial data as tuples and transforms the input into a succession of other tuple sets at each stage of the computation.

An abundance of punctuation?!

After seeing examples of JCascalog, a natural question is, "What's the meaning of all those question marks?" We're glad you asked.

Fields whose names start with a question mark (?) are non-nullable. If JCascalog encounters a tuple with a null value for a non-nullable field, it's immediately filtered from the working dataset. Conversely, field names beginning with an exclamation mark (!) may contain null values.

Additionally, field names starting with a double exclamation mark (!!) are also nullable and are needed to perform outer joins between datasets. For joins involving these kinds of field names, records that do not satisfy the join condition between datasets are still included in the result set, but with null values for these fields where data is not present.

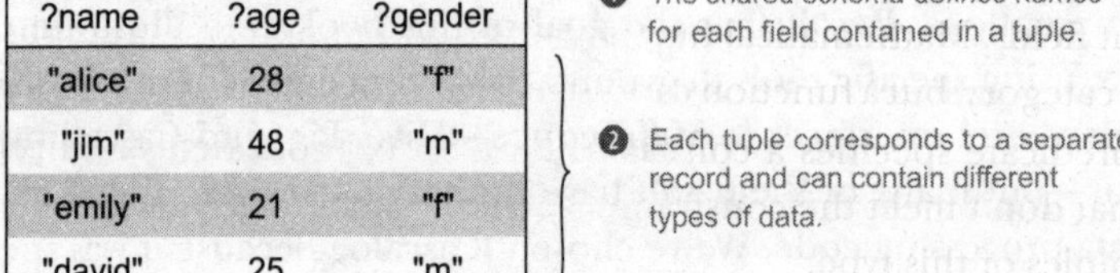

?name	?age	?gender
"alice"	28	"f"
"jim"	48	"m"
"emily"	21	"f"
"david"	25	"m"

❶ The shared schema defines names for each field contained in a tuple.

❷ Each tuple corresponds to a separate record and can contain different types of data.

Figure 7.1 An example set of tuples with a schema describing their contents

AGE	
?person	?age
"alice"	28
"bob"	33
"chris"	40
"david"	25

GENDER	
?person	?gender
"alice"	"f"
"bob"	"m"
"chris"	"m"
"emily"	"f"

FOLLOWS	
?person	?follows
"alice"	"david"
"alice"	"bob"
"bob"	"david"
"emily"	"gary"

INTEGER
?num
-1
0
1
2

Figure 7.2   Example datasets we'll use to demonstrate the JCascalog API: a set of people's ages, a separate set for gender, a person-following relationship (as in Twitter), and a set of integers

The best way to introduce JCascalog is through a variety of examples. Along with the SENTENCE dataset you saw earlier, we'll use a few other in-memory datasets to demonstrate the different aspects of JCascalog. Examples from these datasets are shown in figure 7.2, with the full set available in the source code bundle that accompanies this book.

JCascalog benefits from a simple syntax that's capable of expressing complex queries. We'll examine JCascalog's query structure next.

7.3.2   The structure of a JCascalog query

JCascalog queries have a uniform structure consisting of a destination tap and a subquery that defines the actual computation. Consider the following example, which finds all people from the AGE dataset younger than 30:

```
                                                    The destination tap
Api.execute(new StdoutTap(),  ◄──────────┘
            new Subquery("?person")     ◄─────────── The output fields
              .predicate(AGE, "?person", "?age")  ◄──┐
              .predicate(new LT(), "?age", 30));      Predicates that define
                                                      the desired output
```

Note that instead of expressing *how* to perform a computation, JCascalog uses predicates to describe the desired output. These predicates are capable of expressing all possible operations on tuple sets—transformations, filters, joins, and so forth—and they can be categorized into four main types:

- A *function* predicate specifies a relationship between a set of input fields and a set of output fields. Mathematical functions such as addition and multiplication fall into this category, but a function can also emit multiple tuples from a single input.
- A *filter* predicate specifies a constraint on a set of input fields and removes all tuples that don't meet the constraint. The less-than and greater-than operations are examples of this type.

- An *aggregator* predicate is a function on a group of tuples. For example, an aggregator could compute an average, which emits a single output for an entire group.
- A *generator* predicate is simply a finite set of tuples. A generator can either be a concrete source of data, such as an in-memory data structure or file on HDFS, or it can be the result from another subquery.

Additional example predicates are shown in figure 7.3.

Type	Example	Description
Generator	`.predicate(SENTENCE, "?sentence")`	A generator that creates tuples from the `SENTENCE` dataset, with each tuple consisting of a single field called `?sentence`.
Function	`.predicate(new Multiply(), 2, "?x").out("?z")`	This function doubles the value of `?x` and stores the result as `?z`.
Filter	`.predicate(new LT(), "?y", 50)`	This filter removes all tuples unless the value of `?y` is less than 50.

Figure 7.3 Example generator, function, and filter predicates. We'll discuss aggregators later in the chapter, but they share the same structure.

A key design decision for JCascalog was to make all predicates share a common structure. The first argument to a predicate is the *predicate operation*, and the remaining arguments are parameters for that operation. For function and aggregator predicates, the labels for the outputs are specified using the `out` method.

Being able to represent every piece of your computation via the same simple, consistent mechanism is the key to enabling highly composable abstractions. Despite their simple structure, predicates provide extremely rich semantics. This is best illustrated by examples, as shown in figure 7.4.

As we earlier mentioned, joins between datasets are also expressed via predicates—we'll expand on this next.

Type	Example	Description
Function as filter	`.predicate(new Plus(), 2, "?x").out(6)`	Although `Plus()` is a function, this predicate filters all tuples where the value of `?x` ≠ 4.
Compound filter	`.predicate(new Multiply(), 2, "?a").out("?z")` `.predicate(new Multiply(), 3, "?b").out("?z")`	In concert, these predicates filter all tuples where 2(?a) ≠ 3(?b).

Figure 7.4 The simple predicate structure can express deep semantic relationships to describe the desired query output.

7.3.3 Querying multiple datasets

Many queries will require that you combine multiple datasets. In relational databases, this is most commonly done via a join operation, and joins exist in JCascalog as well.

Suppose you want to combine the AGE and GENDER datasets to create a new set of tuples that contains the age and gender of all people that exist in both datasets. This is a standard inner join on the ?person field, and it's illustrated in figure 7.5.

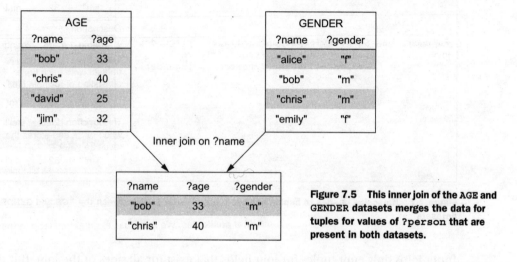

Figure 7.5   This inner join of the AGE **and** GENDER **datasets merges the data for tuples for values of** ?person **that are present in both datasets.**

In a language like SQL, joins are expressed *explicitly.* Joins in JCascalog are implicit based on the variable names. Figure 7.6 highlights the differences.

The way joins work in JCascalog is exactly how joins work in pipe diagrams: tuple sets are joined using the common field names as the join key. In this query, the same field name, ?person, is used as the output of two different generator predicates, AGE and GENDER. Because each instance of the variable must have the same value for any resulting tuples, JCascalog knows that the right way to resolve the query is to do an inner join between the AGE and GENDER datasets.

Language	Query	Description

SQL	`SELECT AGE.person, AGE.age, GENDER.gender`
	`FROM AGE`
	`INNER JOIN GENDER`
	`ON AGE.person = GENDER.person`
		This clause explicitly defines the join condition.

JCascalog	`new Subquery("?person", "?age", "?gender")`
	`   .predicate(AGE, "?person", "?age")`
	`   .predicate(GENDER, "?person", "?gender");`
		By specifying ?person as a field name for both datasets, JCascalog does an implicit join using the shared name.

Figure 7.6   A comparison between SQL and JCascalog syntax for an inner join between the AGE **and** GENDER **datasets**

Join type	Query	Results		

| Left outer join | `new Subquery("?person", "?age", "!!gender")`
   `.predicate(AGE, "?person", "?age")`
   `.predicate(GENDER, "?person", "!!gender");` |

?name	?age	?gender
"bob"	33	"m"
"chris"	40	"m"
"david"	25	null
"jim"	32	null

| Full outer join | `new Subquery("?person", "!!age", "!!gender")`
   `.predicate(AGE, "?person", "!!age")`
   `.predicate(GENDER, "?person", "!!gender");` |

?name	?age	?gender
"alice"	null	"f"
"bob"	33	"m"
"chris"	40	"m"
"david"	25	null
"emily"	null	"f"
"jim"	32	null

Figure 7.7 **JCascalog queries to implement two types of outer joins between the AGE and GENDER datasets**

Inner joins only emit tuples for join fields that exist for all sides of the join. But there are circumstances where you may want results for records that don't exist in one dataset or the other, resulting in a null value for the non-existing data. These operations are called outer joins and are just as easy to do in JCascalog. Consider the join examples in figure 7.7.

As mentioned earlier, for outer joins, JCascalog uses fields beginning with !! to generate null values for non-existing data. In the left outer join, a person must have an age to be included in the result set, with null values being introduced for missing gender data. For the full outer join, all people present in either dataset are included in the results, with null values being used for any missing age or gender data.

Besides joins, there are a few other ways to combine datasets. Occasionally you have two datasets that contain the same type of data, and you want to merge them into a single dataset. For this, JCascalog provides the combine and union functions. The combine function concatenates the datasets together, whereas union will remove any duplicate records during the combining process. Figure 7.8 illustrates the difference between the two functions.

So far you've seen transformations that act on one tuple at a time or that combine datasets together. We'll next cover operations that process groups of tuples.

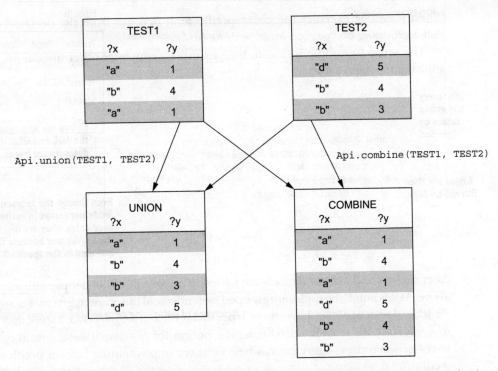

**Figure 7.8 JCascalog provides two different means to merge compatible datasets: `combine` and `union`.
`combine` does a simple aggregation of the two sets, whereas `union` removes any duplicate tuples.**

7.3.4 *Grouping and aggregators*

There are many types of queries where you want to aggregate information for specific groups: "What is the average salary for different professions?" or "What age group writes the most tweets?" In SQL you explicitly state how records should be grouped and the operations to be performed on the resulting sets.

There is no explicit GROUP BY command in JCascalog to indicate how to partition tuples for aggregation. Instead, as with joins, the grouping is implicit based on the desired query output. To illustrate this, let's look at a couple of examples.

The first example uses the Count aggregator to find the number of people each person follows:

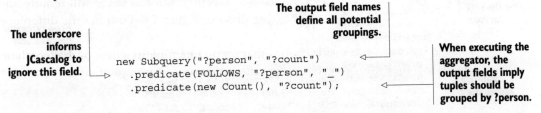

When JCascalog executes the `count` predicate, it deduces from the declared output that a grouping on `?person` must be done first.

The second example is similar, but performs a couple of other operations before applying the aggregator:

This query will group tuples by ?gender. →

Before the aggregator, the AGE and GENDER datasets are joined.

```
new Subquery("?gender", "?count")
    .predicate(GENDER, "?person", "?gender")
    .predicate(AGE, "?person", "?age")
    .predicate(new LT(), "?age", 30)
    .predicate(new Count(), "?count");
```

Tuples are then filtered on ?age.

Even though the ?person and ?age fields were used in earlier predicates, they are discarded by the aggregator because they aren't included in the specified output.

After the AGE and GENDER datasets are joined, JCascalog filters all people with age 30 or above. At this point, the tuples are grouped by gender and the count aggregator is applied.

JCascalog actually supports three types of aggregators: *aggregators, buffers,* and *parallel aggregators.* We're only introducing the notion for now; we'll delve into the differences between these aggregators when we cover implementing custom predicates in section 7.3.6.

We've spoken at length about the different types of JCascalog predicates. Next, let's step through the execution of a query to see how tuple sets are manipulated at different stages of the query's computation.

7.3.5   *Stepping though an example query*

For this exercise, we'll start with two test datasets, as shown in figure 7.9.

We'll use the following query to explain the execution of a JCascalog query, observing how the sets of tuples change at each stage in the execution:

VAL1		VAL2	
?a	?b	?a	?c
"a"	1	"b"	4
"b"	2	"b"	6
"c"	5	"c"	3
"d"	12	"d"	15
"d"	1		

Figure 7.9   Test data for our query-execution walkthrough

Generators for the test datasets →

Multiple aggregators →

```
new Subquery("?a", "?avg")
    .predicate(VAL1, "?a", "?b")
    .predicate(VAL2, "?a", "?c")
    .predicate(new Multiply(), 2, "?b").out("?double-b")
    .predicate(new LT(), "?b", "?c")
    .predicate(new Count(), "?count")
    .predicate(new Sum(), "?double-b").out("?sum")
    .predicate(new Div(), "?sum", "?count").out("?avg")
    .predicate(new Multiply(), 2, "?avg").out("?double-avg")
    .predicate(new LT(), "?double-avg", 50);
```

Pre-aggregator function and filter

Post-aggregator predicates

At the start of a JCascalog query, the generator datasets exist in independent branches of the computation. In the first stage of execution, JCascalog applies functions, filters tuples, and joins datasets until it can no longer do so. A function or filter can be applied if all the input variables for the operation are available. This stage of the query is illustrated in figure 7.10.

Note that some predicates require other predicates to be applied first. In the example, the less-than filter couldn't be applied until after the join was performed.

Eventually this phase reaches a point where no more predicates can be applied because the remaining predicates are either aggregators or require variables that are not yet available. At this point, JCascalog enters the aggregation phase of the query.

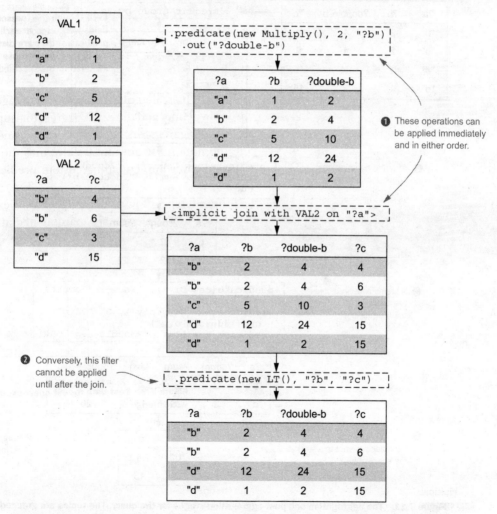

Figure 7.10   The first stage of execution entails applying all functions, filters, and joins where the input variables are available.

JCascalog groups the tuples by any available variables that are declared as output variables for the query and then applies the aggregators to each group of tuples. This is illustrated in figure 7.11.

After the aggregation phase, all remaining functions and filters are applied. The end of this phase drops any variables from the tuples that aren't declared in the output fields for the query.

You've now seen how to use predicates to construct arbitrarily complex queries that filter, join, transform, and aggregate your data. You've seen how JCascalog implements every operation in pipe diagrams and provides a concise way for specifying a

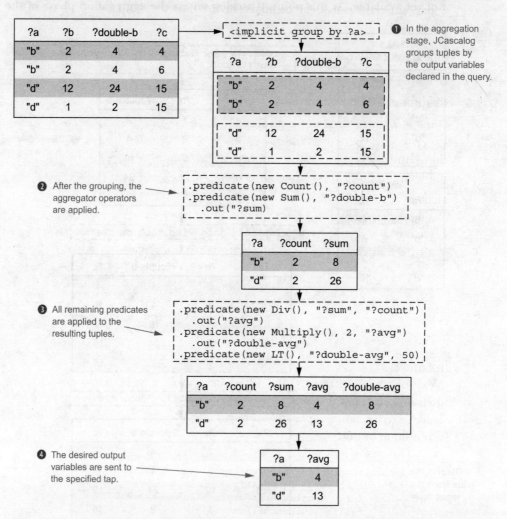

Figure 7.11 The aggregation and post-aggregation stages for the query. The tuples are grouped based on the desired output variables, and then all aggregators are applied. All remaining predicates are then executed, and the desired output is returned.

> **A verbose explanation**
>
> You may have noticed that this example computes an average by doing a count, sum, and division. This was solely for the purposes of illustration—these operations can be abstracted into an Average aggregator, as you saw earlier in this chapter.
>
> You may have also noticed that some variables are never used after a point, yet still remain in the resulting tuple sets. For example, the ?b variable is not used after the LT predicate is applied, but it's still grouped along with the other variables. In reality, JCascalog will drop any variables once they're no longer needed so that they aren't serialized or transferred over the network. This is the optimization mentioned in the previous chapter that can be applied to any pipe diagram.

pipe diagram. We'll next demonstrate how you can implement your own custom filters, functions, and aggregators for use as JCascalog predicates.

7.3.6 *Custom predicate operations*

You'll frequently need to create additional predicate types to implement your business logic. Toward this end, JCascalog exposes simple interfaces to define new filters, functions, and aggregators. Most importantly, this is all done with regular Java code by implementing the appropriate interfaces.

FILTERS

We'll begin with filters. A filter predicate requires a single method named isKeep that returns true if the input tuple should be kept, and false if it should be filtered. The following is a filter that keeps all tuples where the input is greater than 10:

```
public static class GreaterThanTenFilter extends CascalogFilter {
  public boolean isKeep(FlowProcess process, FilterCall call) {
    return call.getArguments().getInteger(0) > 10;          ◁——— Obtains the first
  }                                                                element of the
}                                                                input tuple and
                                                                 treats the value
                                                                 as an integer
```

FUNCTIONS

Next up are functions. Like filters, a function predicate implements a single method—in this case named operate. A function takes in a set of inputs and then emits zero or more tuples as output. Here's a simple function that increments its input value by one:

```
                     public static class IncrementFunction extends CascalogFunction {
Obtains the            public void operate(FlowProcess process, FunctionCall call) {
value from the           int v = call.getArguments().getInteger(0);
input tuple  └▷          call.getOutputCollector().add(new Tuple(v + 1));   ◁—— Emits a new
                       }                                                           tuple with the
                     }                                                             incremented value
```

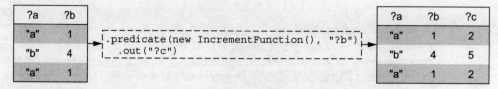

Figure 7.12 The `IncrementFunction` predicate applied to some sample tuples

Figure 7.12 shows the result of applying this function to a set of tuples.

Recall from earlier that a function can act as a filter if it emits zero tuples for a given tuple. Here's a function that attempts to parse an integer from a string, filtering out the tuple if the parsing fails:

```
public static class TryParseInteger extends CascalogFunction {
  public void operate(FlowProcess process, FunctionCall call) {
    String s = call.getArguments().getString(0);
    try {
      int i = Integer.parseInt(s);
      call.getOutputCollector().add(new Tuple(i));
    }
    catch(NumberFormatException e) {}
  }
}
```

Regards input value as a string

Emits value as integer if parsing succeeds

Emits nothing if parsing fails

Figure 7.13 illustrates this function applied to a tuple set. You can observe that one tuple is filtered by the process.

Finally, if a function emits multiple output tuples, each output tuple is appended to its own copy of the input arguments. As an example, here's the `Split` function from word count:

```
public static class Split extends CascalogFunction {
  public void operate(FlowProcess process, FunctionCall call) {
    String sentence = call.getArguments().getString(0);
    for(String word: sentence.split(" ")) {
      call.getOutputCollector().add(new Tuple(word));
    }
  }
}
```

Emits each word as a separate tuple

For simplicity, splits into words using a single whitespace

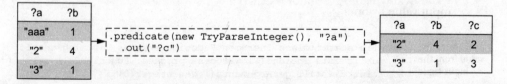

Figure 7.13 The `TryParseInteger` function filters rows where `?a` can't be converted to an integer value.

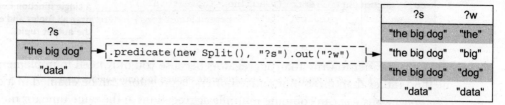

Figure 7.14   The Split function can emit multiple tuples from a single input tuple.

Figure 7.14 shows the result of applying this function to a set of sentences. You can see that each input sentence gets duplicated for each word it contains.

AGGREGATORS

The last class of customizable predicate operations is aggregators. As we mentioned earlier, there are three types of aggregators, each with different properties regarding composition and performance.

Perhaps rather obviously, the first type of aggregator is literally called an *aggregator*. An aggregator looks at one tuple at a time for each tuple in a group, adjusting some internal state for each observed tuple. The following is an implementation of sum as an aggregator:

```
public static class SumAggregator extends CascalogAggregator {
    public void start(FlowProcess process, AggregatorCall call) {
        call.setContext(0);
    }

    public void aggregate(FlowProcess process, AggregatorCall call) {
        int total = (Integer) call.getContext();
        call.setContext(total + call.getArguments().getInteger(0));
    }

    public void complete(FlowProcess process, AggregatorCall call) {
        int total = (Integer) call.getContext();
        call.getOutputCollector().add(new Tuple(total));
    }
}
```

Initializes the aggregator internal state →

Called for each tuple; updates the internal state to store the running sum →

Once all tuples are processed, emits a tuple with the final result ←

The next type of aggregator is called a *buffer*. A buffer receives an iterator to the entire set of tuples for a group. Here's an implementation of sum as a buffer:

```
public static class SumBuffer extends CascalogBuffer {
    public void operate(FlowProcess process, BufferCall call) {
        Iterator<TupleEntry> it = call.getArgumentsIterator();
        int total = 0;
        while(it.hasNext()) {
            TupleEntry t = it.next();
            total+=t.getInteger(0);
        }
```

The tuple set is accessible via an iterator. ←

```
    call.getOutputCollector().add(new Tuple(total)); ◁
  }
}
```
A single function iterates over all tuples and emits the output tuple.

Buffers are easier to write than aggregators because you only need to implement one method rather than three. But unlike buffers, aggregators can be chained in a query. *Chaining* means you can compute multiple aggregations at the same time for the same group. Buffers can't be used along with any other aggregator type, but aggregators can be used with other aggregators.

In the context of the MapReduce framework, both buffers and aggregators rely on reducers to perform the actual computation for these operators. This is illustrated in figure 7.15.

JCascalog packs together as many operations as possible into map and reduce tasks, but these aggregator operators are solely performed by reducers. This necessitates a network-intensive approach because all data for the computation must flow from the mappers to the reducers. Furthermore, if there were only a single group (such as if you were counting the number of tuples in a dataset), all the tuples would have to be sent to a single reducer for aggregation, defeating the purpose of using a parallel computation system.

Fortunately, the last type of aggregator operation can do aggregations more scalably and efficiently. These aggregators are analogous to *combiner aggregators* from pipe diagrams, though in JCascalog they're called *parallel aggregators*. A parallel aggregator performs an aggregation incrementally by doing partial aggregations in the map tasks.

Figure 7.16 shows the division of labor for sum when implemented as a parallel aggregator. Not every aggregator can be implemented as a parallel aggregator, but when it's possible, you can achieve huge performance gains by avoiding all that network I/O.

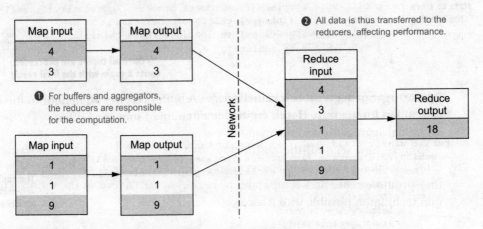

Figure 7.15 Execution of sum aggregator and sum buffer at the MapReduce level

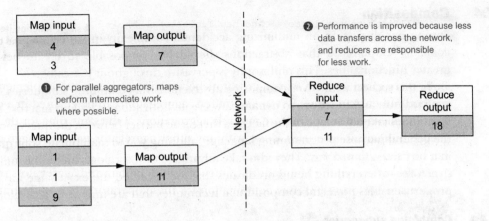

Figure 7.16 Execution of a sum parallel aggregator at the MapReduce level

To write your own parallel aggregator, you must implement two functions:

- The init function maps the arguments from a single tuple to a partial aggregation for that tuple.
- The combine function specifies how to combine two partial aggregations into a single aggregation value.

The following code implements sum as a parallel aggregator:

For sum, the partial aggregation is just the value in the argument.

```
public static class SumParallel implements ParallelAgg {
    public void prepare(FlowProcess process, OperationCall call) {}

    public List<Object> init(List<Object> input) {
        return input;
    }

    public List<Object> combine(List<Object> input1,
        List<Object> input2) {
        int val1 = (Integer) input1.get(0);
        int val2 = (Integer) input2.get(0);
        return Arrays.asList((Object) (val1 + val2));
    }
}
```

To combine two partial aggregations, simply sum the values.

Parallel aggregators can be chained with other parallel aggregators or regular aggregators. But when chained with regular aggregators, parallel aggregators are unable to do partial aggregations in the map tasks and will act like regular aggregators.

You've now seen all the abstractions that comprise JCascalog subqueries: predicates, functions, filters, and aggregators. The power of these abstractions lies in how they promote reuse and composability. Let's now take a look at the various composition techniques possible with JCascalog.

7.4   Composition

During our discussion on minimizing accidental complexity in your data-processing code, we emphasized that abstractions should be composable to create new and greater functionalities. This philosophy is pervasive throughout JCascalog.

In this section we'll cover composing abstractions via combining subqueries, predicate macros, and functions to dynamically create both subqueries and macros. These techniques take advantage of the fact that there's no barrier between the query tool and the general-purpose programming language, allowing you to manipulate your queries in a very fine-grained way. They also take advantage of JCascalog's incredibly uniform structure—of everything being predicates that are specified the exact same way. This property enables powerful compositional techniques that are unique to JCascalog.

7.4.1   Combining subqueries

Subqueries are the basic unit of abstraction in JCascalog, for they represent an arbitrary view on any number of data sources. One of the most powerful features of subqueries is that they can be addressed as data sources for other subqueries. Just as you break down a large program into many functions, this allows you to similarly deconstruct large queries.

Let's look at an example to find all the records from the FOLLOWS dataset where each person in the record follows more than two people:

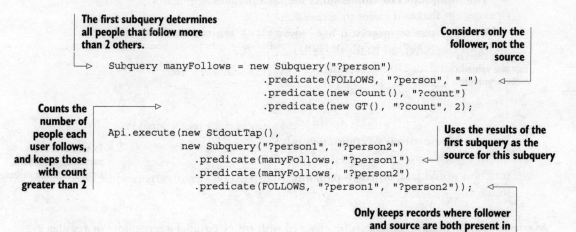

Subqueries are lazy—nothing is computed until Api.execute is called. In the previous example, even though the manyFollows subquery is defined first, no MapReduce jobs are launched until the Api.execute call is made.

Here's another example of a query that requires multiple subqueries. This query extends word count by finding the number of words that exist for each computed word count:

```
Subquery wordCount = new Subquery("?word", "?count")
                       .predicate(SENTENCE, "?sentence")
                       .predicate(new Split(), "?sentence").out("?word")
                       .predicate(new Count(), "?count");
```
⟵ **The basic word count subquery**

```
Api.execute(new StdoutTap(),
            new Subquery("?count", "?num-words")
            .predicate(wordCount, "_", "?count")
            .predicate(new Count(), "?num-words"));
```
⟵ **The second subquery only requires the count for each word.**

⟵ **Determines the number of words for each count value**

Combining subqueries is a powerful paradigm for expressing complex operations using simple components. This power is made more accessible because functions can generate subqueries directly, as we'll discuss next.

7.4.2 Dynamically created subqueries

One of the most common techniques when using JCascalog is to write functions that create subqueries dynamically. That is, you write regular Java code that constructs a subquery according to some parameters. You've previously witnessed the advantages of using subqueries as data sources for other subqueries, and generating subqueries dynamically makes it easier to access these benefits.

For example, suppose you have text files on HDFS representing transaction data: an ID for the buyer, an ID for the seller, a timestamp, and a dollar amount. The data is JSON-encoded and looks like this:

```
{"buyer": 123, "seller": 456, "amt": 50, "timestamp": 1322401523}
{"buyer": 1009, "seller": 12, "amt": 987, "timestamp": 1341401523}
{"buyer": 2, "seller": 98, "amt": 12, "timestamp": 1343401523}
```

You may have a variety of computations you want to run on this data, but each of your queries shares a common need to parse the data from the text files. A useful utility function would take an HDFS path and return a subquery that parses the data at that location:

The subquery needs a Cascalog function to perform the actual parsing.

An external library converts the JSON to a map.

The desired map values are translated into a single tuple.

```
public static class ParseTransactionRecord extends CascalogFunction {  ⟵
    public void operate(FlowProcess process, FunctionCall call) {
        String line = call.getArguments().getString(0);
    ⟶  Map parsed = (Map) JSONValue.parse(line);
    ⟶  call.getOutputCollector().add(new Tuple(parsed.get("buyer"),
                                              parsed.get("seller"),
                                              parsed.get("amt"),
                                              parsed.get("timestamp")));
        }
    }
```

Generates a tap from the provided HDFS path

A regular Java function dynamically generates the subquery.

```
public static Subquery parseTransactionData(String path) {
  return new Subquery("?buyer", "?seller", "?amt", "?timestamp")
    .predicate(Api.hfsTextline(path), "?line")
    .predicate(new ParseTransactionRecord(), "?line")
    .out("?buyer", "?seller", "?amt", "?timestamp");
}
```

Calls the custom JSON parsing function

Once it's defined, you can use this abstraction for any query over the dataset. For example, here's a query that computes the number of transactions for each buyer:

```
public static Subquery buyerNumTransactions(String path) {
  return new Subquery("?buyer", "?count")
    .predicate(parseTransactionData(path), "?buyer", "_", "_", "_")
    .predicate(new Count(), "?count");
}
```

Disregards all fields but the buyer

This is a very simple example of creating subqueries dynamically, but it illustrates how subqueries can be composed together in order to abstract away pieces of a more complicated computation. Let's look at another example in which the number of predicates in a subquery is dynamic based on the arguments.

Suppose you have a set of retweet data with each record denoting a retweet of some other tweet, and you want to find all chains of retweets of a certain length. That is, for a chain of length 4, you want to know all retweets of retweets of retweets of tweets.

The original dataset consists of pairs of tweet identifiers. Notice that you can transform these pairs into chains of length 3 by joining the dataset with itself. Similarly, you can then find chains of length 4 by joining the length 3 chains with the original pairs. To illustrate, here's a query that returns chains of length 3, given an input generator of pairs:

```
public static Subquery chainsLength3(Object pairs) {
  return new Subquery("?a", "?b", "?c")
    .predicate(pairs, "?a", "?b")
    .predicate(pairs, "?b", "?c");
}
```

An additional join finds all chains of length 4:

```
public static Subquery chainsLength4(Object pairs) {
  return new Subquery("?a", "?b", "?c", "?d")
    .predicate(pairs, "?a", "?b")
    .predicate(pairs, "?b", "?c")
    .predicate(pairs, "?c", "?d");
}
```

To generalize this process to find chains of any length, you need a function that generates a subquery with the correct number of predicates and variables. This can be accomplished by writing some fairly simple Java code:

```
public static Subquery chainsLengthN(Object pairs, int n) {
   List<String> genVars = new ArrayList<String>();
   for(int i=0; i<n; i++) {
      genVars.add(Api.genNullableVar());     ←──── Generates
   }                                                unique nullable
                                                    output variables
   Subquery ret = new Subquery(genVars);
   for(int i=0; i<n-1; i++) {
      ret = ret.predicate(pairs, genVars.get(i), genVars.get(i+1));   ←──
   }
   return ret;                                          Loops to define the
}                                                       required number of joins
```

An interesting note about this function is that it's not specific to retweet data: it can take any subquery or source of data containing pairs and return a subquery that computes chains.

Let's look at one more example of a dynamically created subquery. Suppose you want to draw a random sample of *N* elements from a dataset of unknown size. The simplest strategy to accomplish this in a distributed and scalable way is with the following algorithm:

1. Generate a random number for every element.
2. Find the *N* elements with the smallest random numbers.

JCascalog has a built-in aggregator named `Limit` for performing the second step. `Limit` uses a strategy similar to parallel aggregators where it finds the smallest *N* elements on each map task, and then combines the results from all the map tasks to find the *N* smallest elements overall. The following code implements this strategy to draw a random sample:

Introspects the input dataset to
determine the correct number of
input and output fields

```
                    public static Subquery fixedRandomSample(Object data, int n) {
Generates              List<String> inputVars = new ArrayList<String>();
separate fields        List<String> outputVars = new ArrayList<String>();
for input and          for(int i=0; i < Api.numOutFields(data); i++) {
output variables         inputVars.add(Api.genNullableVar());
                         outputVars.add(Api.genNullableVar());
                       }                                    Creates a separate field to
                                                            hold the random values

                       String randVar = Api.genNullableVar();   ←──
Uses the               return new Subquery(outputVars)
JCascalog                .predicate(data, inputVars)
RandLong                 .predicate(new RandLong(), randVar)    Performs secondary sorting
function to              .predicate(Option.SORT, randVar)       on the random values
append each              .predicate(new Limit(n), inputVars).out(outputVars);   ←──
input tuple with     }
a random value
                                                            Uses the Limit aggregator to find N
                                                            random tuples from the dataset
```

This algorithm is very scalable: it parallelizes the computation of the fixed sample without ever needing to centralize all the records in one place.

When writing JCascalog queries, you'll notice that certain combinations of predicates are frequently used together. In these situations it's simpler and more efficient to express the collective functionality with a single operation. We'll next delve into how JCascalog supports this ability by the use of predicate macros.

7.4.3   Predicate macros

A predicate macro is an operation that JCascalog expands to another set of predicates. Because JCascalog represents all operations as predicates, predicate macros can create powerful abstractions by composing predicates together, whether they're aggregators, filters, or functions.

You've already seen one example of a predicate macro with the definition of Average at the beginning of this chapter. Let's look at that definition once more:

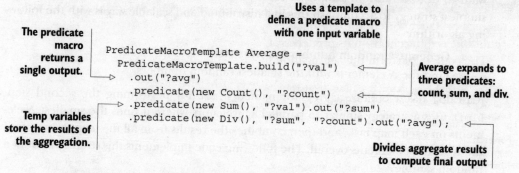

Average consists of three predicates composed together: a count aggregation, a sum aggregation, and a division function. Figure 7.17 demonstrates how Average is called and its resulting expansion.

The definition of Average uses a JCascalog template to specify the predicates this particular predicate macro should be expanded to. But not everything can be specified with

```
new Subquery("?result")
  .predicate(INTEGER, "?n")
  .predicate(Average, "?n").out("?result");
```

Example source code using the Average predicate macro.

```
new Subquery("?result")
  .predicate(INTEGER, "?n")
  .predicate(new Count(), "?count_gen1")
  .predicate(new Sum(), "?n").out("?sum_gen2")
  .predicate(new Div(), "?sum_gen2", "?count_gen1")
  .out("?result");
```

Behind the scenes, JCascalog expands the macro into its constituent predicates using unique field names so as not to conflict with the surrounding subquery.

Figure 7.17   Predicate macros provide powerful abstractions for writing simple queries that JCascalog automatically expands into the constituent predicates.

a template. For example, suppose you wanted to create a predicate macro that computes the number of distinct values for a given set of variables, like so:

```
new Subquery("?distinct-followers-count")
    .predicate(FOLLOWS, "?person", "_")
    .predicate(new DistinctCount(), "?person")
    .out("?distinct-followers-count");
```

The desired macro counts the number of distinct followers.

This subquery determines the number of distinct users that follow at least one other person. Unlike calculating the average of a single variable, you could potentially calculate distinct counts for variable sets of any size. You can't use templates because they only support fixed sets of input and output variables. Let's look at another way to define predicate macros to achieve this functionality.

First, you need to define an aggregator that performs the actual computation. This aggregator must work even if the number of tuples for a group is so large that it could not be contained in memory. To solve this problem, you can make use of a feature called *secondary sorting* that sorts the group of tuples before being processed by the aggregator. Once sorted, the aggregator only increments the distinct count if the current tuple is different from its predecessor.

The code to perform the aggregation follows:

```
public static class DistinctCountAgg extends CascalogAggregator {
    static class State {
        int count = 0;
        Tuple last = null;
    }

    public void start(FlowProcess process, AggregatorCall call) {
        call.setContext(new State());
    }

    public void aggregate(FlowProcess process, AggregatorCall call) {
        State s = (State) call.getContext();
        Tuple t = call.getArguments().getTupleCopy();
        if(s.last==null || !s.last.equals(t)) {
            s.count++;
        }
        s.last = t;
    }

    public void complete(FlowProcess process, AggregatorCall call) {
        State s = (State) call.getContext();
        call.getOutputCollector().add(new Tuple(s.count));
    }
}
```

Internal state to track the current count and the previously seen tuple

For each group, initializes the tracking state

When processing a tuple, retrieves the current state

Increases the distinct count only if the current tuple differs from the previous one

Always updates the last seen tuple in the state

When all tuples of the group have been processed, emits the distinct count

`DistinctCountAgg` contains the logic to compute the unique count given a sorted input; unsurprisingly, JCascalog has an `Option.SORT` predicate to specify how to sort the tuples for each group. The following code demonstrates how you define the sort and compute the distinct count by hand:

```
public static Subquery distinctCountManual() {
  return new Subquery("?distinct-followers-count")
    .predicate(FOLLOWS, "?person", "_")
    .predicate(Option.SORT, "?person")           ◄──── Sorts the tuple
    .predicate(new DistinctCountAgg(), "?person")       by ?person field
    .out("?distinct-followers-count");
```

Of course, you would much prefer a predicate macro here so that you don't have to specify the sort and aggregator each time you want to do a distinct count. The most general form of a predicate macro is a function that takes a list of input fields and a list of output fields and then returns a set of predicates. The following is the definition of DistinctCount as a regular PredicateMacro:

> The input and output fields are determined when the macro is used within a subquery.

```
public static class DistinctCount implements PredicateMacro {
  public List<Predicate> getPredicates(Fields inFields,
                                       Fields outFields) {   ◄────
    List<Predicate> ret = new ArrayList<Predicate>();
    ret.add(new Predicate(Option.SORT, inFields));      ◄──── Groups are sorted
    ret.add(new Predicate(new DistinctCountAgg(),             by the provided
                   inFields,                                  input fields.
                   outFields));                    ◄────
    return ret;
  }                    For this macro, the distinct count emits
}                      a single field, but the general macro
                       form supports multiple outputs.
```

7.4.4   *Dynamically created predicate macros*

You previously saw how regular Java functions can dynamically create subqueries, so it's no great surprise that you can do the same with predicate macros. This is an extremely powerful technique that showcases the advantages of having your data-processing tool be a library for your general-purpose programming language.

Consider the following query:

```
new Subquery("?x", "?y", "?z")                    Reads a dataset
  .predicate(TRIPLETS, "?a", "?b", "?c")    ◄──── containing triples
  .predicate(new IncrementFunction(), "?a").out("?x")   of numbers
  .predicate(new IncrementFunction(), "?b").out("?y")  ◄──
  .predicate(new IncrementFunction(), "?c").out("?z");    Returns a new triplet
                                                          where each field is
                                                          incremented
```

Although it's a simple query, there's considerable repetition because it must explicitly apply IncrementFunction to each field from the input data. It would be nice to be able to eliminate this repetition, like so:

```
new Subquery("?x", "?y", "?z")
    .predicate(TRIPLETS, "?a", "?b", "?c")
    .predicate(new Each(new IncrementFunction()), "?a", "?b", "?c")
    .out("?x", "?y", "?z");
```

Rather than repeatedly using `IncrementFunction`, the `Each` predicate macro applies the function to the specified input fields and generates the desired output. The expansion of the predicate macro matches the three separate predicates in the original query. Here's the `Each` predicate macro:

```
public static class Each implements PredicateMacro {
  Object _op;

  public Each(Object op) {              Each is parameterized
    _op = op;                  ◁───────  with the predicate
  }                                      operation to use.

  public List<Predicate> getPredicates(Fields inFields,
                                       Fields outFields) {
    List<Predicate> ret = new ArrayList<Predicate>();
    for(int i=0; i<inFields.size(); i++) {
      Object in = inFields.get(i);
      Object out = outFields.get(i);                 The predicate macro
      ret.add(new Predicate(_op,                     creates a predicate
                      Arrays.asList(in),             for each given input/
                      Arrays.asList(out)));  ◁─────  output field pair.
    }
    return ret;
  }
}
```

Let's look at another example of a dynamic predicate macro. We earlier defined `IncrementFunction` as its own function that increments its argument, but in reality it's simply the `Plus` function with one argument set to 1. It would be useful to have a predicate macro that abstracts away the partial application of a predicate operation. You could then define the `Increment` operation like this:

```
Object Increment = new Partial(new Plus(), 1);
```

As you can see, `Partial` is a predicate macro that fills in some of the input fields. It allows you to rewrite the query that increments the triplets like so:

```
new Subquery("?x", "?y", "?z")
    .predicate(TRIPLETS, "?a", "?b", "?c")
    .predicate(new Each(new Partial(new Plus(), 1)), "?a", "?b", "?c")
    .out("?x", "?y", "?z");
```

After expanding all the predicate macros, this query translates to the following:

```
new Subquery("?x", "?y", "?z")
    .predicate(TRIPLETS, "?a", "?b", "?c")
    .predicate(new Plus(), 1, "?a").out("?x")
    .predicate(new Plus(), 1, "?b").out("?y")
    .predicate(new Plus(), 1, "?c").out("?z");
```

The definition of `Partial` is straightforward:

```
public static class Partial implements PredicateMacro {
  Object _op;
  List<Object> _args;

  public Partial(Object op, Object... args) {
    _op = op;
    _args = Arrays.asList(args);
  }

  public List<Predicate> getPredicates(Fields inFields,
                                       Fields outFields) {
    List<Predicate> ret = new ArrayList<Predicate>();
    List<Object> input = new ArrayList<Object>();
    input.addAll(_args);
    input.addAll(inFields);
    ret.add(new Predicate(_op, input, outFields));
    return ret;
  }
}
```

The predicate macro simply prepends any provided input fields to the input fields specified when the subquery is created. As you can see, dynamic predicate macros give you great power to manipulate the construction of your subqueries.

7.5   *Summary*

The way you express your computations is crucially important if you want to avoid complexity, prevent bugs, and increase productivity. The main techniques for fighting complexity are abstraction and composition, and it's important that your data-processing tool encourage these techniques rather than make them difficult.

In the next two chapters, we'll reinforce the concepts of the batch layer by building out the batch layer for SuperWebAnalytics.com. SuperWebAnalytics.com is a more sophisticated and realistic example that's intended to really demonstrate the intricacies of batch computation in terms of architecture, algorithms, and implementation.

An example batch layer: Architecture and algorithms

This chapter covers

- Building a batch layer from end to end
- Practical examples of precomputation
- Iterative graph algorithms
- HyperLogLog for efficient set-cardinality operations

You've now learned all the pieces of the batch layer: formulating a schema for your data, storing a master dataset, and running computations at scale with a minimum of complexity. In this chapter you'll tie these pieces together into a coherent batch layer. No new theory is introduced in this chapter—our goal is to reinforce the concepts of the previous chapters by going through a batch layer design from start to finish. There is great value in understanding how the theory maps to a non-trivial example.

Specifically, you'll learn how to create the batch layer for our running example of SuperWebAnalytics.com. SuperWebAnalytics.com is complex enough to require a fairly sophisticated batch layer, but not so complex as to lose you in the details.

You'll see that the various batch layer abstractions fit together nicely and that the resulting batch layer for SuperWebAnalytics.com is quite elegant.

After reviewing the product requirements for SuperWebAnalytics.com, we'll give a broad overview of what the batch layer must accomplish and what should be precomputed for each batch view. In this chapter you'll see the architecture and algorithms for the batch layer (using pipe diagrams), and in the next chapter you'll see them implemented in code using specific tools. Throughout the chapter, keep in mind the flexibility of the batch layer. We'll cover the processing workflow for three example batch views, but it's very easy to extend the batch layer to compute new views. This means the batch layer is inherently prepared to adapt to changing customer and application requirements.

8.1   Design of the SuperWebAnalytics.com batch layer

You'll build the batch layer for SuperWebAnalytics.com to support the computation of three types of queries. Recall that the goal of the batch layer is to precompute views so that the specified queries can be satisfied with low latency. After introducing the queries that SuperWebAnalytics.com will support, we'll discuss the batch views needed to answer them.

8.1.1   Supported queries

SuperWebAnalytics.com will support three distinct types of queries:

- *Pageview counts by URL sliced by time*—"What were the pageviews for each day over the past year?" and "How many pageviews have there been in the past 12 hours?"
- *Unique visitors by URL sliced by time*—"How many unique users frequented this domain in 2010?" and "How many unique people visited this domain each hour for the past three days?"
- *Bounce-rate analysis*—"What percentage of people visit the page without visiting any other pages on this website?"

The way people are modeled makes the second query type more challenging. Recall that the SuperWebAnalytics.com schema represents a person as either the user ID of a logged-in user or via a cookie identifier from the browser. A single person could therefore visit the same site under different identifiers—their cookie may change if they clear the cookie, or the user could register with multiple user IDs.

The schema handles this multiplicity by defining *equiv* edges that indicate when two different user representations are actually the same person. The equiv graph for a person can be arbitrarily complex, as shown in figure 8.1. Accurately computing this second query type requires that you must analyze the data to determine which pageviews belong to one person using different identifiers.

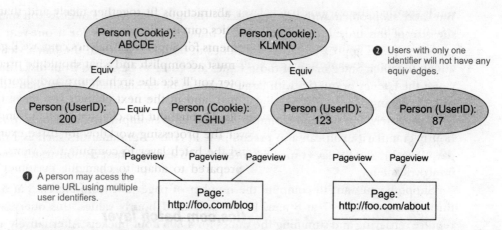

Figure 8.1   Examples of different pageviews for the same person being captured using different identifiers

8.1.2   Batch views

Next we'll review the batch views needed to satisfy each query. The key to each batch view is striking a balance between the size of the precomputed views and the amount of on-the-fly computation required at query time.

PAGEVIEWS OVER TIME

You want to be able to retrieve the number of pageviews for a URL for any time range down to the granularity of an hour. As mentioned in chapter 4, precomputing the pageview counts for every possible time range is infeasible, as that would require an unmanageable 380 million precomputed values for every URL for each year covered by the dataset. Instead, you can precompute a smaller number and require more computation to be done at query time.

The simplest approach is to precompute the number of pageviews for each URL for every hour bucket. This would result in a batch view that looks like figure 8.2. To resolve a query, you retrieve the value for every hour bucket in the time range, and sum the values together.

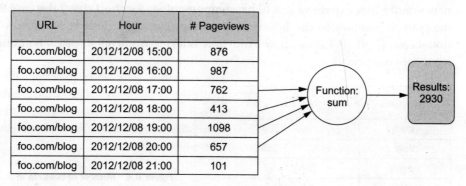

Figure 8.2   Precomputing pageviews with an hourly granularity

But there's a problem with this approach—the query becomes slower as you increase the size of the time range. Finding the number of pageviews for a one-year time period requires approximately 8,760 values to be retrieved from the batch view and added together. Since many of those values are going to be served from disk, this can cause the latency of queries with large ranges to be substantially higher than queries with small ranges.

Fortunately, the solution is simple. Instead of precomputing values only using an hourly granularity, you can also precompute at coarser granularities such as 1-day, 7-day (1-week), and 28-day (1-month) intervals. An example best demonstrates how this improves latency.

Suppose you want to compute the number of pageviews from March 3 at 3 a.m. through September 17 at 8 a.m. If you only used hourly values, this query would require retrieving and summing the values for 4,805 hour buckets. Alternatively, using coarser granularities can substantially reduce the number of retrieved values. The idea is to retrieve values for each month between March 3 and September 17, and then add or subtract values for more refined intervals to get the desired range. This idea is illustrated in figure 8.3.

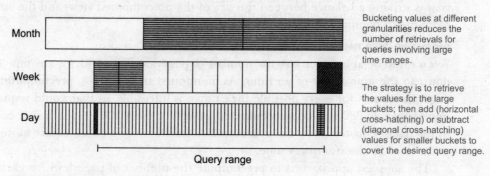

Bucketing values at different granularities reduces the number of retrievals for queries involving large time ranges.

The strategy is to retrieve the values for the large buckets; then add (horizontal cross-hatching) or subtract (diagonal cross-hatching) values for smaller buckets to cover the desired query range.

Figure 8.3   Optimizing pageviews over large query ranges using coarser granularities

For this query, only 26 values need to be retrieved—almost a 200x improvement! You may wonder how expensive it is to precompute values for the 1-day, 7-day, and 28-day intervals in addition to the hourly buckets. Astonishingly, there is hardly any additional cost. Figure 8.4 shows how many time buckets are needed for each granularity for a one-year period.

Granularity	Number of buckets in 1 year
hourly	8760
daily	~ 365
weekly	~ 52
monthly	~ 13

Figure 8.4   Number of buckets in a one-year period for each granularity

Adding up the numbers, the 1-day, 7-day, and 28-day buckets require an additional 430 values to be precomputed for every URL for a one-year period. That's only a 5% increase in precomputation for a 200x reduction in the query-time work for large ranges—a more than acceptable trade-off.

UNIQUE VISITORS OVER TIME

The next query type determines the number of unique visitors for a specified time interval. This seems like it should be similar to pageviews over time, but there is one key difference: unique counts are not additive. Whereas you can get the total number of pageviews for a two-hour period by adding the values for the individual hours together, you can't do the same for this query type. This is because a unique count represents the size of a *set* of elements, and there may be overlap between the sets for each hour. If you simply added the counts for the two hours together, you'd double-count the people who visited the URL in both time intervals.

The only way to compute the number of uniques with perfect accuracy over any time range is to compute the unique count on the fly. This requires random access to the set of visitors for each URL for each hour time bucket. This is doable but expensive, as essentially your entire master dataset must be indexed. Alternatively, you can use an approximation algorithm that sacrifices some accuracy to vastly decrease the amount of data to be indexed in the batch view. An example of an approximation algorithm for distinct counting is the HyperLogLog algorithm. For every URL and hour bucket, HyperLogLog only requires information on the order of 1 KB to estimate set cardinalities of up to one billion with a maximum 2% error rate.[1]

Although it's an intriguing algorithm, we want to avoid becoming sidetracked with the details of HyperLogLog. Instead, let's treat it as a black box and focus on its interface:

```
interface HyperLogLog {
  long size();
  void add(Object o);
  HyperLogLog merge(HyperLogLog... otherSets);
}
```

Each `HyperLogLog` object represents a set of elements and supports adding new elements to the set, merging with other HyperLogLog sets, and retrieving the size of the set. Using HyperLogLog makes the uniques-over-time query very similar to the pageviews-over-time query. The key differences are that a relatively larger value is computed for each URL and time bucket, and the HyperLogLog merge function is used to combine time buckets instead of summing counts together. As with pageviews over time, HyperLogLog sets for 1-day, 7-day, and 28-day granularities are created to reduce the amount of work to be done at query time.

---

[1] The HyperLogLog algorithm is described in a research paper titled "HyperLogLog: the analysis of a near-optimal cardinality estimation algorithm" by Philippe Flajolet, Éric Fusy, Olivier Gandouet, and Frédéric Meunier, available at http://algo.inria.fr/flajolet/Publications/FlFuGaMe07.pdf.

BOUNCE-RATE ANALYSIS

The final query type is to determine the bounce rate for every domain. The batch view for this query is simple: a map from each domain to the number of bounced visits and the total number of visits. The bounce rate is simply the ratio of these two values.

The key to precomputing these values is defining what exactly constitutes a visit. We'll define two pageviews as being part of the same visit if they are from the same user to the same domain and are separated by less than half an hour. A visit is considered a bounce if it only contains one pageview.

8.2   *Workflow overview*

Now that the specific requirements for the batch views are understood, we can define the batch layer workflow at a high level. The basis of the workflow is illustrated in figure 8.5.

At the start of the batch layer workflow is a single folder on the distributed filesystem that contains the master dataset. The first step is simply to take any new data that has accumulated since the last time the batch layer ran and append it to the master dataset.

The next two steps normalize the data in preparation for computing the batch views. The first normalization step accounts for the fact that different URLs can refer

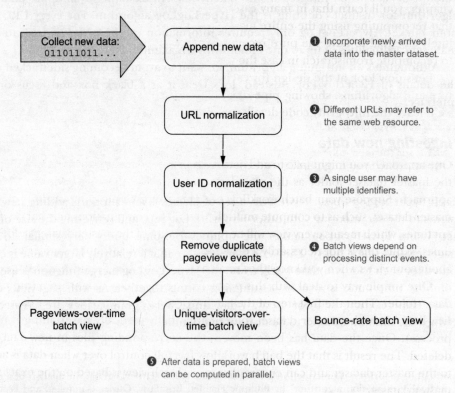

Figure 8.5   Batch workflow for SuperWebAnalytics.com

to the same resource. For example, the distinct URLs www.mysite.com/blog/1?utm=1 and http://mysite.com/blog/1 refer to the same location. This first normalization step transforms all URLs to a standard format so that future computations can correctly aggregate the data.

The second normalization step is needed because data for the same person may exist under different user identifiers. In order to support queries about visits and visitors, you must select a single identifier for each person. This latter normalization step processes the equiv graph to accomplish this task. Since the batch views only make use of the pageviews data, only the pageview edges will be converted to use these selected user IDs.

The next step deduplicates the pageview events. Recall from chapter 2 the advantages of having your data units contain enough information to make them uniquely identifiable. In problematic scenarios (such as network partitioning), it's common to register the same pageview multiple times to ensure that the event is recorded. Deduplicating the pageviews is necessary to compute the batch views, as they depend on the distinct events in the dataset.

The final step is to use the normalized data to compute the batch views described in the previous section. Note that this workflow is a pure recomputation workflow—every time new data is added, the batch views are recomputed from scratch. In a later chapter, you'll learn that in many cases you can incrementalize the batch layer such that recomputing using the entire master dataset is not always required. But it's absolutely essential to have the pure recomputation workflow defined, because you need to recompute from scratch in case the views become corrupted.

Let's now look at the design for each step in more detail. We'll focus on architecture and algorithms, showing pipe diagrams for every data-transformation step, and we'll leave the nitty-gritty code details for next chapter.

8.3 Ingesting new data

One approach you might take to add data to the master dataset is to insert new files into the master dataset folder as the new data comes in. But there's a problem with this approach. Suppose your batch workflow needs to run multiple computations over the master dataset, such as to compute multiple views. The computations may start at different times, which means every view will be representative of the master dataset at different times. While this is not necessarily a deal-breaker, we think it's much simpler to reason about your views when you know they're all based on the exact same master dataset.

One simple way to deal with this problem is to have new data written into a new-data/ folder. Then the first step of the batch workflow is to move whatever data was in new-data/ into the master dataset folder (potentially vertically partitioning it in the process). Once the data has been moved, the corresponding files in new-data/ are deleted. The result is that the batch workflow has full control over when data is added to the master dataset and can ensure that every batch view is based on the exact same master dataset.

8.4   URL normalization

The next step of the workflow is to normalize all of the URLs in the master dataset. The query to accomplish this task requires a custom function that implements the normalization logic. Normalization can involve stripping URL parameters, adding *http://* to the beginning, removing trailing slashes, and so on. Most importantly, all the normalization logic is self-contained in a single function and can operate on every URL independently.

The pipe diagram for this computation is extremely simple and is shown in figure 8.6. As you can see, all it has to do is run a function on each data unit.

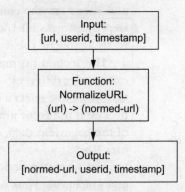

Figure 8.6   URL-normalization pipe diagram

Extracting fields from objects in pipe diagrams

Generally your data is packaged into objects containing the fields you care about. For example, a `Pageview` object contains the fields `url`, `timestamp`, and `userid`. When using a real-world implementation of pipe diagrams, your computation starts with a single field containing your object, and you run a function on that object to extract the fields you want to manipulate (to join on, group on, use as arguments to functions, and so on). For conciseness, in this chapter we'll typically skip the extraction step and start the pipe diagram with the input being the constituent fields of the object being manipulated.

8.5   User-identifier normalization

The next step is to select a single user identifier for each person. This is the most sophisticated portion of the workflow, as it involves a fully distributed iterative graph algorithm. Despite its complexity, it only requires a few small pipe diagrams to solve it. With the appropriate tooling, you can implement it in only about 100 lines of code (as will be demonstrated in the next chapter).

User IDs are marked as belonging to the same person via equiv edges. If you were to visualize these edges from a dataset, you'd see numerous independent subgraphs, as shown in figure 8.7.

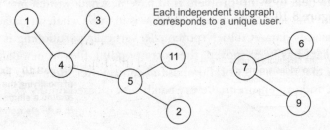

Each independent subgraph corresponds to a unique user.

Figure 8.7   Example equiv graph

User ID	Mapped user ID
2	1
3	1
4	1
5	1
11	1
7	6
9	6

❶ If a user has multiple IDs, map the extraneous IDs to the minimum value for the user.

❷ Only need to store remapped IDs, so selected IDs (1, 6) are omitted.

Figure 8.8 Mapping from user IDs to a single identifier for each set

Each subgraph represents a unique user. For each person, you need to select a single identifier and create a mapping from the other IDs to this identifier, as shown in figure 8.8.

You'll accomplish this by transforming the original equiv graph to the form depicted in figure 8.8. For this example, the transformation is shown in figure 8.9, where every user ID associated with a person maps to a single ID uniquely chosen for that person.

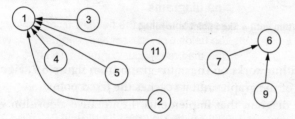

Figure 8.9 Original equiv graph transformed so that all nodes in a set point to a single node

This idea must be translated into a concrete algorithm that runs scalably using batch computation. All of our previous examples of batch computation involved executing a single pipe diagram a single time to generate the desired output. For this algorithm, however, it's impossible to get the desired results in a single step. Instead, you must take an iterative approach where each step modifies the graph to a state closer to the desired structure shown in figure 8.9. Once you've defined the iterative step, you execute it repeatedly until no further progress is made. This is known as reaching a *fixed point* where the resulting output is the same as the input. When this point is reached, the graph has attained the desired state.

At each iteration, the algorithm will examine the neighbors for each node in the graph. It will determine the smallest ID among the connected nodes, and then ensure that each edge points to the node with this minimum value. This process is illustrated for a single node in figure 8.10.

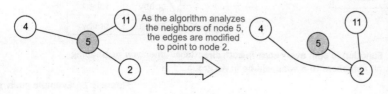

As the algorithm analyzes the neighbors of node 5, the edges are modified to point to node 2.

Figure 8.10 Example of modifying the edges around a single node in a single iteration

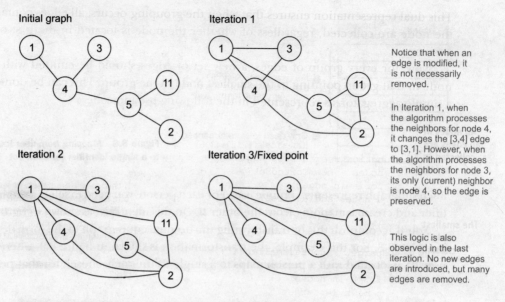

Notice that when an edge is modified, it is not necessarily removed.

In Iteration 1, when the algorithm processes the neighbors for node 4, it changes the [3,4] edge to [3,1]. However, when the algorithm processes the neighbors for node 3, its only (current) neighbor is node 4, so the edge is preserved.

This logic is also observed in the last iteration. No new edges are introduced, but many edges are removed.

Figure 8.11   Iterating the algorithm until a fixed point is reached

You can see how this algorithm works on the equiv graph from figure 8.7. Figure 8.11 shows the transformations of the graph until it reaches the fixed point.

Let's formulate a pipe diagram that implements the iterative algorithm you just saw. The input to the algorithm is a set of 2-tuples of person IDs representing equiv edges.

The first requirement of the iterative algorithm is to determine the immediate neighbors for each node. You could try grouping the tuples by their first element, but this would exclude edges where the given node is stored in the last element. So the first step is to emit every edge in both directions using a function we'll call BidirectionalEdges. That way, when grouping by the first element, you get every edge that node exists in. BidirectionalEdges is illustrated in figure 8.12.

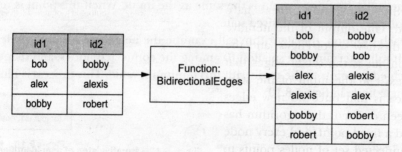

Figure 8.12   Function to emit every edge in both directions. When you're grouping by id1 or id2, all neighbors to a node will be in its group.

This dual representation ensures that when the grouping occurs, all edges containing the node are collected, regardless of whether the node is located in the first or last position.

Now, for every group of edges, a new set of edges should be emitted with each node in that group pointing to the smallest node in the group. This can be done with a simple aggregator, as represented in the following pseudo-code:

All nodes in all edges are collected in a set.

The smallest node is chosen.

```
function userid-step-aggregator(grouped-node, edges) {
    nodes = new SortedSet()
    for(e in edges) {
        nodes.add(e.first)
        nodes.add(e.second)
    }
    target = nodes.smallest()
    isNewEdges = grouped != target && nodes.size() > 2
    for(n in nodes) {
        if(n != target) {
            emit(n, target, isNewEdges)
        }
    }
}
```

If this condition is met, at least one new edge is being emitted. This information will be used later to determine when to stop running the iterative step.

For every node except the chosen node, a new edge is emitted to the chosen node.

When the grouped node is the smallest among its neighbors, then the emitted edges are unchanged. Otherwise, if the node has more than one neighbor, then some edges will be modified to point to the smallest identifier. With the `BidirectionalEdges` function and the aggregator complete, the pipe diagram for the iterative step is simple, as shown in figure 8.13.

The iterative step needs to be run repeatedly until no edges have changed. One output of the iterative step is the new set of edges, and the other output is the set of edges that didn't exist in the input of the step. The idea is that once no new edges have been emitted, the algorithm has reached a fixed point, and every node in a connected set of nodes points to the smallest node in that set.

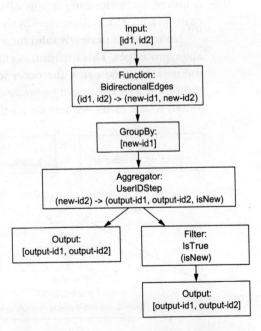

Figure 8.13 Iterative step of user-identifier normalization

To complete this algorithm, the iterative step must be wrapped in a loop until it reaches a fixed point, as illustrated by the following pseudo-code:

> **startingEdges represents a set of edges that is stored on your computation cluster. It's not explicitly represented within this controller program.**

Runs until no new edges are emitted

```
function userid-normalization(startingEdges) {
  isNewEdges = true
  while(isNewEdges) {
    [nextEdges, newEdges] = runNormalizationStep(startingEdges)
    isNewEdges = !newEdges.isEmpty()
  }
}
```

> **runNormalizationStep wraps the previous pipe diagram and returns the new set of edges and the brand new edges.**

In practice, code like this would run on a single machine, whereas runNormalization-Step would invoke a job to execute in parallel on your distributed computation cluster. When using a distributed filesystem to store inputs and outputs, a little more code is necessary to coordinate the file paths, as is shown in the next chapter. This code captures the gist of the algorithm, though.

The last requirement to complete this workflow step is to change the person IDs in the pageview data to use the selected user identifiers. This transformation can be achieved by performing a join of the pageview data with the final iteration of the equiv graph. This is illustrated by the pipe diagram in figure 8.14.

Note that it's perfectly valid for a person ID to exist in the pageview data but not in any equiv edges. This situation occurs when only one identifier was ever recorded for the user. In these cases, the outer join ensures these person IDs aren't filtered from the results and will join those pageviews to a null value. The chosen person ID is the joined ID if it exists—otherwise it's the original person ID.

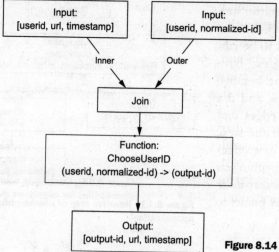

Figure 8.14   Final step of user-identifier normalization

And that's all there is to user-identifier normalization. Although it's a more difficult computation problem, only a few pipe diagrams and some pseudo-code were needed to express the algorithm.

8.6 Deduplicate pageviews

The final preparation step prior to computing the batch views is deduplicating the pageview events. The pipe diagram for this is trivial and is shown in figure 8.15.

8.7 Computing batch views

The data is now ready to compute the batch views, as designed in the beginning of the chapter. This computation step will generate unindexed records; in a later chapter, you'll learn how to index the batch views so they can be queried in a random-access manner.

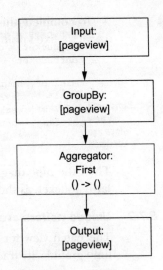

Figure 8.15 Deduplication pipe diagram

8.7.1 Pageviews over time

As outlined earlier, the pageviews-over-time batch view should aggregate the pageviews for each URL at hourly, daily, 7-day, and 28-day granularities. The approach you'll take is to first aggregate the pageviews at an hourly granularity. This will reduce the size of the data by many orders of magnitude. Afterward, you'll roll up the hourly values to obtain the counts for the larger buckets. The latter operations will be much faster due to the smaller size of the input.

Let's start with the pipe diagram to compute the number of pageviews at the hourly granularity. First, the timestamp in each pageview must be converted to an hour bucket, and then the pageviews can be counted for every URL and bucket group. This pipe diagram is shown in figure 8.16.

Next, let's take a look at the pipe diagram to generate pageview counts at all granularities based on the hourly granularities. The core of this pipe diagram is a function to emit the bucket for each granularity for each hourly pageview count, like so:

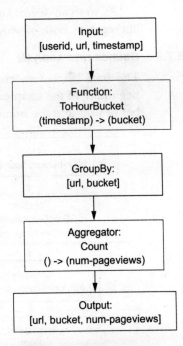

Figure 8.16 Computing hourly granularities for pageviews over time

```
function emitGranularities(hourBucket) {
    dayBucket = hourBucket / 24;
    weekBucket = dayBucket / 7;
    monthBucket = dayBucket / 28;

    emit("h", hourBucket)
    emit("d", dayBucket)
    emit("w", weekBucket)
    emit("m", monthBucket)
    }
}
```

The function emits four 2-tuples for each input.

The first element is either h, d, w, or m to indicate the hour, day, week, or month granularity; the second element is the numerical value of the time bucket.

Then the pipe diagram simply has to sum the pageview counts for each URL/granularity/bucket, as shown in figure 8.17.

8.7.2   Unique visitors over time

The batch view for unique visitors over time contains a HyperLogLog set for every time granularity tracked for every URL. It's essentially the same computation that was done to compute pageviews over time, except instead of aggregating counts, you aggregate HyperLogLog sets.

The combined pipe diagram for computing both the hourly HyperLogLog sets as well as the HyperLogLog sets for the higher granularities is shown in figure 8.18.

As you can see, it only requires `ConstructHyperLogLog` and `MergeHyperLogLog` aggregators, both of which are easy to write.

8.7.3   Bounce-rate analysis

The final batch view computes the bounce rate for each URL. As outlined in the beginning of the chapter, you'll compute two values for each domain: the total number of visits and the number of bounced visits.

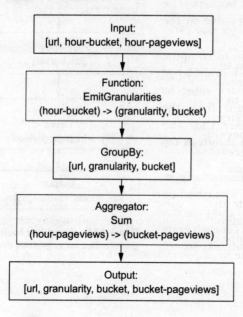

Figure 8.17   Pageviews over time for all granularities

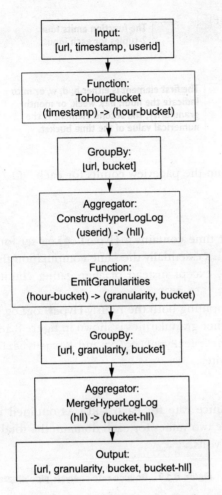

Figure 8.18 Uniques-over-time pipe diagram

The key part of this query is tracing each visit a person made as they browsed the internet. An easy way to accomplish this is to examine all the pageviews a person made for a particular domain, sorted by chronological order. You can then use the time difference between successive pageviews to determine whether they belong to the same visit. If a visit contains only one pageview, it counts as a bounced visit.

Let's call an aggregator that does this AnalyzeVisits. After looking at all of a user's pageviews on a domain, AnalyzeVisits emits two fields: the total number of visits made by that user on that domain, and the number of those visits that were bounces.

The pipe diagram for bounce-rate analysis is shown in figure 8.19. As you can see, this is a more sophisticated computation because it requires multiple aggregations—but it's still easily represented via a pipe diagram.

And that's it! That completes the workflow and algorithms for the batch layer of SuperWebAnalytics.com.

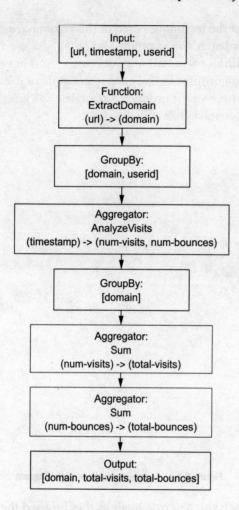

Figure 8.19   **Bounce-rate-analysis pipe diagram**

8.8   *Summary*

The batch layer for SuperWebAnalytics.com contains sophisticated logic, yet it's very straightforward to implement. This is entirely due to the batch layer's nature of computing functions on all your data. When you can look at all your data at once—and you aren't constrained by the limitations of incremental algorithms—building systems is both simple and easy. Batch computation also gives you great flexibility. It's really easy to extend the batch layer to compute new views: each stage of the workflow is free to run an arbitrary function on all the data.

As we've indicated a few times, what you developed in this chapter is a recomputation-based workflow where the batch views are always recomputed from scratch. There is a large class of problems for which you can incrementalize the batch layer and make it much more resource-efficient without adding too much complexity. You'll see how to do this in chapter 18.

We wish to emphasize that none of the techniques used in this chapter are specific to any toolset, so regardless of what batch computation and batch storage systems you're using, the workflow and algorithms presented will not change. And in practice, the mapping from the workflow and algorithms to real code is straightforward as well. You'll see this in the next chapter where you'll produce a complete working implementation of the SuperWebAnalytics.com batch layer.

An example batch layer:
Implementation

9

This chapter covers

- Ingesting new data into the master dataset
- Managing the details of a batch workflow
- Integrating Thrift-based graph schemas, Pail, and JCascalog

In the last chapter you saw the architecture and algorithms for the batch layer for SuperWebAnalytics.com. Let's now translate that to a complete working implementation using the tools you've learned about like Thrift, Pail, and JCascalog. In the process, you'll see that the code matches the pipe diagrams and workflows developed in the previous chapter very closely. This is a sign that the abstractions used are sound, because you can write code similar to how you think about the problems.

As always happens with real-world tools, you'll encounter friction from artificial complexities of the tooling. In this case, you'll see certain complexities arise from Hadoop's limitations regarding small files, and those complexities will have to be worked around. There's great value in understanding not just the ideal workflow and algorithms, but the nuts and bolts of implementing them in practice.

156

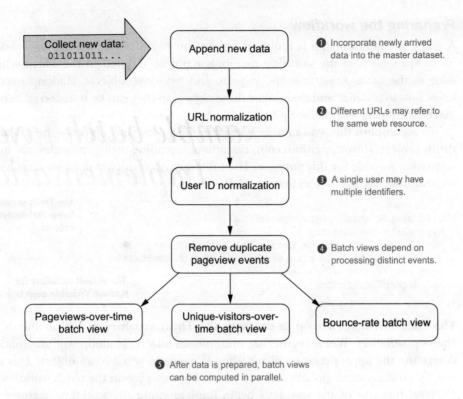

Figure 9.1   Batch workflow for SuperWebAnalytics.com

The workflow developed in the previous chapter is repeated in figure 9.1. You're encouraged to look back at the previous chapter to refresh your memory on what each step of the workflow does.

9.1   Starting point

Before implementing the workflow, let's quickly review what has been developed up to this point for SuperWebAnalytics.com. So far you've implemented the very core of the batch layer: a strong schema representing the data model and the ability to store that data in a distributed filesystem. You used Thrift to create a graph schema—people and pages are represented as nodes, pageviews are edges between people and pages, and other information is stored as properties of the nodes.

You used the Pail library to interface with HDFS—Pail provides you an easy interface for vertically partitioning the data, selecting the file format, and managing basic operations like appends between datasets. A `PailStructure` was created to allow SuperWebAnalytics.com `Data` objects to be stored inside pails, optionally partitioned by edge or property type.

9.2   Preparing the workflow

A quick preparation step is required before you begin implementing the workflow itself. Many parts of the workflow manipulate objects defined in the Thrift schema, such as the `Data`, `PageViewEdge`, `PageID`, and `PersonID` objects. Hadoop needs to know how to serialize and deserialize these objects so they can be transferred between machines during MapReduce jobs.

To accomplish this, you must register a serializer for your objects—the cascading-thrift project (https://github.com/cascading/cascading-thrift) provides an implementation suitable for this purpose. The following code snippet demonstrates how to register it for the batch workflow:

```
public static void setApplicationConf() {
  Map conf = new HashMap();
  String sers = "backtype.hadoop.ThriftSerialization," +    ◁
      "org.apache.hadoop.io.serializer.WritableSerialization";    ◁
  conf.put("io.serializations", sers);
  Api.setApplicationConf(conf);
}
```

The Thrift serializer for SuperWebAnalytics.com objects

The default serializer for Hadoop Writable objects

This code instructs Hadoop to use both the Thrift serializer as well as the default Hadoop serializer. When registering multiple serializers, Hadoop will automatically determine the appropriate serializer when it needs to serialize an object. This code sets the configuration globally and will be used by every job in the batch workflow.

With that out of the way, let's begin implementing the workflow, starting with ingesting new data.

9.3   Ingesting new data

You saw how, in the design of the workflow, it was important to separate the master dataset from new data coming in. This prevents new data from being inserted into the master dataset while the batch workflow is running, avoiding the possibility of separate views being representative of slightly different master datasets.

So the first step of the workflow is to take the data in new-data/, add it to the master dataset pail, and remove that data from new-data/. Although this is straightforward in concept, there may be synchronization issues. Omitting the details of the actual append for a moment, suppose you tried the following:

```
// do not use!
public static void badNewDataAppend(Pail masterPail, Pail newDataPail)
    throws IOException {
  appendNewDataToMasterDataPail(masterPail, newDataPail);
  newDataPail.clear();
}
```

This seems simple enough, but there's a hidden race condition in this code. While the append is running, more data may be written into the new-data pail. If you clear the new-data pail after the append finishes, you'll also delete any new data that was written while the append job was running.

Fortunately there's an easy solution. Pail provides `snapshot` and `deleteSnapshot` methods to solve this problem. The `snapshot` method stores a snapshot of the pail in a new location, whereas `deleteSnapshot` removes from the original pail only the data that exists in the snapshot. With these methods, the following code ensures that the only data removed is data that was successfully appended to the master dataset pail:

/tmp/swa is used as a temporary workspace throughout the batch workflow.

Takes a snapshot of the new-data pail

```
public static void ingest(Pail masterPail, Pail newDataPail)
    throws IOException {
  FileSystem fs = FileSystem.get(new Configuration());
  fs.delete(new Path("/tmp/swa"), true);
  fs.mkdirs(new Path("/tmp/swa"));

  Pail snapshotPail = newDataPail.snapshot("/tmp/swa/newDataSnapshot");
  appendNewDataToMasterDataPail(masterPail, snapshotPail);
  newDataPail.deleteSnapshot(snapshotPail);
}
```

Appends data from the snapshot to the master dataset

After the append, deletes only the data that exists in the snapshot

Note that this code also creates a temporary working space at /tmp/swa. Many stages of the workflow will require a space for intermediate data, and it's opportune to initialize this staging area before the first step executes.

We're not yet done, as we must look at the details of implementing the `appendNewDataToMasterDataPail` function. One difference between the new-data/ pail and the master dataset pail is that the master dataset is vertically partitioned by property or edge type. The new-data/ pail is just a dumping ground for new data, so each file within it may contain data units of all property types and edges. Before this data can be appended to the master dataset, it must first be reorganized to be consistent with the structure used for the master dataset pail. This process of reorganizing a pail to have a new structure is called *shredding*.

To shred a pail, you must be able to write to and read from pails via JCascalog queries. Before we implement shredding, let's see how you can integrate JCascalog and pails. Recall that in JCascalog, the abstraction for reading and writing data is called a *tap*. The dfs-datastores project (https://github.com/nathanmarz/dfs-datastores) provides a `PailTap` implementation so that pails can be used as input and output for JCascalog queries. When used as a source, a `PailTap` inspects the pail and automatically deserializes the records it contains.

The following code creates a tap to read all the data from a pail as a source for a query:

The snapshot is a SuperWebAnalytics.com pail, so the tap will emit Thrift Data objects.

The tap emits the file containing the record and the record itself; the filename isn't needed in the workflow, and so can be ignored.

```
public static void pailTapUsage() {
  Tap source = new PailTap("/tmp/swa/snapshot");
  new Subquery("?data").predicate(source, "_", "?data");
}
```

A `PailTap` also supports reading a subset of the data within the pail. For pails using the `SplitDataPailStructure` from chapter 3, you can construct a `PailTap` that reads only the equiv edges contained in the pail:

> **The attributes are an array of lists; each list contains the directory path of a subfolder to be used as input.**

> **Relays custom configurations to the PailTap**

> **Creates a list containing the relative path of the equiv edges**

> **Creates the tap with the specified options**

```
PailTapOptions opts = new PailTapOptions();
opts.attrs = new List[] {
  new ArrayList<String>() {{
    add("" + DataUnit._Fields.EQUIV.getThriftFieldId());
  }}
};
Tap equivs = new PailTap("/tmp/swa/snapshot", opts);
```

This functionality is needed quite often, so it should be wrapped into a function for future use:

> **Multiple subfolders can be specified as input to the tap.**

```
public static PailTap attributeTap(String path,
                                   final DataUnit._Fields... fields) {
  PailTapOptions opts = new PailTapOptions();
  opts.attrs = new List[] {
    new ArrayList<String>() {{
      for(DataUnit._Fields field: fields) {
        add("" + field.getThriftFieldId());
      }
    }}
  };
  return new PailTap(path, opts);
}
```

When sinking data from queries into brand-new pails, you must declare the type of records you'll be writing to the `PailTap`. You do this by setting the `spec` option to contain the appropriate `PailStructure`. To create a pail that shreds the data units by attribute, you can use `SplitDataPailStructure` from chapter 5:

```
public static PailTap splitDataTap(String path) {
  PailTapOptions opts = new PailTapOptions();
  opts.spec =
    new PailSpec((PailStructure) new SplitDataPailStructure());
  return new PailTap(path, opts);
}
```

Now you can use `PailTap` and JCascalog to implement the shredding part of the workflow. Your first attempt to shred might look something like this:

```
// do not use!
public static void badShred() {
  PailTap source = new PailTap("/tmp/swa/snapshot");
  PailTap sink = splitDataTap("/tmp/swa/shredded");

  Api.execute(sink,
              new Subquery("?data").predicate(source, "_", "?data"));
}
```

Logically this query is correct. But when you attempt to run this query on a massive input dataset on HDFS, you'll encounter strange issues like namenode errors and file handle limits. These are limitations within Hadoop itself. The problem with the query is that it creates countless small files, and as discussed in chapter 7, Hadoop doesn't play well with an enormous number of small files.

To understand why this happens, you have to understand how the query executes. This query doesn't involve aggregations or joins, so it executes as a map-only job that skips the reduce stage. Normally this is highly desirable, as the reduce step is the far more expensive step. But suppose your schema has 100 different edge and property types. A single map task could therefore create 100 separate output files—one for each record type. If processing your input data requires 10,000 mappers (roughly 1.5 TB of data stored in 128-MB blocks), then the output will consist of approximately one million files, which is too many for Hadoop to handle.

You can solve this problem by artificially introducing a reduce step into the computation. Unlike mappers, you can explicitly control the number of reducers via the job configuration. If you ran this hypothetical job on 1.5 TB of data with 100 reducers, you'd generate a much more manageable 10,000 files. The following code includes an "identity aggregator" to force the query to perform a reduce step:

```
public static Pail shred() throws IOException {
    PailTap source = new PailTap("/tmp/swa/snapshot");
    PailTap sink = splitDataTap("/tmp/swa/shredded");

    Subquery reduced = new Subquery("?rand", "?data")
        .predicate(source, "_", "?data-in")
        .predicate(new RandLong())
          .out("?rand")
      .predicate(new IdentityBuffer(), "?data-in")
          .out("?data");

    Api.execute(sink,
                new Subquery("?data").predicate(reduced, "_","?data"));

    Pail shreddedPail = new Pail("/tmp/swa/shredded");
    shreddedPail.consolidate();
    return shreddedPail;
}
```

Assigns a random number to each record *(annotation pointing to `.out("?rand")`)*

Uses an identity aggregator to get each data record to the reducer *(annotation pointing to `.predicate(new IdentityBuffer(), "?data-in")`)*

After the reduce stage, projects out the random number *(annotation pointing to `Api.execute(sink,`)*

Consolidates the shredded pail to further reduce the number of files *(annotation pointing to `shreddedPail.consolidate();`)*

Now that the data is shredded and the number of files has been minimized, you can finally append it to the master dataset pail:

```
public static void appendNewData(Pail masterPail,
                                 Pail snapshotPail) throws IOException {
    Pail shreddedPail = shred();
    masterPail.absorb(shreddedPail);
}
```

Once the new data is ingested into the master dataset, you can begin normalizing the data.

9.4   URL normalization

The next step is to normalize all URLs in the master dataset to their canonical form. Although normalization can involve many things, including stripping URL parameters, adding *http://* to the beginning, and removing trailing slashes, we'll provide only a rudimentary implementation here for demonstration purposes:

The function takes a Data object and emits a normalized Data object.

The input object is cloned so it can be safely modified.

```
public static class NormalizeURL extends CascalogFunction {

  public void operate(FlowProcess process, FunctionCall call) {
    Data data = ((Data) call.getArguments().getObject(0)).deepCopy();
    DataUnit du = data.get_dataunit();

    if(du.getSetField() == DataUnit._Fields.PAGE_VIEW) {
      normalize(du.get_page_view().get_page());
    }
    call.getOutputCollector().add(new Tuple(data));
  }

  private void normalize(PageID page) {
    if(page.getSetField() == PageID._Fields.URL) {
      String urlStr = page.get_url();
      try {
        URL url = new URL(urlStr);
        page.set_url(url.getProtocol() + "://" + url.getHost()
            + url.getPath());
      } catch(MalformedURLException e) {}
    }
  }
}
```

For the supported batch views, only pageview edges need to be normalized.

Pageviews are normalized by extracting standard components from the URL.

You can use this function to create a normalized version of the master dataset. Recall the pipe diagram for URL normalization, as shown in figure 9.2.

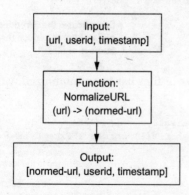

Figure 9.2   URL-normalization pipe diagram

Translating this pipe diagram to JCascalog is done with the following code:

```
public static void normalizeURLs() {
    Tap masterDataset = new PailTap("/data/master");
    Tap outTap = splitDataTap("/tmp/swa/normalized_urls");
    Api.execute(outTap,
            new Subquery("?normalized")
                .predicate(masterDataset, "_", "?raw")
                .predicate(new NormalizeURL(), "?raw")
                  .out("?normalized"));
}
```

9.5 *User-identifier normalization*

Let's now implement the most involved part of the workflow: user-identifier normalization. Recall that this is an iterative graph algorithm that operates as shown in figure 9.3.

Ordering Thrift data types

You may recall that instead of integers, `PersonIDs` are actually modeled as Thrift unions:

```
union PersonID {
  1: string cookie;
  2: i64 user_id;
}
```

Fortunately, Thrift provides a natural ordering for all Thrift structures, which can be used to determine the "minimum" identifier. The user-identifier normalization algorithm in this section takes advantage of this feature of Thrift.

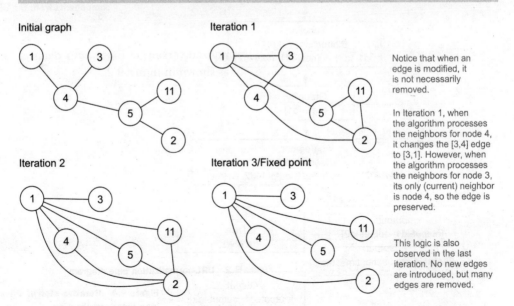

Initial graph

Iteration 1

Notice that when an edge is modified, it is not necessarily removed.

In Iteration 1, when the algorithm processes the neighbors for node 4, it changes the [3,4] edge to [3,1]. However, when the algorithm processes the neighbors for node 3, its only (current) neighbor is node 4, so the edge is preserved.

Iteration 2

Iteration 3/Fixed point

This logic is also observed in the last iteration. No new edges are introduced, but many edges are removed.

Figure 9.3 Iterating the algorithm until a fixed point is reached

You can now begin implementing the iterative algorithm. The output of each iteration will be stored in a new folder on the distributed filesystem, using the template /tmp/swa/equivs{iteration number} for the path. These outputs will consist of 2-tuples of PersonIDs.

The following code creates the initial dataset by transforming the equiv edge objects stored in the master dataset:

```
public static class EdgifyEquiv extends CascalogFunction {
  public void operate(FlowProcess process, FunctionCall call) {
    Data data = (Data) call.getArguments().getObject(0);
    EquivEdge equiv = data.get_dataunit().get_equiv();
    call.getOutputCollector()
        .add(new Tuple(equiv.get_id1(), equiv.get_id2()));
  }
}
```

A custom function to extract the identifiers from the equiv edges

```
public static void initializeUserIdNormalization() throws IOException {
  Tap equivs = attributeTap("/tmp/swa/normalized_urls",
                            DataUnit._Fields.EQUIV);
  Api.execute(Api.hfsSeqfile("/tmp/swa/equivs0"),
              new Subquery("?node1", "?node2")
                 .predicate(equivs, "_", "?data")
                 .predicate(new EdgifyEquiv(), "?node1", "?node2"));
}
```

The initialized data is stored as iteration 0.

The pipe diagram for the iterative step is repeated in figure 9.4.

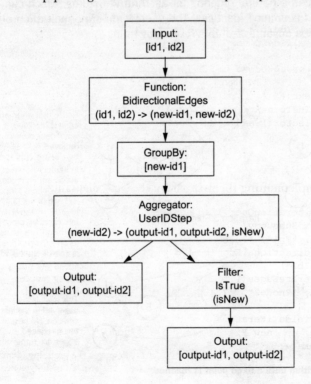

Figure 9.4 Iterative step of user-identifier normalization

Recall that edges must be emitted in both directions so that all neighbors of a node can be grouped together. The following custom function emits edges in both orientations:

Filters any edges that connect a node to itself

```
public static class BidirectionalEdge extends CascalogFunction {
  public void operate(FlowProcess process, FunctionCall call) {
    Object node1 = call.getArguments().getObject(0);
    Object node2 = call.getArguments().getObject(1);
    if(!node1.equals(node2)) {
      call.getOutputCollector().add(new Tuple(node1, node2));
      call.getOutputCollector().add(new Tuple(node2, node1));
    }
  }
}
```

Emits edges using both [a, b] and [b, a] orderings

Once they're grouped, you need a custom aggregator to implement the algorithm logic and denote which edges are new:

Gets the node used for grouping tuples

```
public static class IterateEdges extends CascalogBuffer {
  public void operate(FlowProcess process, BufferCall call) {
    PersonID grouped = (PersonID) call.getGroup().getObject(0);
    TreeSet<PersonID> allIds = new TreeSet<PersonID>();
    allIds.add(grouped);

    Iterator<TupleEntry> it = call.getArgumentsIterator();
    while(it.hasNext()) {
      allIds.add((PersonID) it.next().getObject(0));
    }

    Iterator<PersonID> allIdsIt = allIds.iterator();
    PersonID smallest = allIdsIt.next();
    boolean progress =
      allIds.size() > 2 && !grouped.equals(smallest);

    while(allIdsIt.hasNext()) {
      PersonID id = allIdsIt.next();
      call.getOutputCollector().add(new Tuple(smallest, id, progress));
    }
  }
}
```

The TreeSet contains the node and all of its neighbors.

A TreeSet is sorted, so the first element is the smallest.

If the grouped node is not the smallest and is connected to at least two other nodes, then a new edge will be created.

Emits the edges generated during this iteration

Finally, here's the code implementing the first part of the pipe diagram:

The source tap emits the tuples of PersonIDs from the previous iteration.

```
public static Subquery iterationQuery(Tap source) {
  Subquery iterate = new Subquery("?b1", "?node1", "?node2", "?is-new")
    .predicate(source, "?n1", "?n2")
    .predicate(new BidirectionalEdge(), "?n1", "?n2")
      .out("?b1", "?b2")
    .predicate(new IterateEdges(), "?b2")
      .out("?node1", "?node2", "?is-new");

  iterate = Api.selectFields(iterate,
                             new Fields("?node1", "?node2", "?is-new"));
  return (Subquery) iterate;
}
```

From the declared output of the query, JCascalog groups tuples using ?b1.

Removes the grouping identifier because it's no longer needed

This subquery addresses the logic of the algorithm; completing the iterative step requires adding the appropriate source and sink taps and executing the query:

All edges are emitted to the output of the iterative step.

```
public static Tap userIdNormalizationIteration(int i) {
    Tap source = (Tap) Api.hfsSeqfile("/tmp/swa/equivs" + (i - 1));
    Tap sink = (Tap) Api.hfsSeqfile("/tmp/swa/equivs" + i);
    Tap progressSink = (Tap) Api.hfsSeqfile("/tmp/swa/equivs" + "-new");

    Subquery iteration = iterationQuery(source);
    Subquery newEdgeSet = new Subquery("?node1", "?node2")
        .predicate(iteration, "?node1", "?node2", "_")
        .predicate(Option.DISTINCT, true);
    Subquery progressEdges = new Subquery(?node1", "?node2")
        .predicate(iteration, "?node1", "?node2", true);

    Api.execute(Arrays.asList(sink, progressSink),
                Arrays.asList(newEdgeSet, progressEdges));

    return progressEdgesSink;
}
```

Avoids writing duplicate edges to the sink

Executes both newEdgeSet and progressEdges queries in parallel

New edges are additionally stored in a separate path.

Only the new edges in this iteration are written to the progress sink.

In addition to storing all the edges as input for the next iteration, the iterative step also stores the new edges in a separate folder. This provides an easy way to determine if the current iteration generated any new edges; if not, the fixed point has been reached. The following code implements the iterative loop and this termination logic.

Tracks the current iteration

```
public static int userIdNormalizationiterationLoop() {
    int iter = 1;
    while(true) {
        Tap progressEdgesSink = userIdNormalizationIteration(iter);
        FlowProcess flowProcess = new HadoopFlowProcess(new JobConf());
        if(!flowProcess.openTapForRead(progressEdgesSink).hasNext()) {
            return iter;
        }
        iter++;
    }
}
```

The last iteration determines the path of the final output.

If new edges were generated, increases the counter and loop

Terminates if no new edges were generated during this iteration

The next step is to update the PersonIDs in the pageview data with the new normalized PersonIDs. The pipe diagram to accomplish this is repeated in figure 9.5 and involves a join.

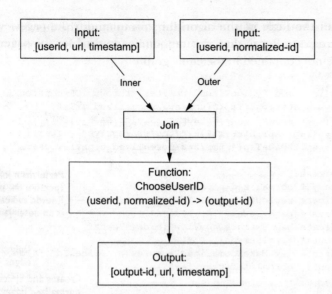

Figure 9.5 Final step of user-identifier normalization

A couple of custom functions are needed before you can execute this join. First, you must unravel the Thrift pageview objects to extract the necessary fields:

Extracts the relevant parameters from PageViewEdge objects →
Emits the URL, PersonID, and timestamp of the pageview →

```
public static class ExtractPageViewFields extends CascalogFunction {
  public void operate(FlowProcess process, FunctionCall call) {
    Data data = (Data) call.getArguments().getObject(0);
    PageViewEdge pageview = data.get_dataunit().get_page_view();
    if(pageview.get_page().getSetField() == PageID._Fields.URL) {
      call.getOutputCollector().add(
        new Tuple(pageview.get_page().get_url(),
                  pageview.get_person(),
                  data.get_pedigree().get_true_as_of_secs())); ←
    }
  }
}
```

Although the timestamp is not immediately required, this function will be reused in other parts of the workflow.

The second required function takes a pageview `Data` object and the new `PersonID`, and it returns a new pageview `Data` object with an updated `PersonID`:

newId may be null if the PersonID in the pageview is not part of the equiv graph.

Clones the Data object so it can be modified safely →

```
public static class MakeNormalizedPageview extends CascalogFunction {
  public void operate(FlowProcess process, FunctionCall call) {
    PersonID newId = (PersonID) call.getArguments().getObject(0); ←
    Data data = ((Data) call.getArguments().getObject(1)).deepCopy();
    if(newId != null) {
      data.get_dataunit().get_page_view().set_person(newId);
    }
    call.getOutputCollector().add(new Tuple(data)); ←
  }
}
```

Emits the potentially modified pageview Data object

With these two functions, you can now perform the join to modify the pageviews to use the normalized `PersonIDs`. Recall that an outer join is required for the pageviews with `PersonIDs` that are not contained in the equiv graph:

```
public static void modifyPageViews(int iter) throws IOException {
    Tap pageviews = attributeTap("/tmp/swa/normalized_urls",
                                     DataUnit._Fields.PAGE_VIEW);
    Tap newIds = (Tap) Api.hfsSeqfile("/tmp/swa/equivs" + iter);
    Tap result = splitDataTap("/tmp/swa/normalized_pageview_users");

    Api.execute(result,
       new Subquery("?normalized-pageview")
         .predicate(newIds, "!!newId", "?person")
         .predicate(pageviews, "_", "?data")
         .predicate(new ExtractPageViewFields("?data")
            .out("_", "?person", "_")
         .predicate(new MakeNormalizedPageview(), "!!newId", "?data")
         .out("?normalized-pageview"));
}
```

Uses the final output from the iterative loop → lines 3–5

Joins on the user identifier in the pageview → `ExtractPageViewFields`

Performs a join on ?person; the prefix of !!newId indicates this is an outer join

Creates and emits new normalized pageview

The last task is to define a wrapper function to execute the distinct phases of this workflow step:

```
public static void normalizeUserIds() throws IOException {
  initializeUserIdNormalization();
  int numIterations = userIdNormalizationiterationLoop();
  modifyPageViews(numIterations);
}
```

That concludes the user-identifier normalization portion of the workflow. This is a great example of the benefit of specifying the MapReduce computations using a library of your general-purpose programming language. A significant part of the logic, such as the iteration and fixed-point checking, was written as normal Java code. You should also note how closely the code followed the pipe diagrams and pseudo-code laid out in the previous chapter. This is a great sign that you're working at the right level of abstraction.

9.6   *Deduplicate pageviews*

The next step is to deduplicate pageviews in preparation for computing batch views. This code is so trivial that we'll skip the pipe diagram and go straight to the code:

```
public static void deduplicatePageviews() {
    Tap source = attributeTap("/tmp/swa/normalized_pageview_users",
                                   DataUnit._Fields.PAGE_VIEW);
    Tap outTap = splitDataTap("/tmp/swa/unique_pageviews");

    Api.execute(outTap,
            new Subquery("?data")
              .predicate(source, "?data")
              .predicate(Option.DISTINCT, true));
}
```

Restricts source tap to only read pageviews from the pail

The distinct predicate removes all duplicate pageview objects.

JCascalog's `Option.DISTINCT` predicate is a convenience that inserts the grouping and aggregation necessary to distinguish the tuples.

9.7 Computing batch views

With the pageviews now normalized and deduplicated, let's now go through the code to compute the batch views.

9.7.1 Pageviews over time

The computation for pageviews over time is split into two pieces: first the pageviews are counted at the hourly granularity, and then the hourly counts are rolled up into all the desired granularities.

The pipe diagram for the first part is repeated in figure 9.6.

First, let's write the function that determines the hour bucket for a timestamp:

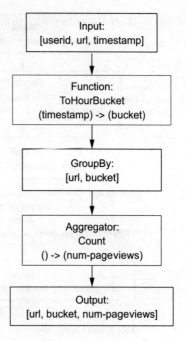

Figure 9.6 Computing hourly granularities for pageviews over time

```java
public static class ToHourBucket extends CascalogFunction {
    private static final int HOUR_IN_SECS = 60 * 60;

    public void operate(FlowProcess process, FunctionCall call) {
        int timestamp = call.getArguments().getInteger(0);
        int hourBucket = timestamp / HOUR_IN_SECS;
        call.getOutputCollector().add(new Tuple(hourBucket));
    }
}
```

With this function, it's a very standard JCascalog query to determine the hourly counts:

```java
public static Subquery hourlyRollup() {
    Tap source = new PailTap("/tmp/swa/unique_pageviews");
    return new Subquery("?url", "?hour-bucket", "?count")
            .predicate(source, "?pageview")
            .predicate(new ExtractPageViewFields(), "?pageview")
                .out("?url", "_", "?timestamp")
            .predicate(new ToHourBucket(), "?timestamp")
                .out("?hour-bucket")
            .predicate(new Count(), "?count");
}
```

Reuses the pageview extraction code from earlier ◁────

Groups by ?url and ?hour-bucket └─▷

As usual, the mapping between pipe diagram and JCascalog code is very direct.

The pipe diagram for the second part of the computation is shown in figure 9.7.

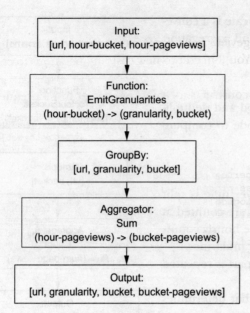

Input:
[url, hour-bucket, hour-pageviews]

↓

Function:
EmitGranularities
(hour-bucket) -> (granularity, bucket)

↓

GroupBy:
[url, granularity, bucket]

↓

Aggregator:
Sum
(hour-pageviews) -> (bucket-pageviews)

↓

Output:
[url, granularity, bucket, bucket-pageviews]

Figure 9.7   Pageviews over time for all granularities

Let's start with the function to emit all the granularities for a given hour bucket:

```
public static class EmitGranularities extends CascalogFunction {
  public void operate(FlowProcess process, FunctionCall call) {
    int hourBucket = call.getArguments().getInteger(0);
    int dayBucket = hourBucket / 24;
    int weekBucket = dayBucket / 7;
    int monthBucket = dayBucket / 28;

    call.getOutputCollector().add(new Tuple("h", hourBucket));
    call.getOutputCollector().add(new Tuple("d", dayBucket));
    call.getOutputCollector().add(new Tuple("w", weekBucket));
    call.getOutputCollector().add(new Tuple("m", monthBucket));
  }
}
```

The function emits four 2-tuples for each input.

The first element is either h, d, w, or m to indicate the hour, day, week, or month granularity; the second element is the numerical value of the time bucket.

With this function, computing the rollups for all the granularities is easy:

```
public static Subquery pageviewBatchView() {
  Subquery pageviews =
    new Subquery("?url", "?granularity", "?bucket", "?total-pageviews")
      .predicate(hourlyRollup(), "?url", "?hour-bucket", "?count")
      .predicate(new EmitGranularities(), "?hour-bucket")
        .out("?granularity", "?bucket")
      .predicate(new Sum(), "?count").out("?total-pageviews");
  return pageviews;
}
```

Executes the hourly counts subquery

Emits the buckets for all granularities

Sums the pageview counts by url, granularity, and bucket

9.7.2 *Uniques over time*

Uniques over time is similar to pageviews over time, except instead of counting, you need to create HyperLogLog sets. You'll need two new custom operations to compute this batch view.

The first is an aggregator that constructs a HyperLogLog set from a sequence of user identifiers:

> The function generates a HyperLogLog set for a set of visitors.

```
public static class ConstructHyperLogLog extends CascalogBuffer {
   public void operate(FlowProcess process, BufferCall call) {
      HyperLogLog hll = new HyperLogLog(8192);
      Iterator<TupleEntry> it = call.getArgumentsIterator();
      while(it.hasNext()) {
         TupleEntry tuple = it.next();
         hll.offer(tuple.getObject(0));
      }
      try {
         call.getOutputCollector().add(new Tuple(hll.getBytes()));
      } catch (IOException e) {
         throw new RuntimeException(e);
      }
   }
}
```

> Constructs a HyperLogLog set using I KB of storage

> Adds all objects to the set

> Emits the storage bytes of the HyperLogLog object

The next function is another custom aggregator that combines the HyperLogLog sets for hourly granularities into HyperLogLog sets for coarser intervals:

```
public static class MergeHyperLogLog extends CascalogBuffer {
   public void operate(FlowProcess process, BufferCall call) {
      Iterator<TupleEntry> it = call.getArgumentsIterator();
      HyperLogLog merged = null;
      try {
         while(it.hasNext()) {
            TupleEntry tuple = it.next();
            byte[] serialized = (byte[]) tuple.getObject(0);
            HyperLogLog hll = HyperLogLog.Builder.build(serialized);
            if(merged == null)
               merged = hll; {
            } else {
               merged = (HyperLogLog) merged.merge(hll); {
            }
         }
         call.getOutputCollector().add(new Tuple(merged.getBytes()));
      } catch (Exception e) {
         throw new RuntimeException(e);
      }
   }
}
```

> Creates a new HyperLogLog set to contain the merged results

> Reconstructs a HyperLogLog set from storage bytes

> Merges the current set into the results

> Emits the storage bytes for merged set

The following listing uses these operations to compute the batch view. Note the similarity to the pageviews-over-time query:

```
public static void uniquesView() {
    Tap source = new PailTap("/tmp/swa/unique_pageviews");

    Subquery hourlyUniques =
        new Subquery("?url", "?hour-bucket", "?hyper-log-log")
            .predicate(source, "?pageview")
            .predicate(new ExtractPageViewFields(), "?pageview")
                .out("?url", "?user", "?timestamp")
            .predicate(new ToHourBucket(), "?timestamp")
                .out("?hour-bucket")
            .predicate(new ConstructHyperLogLog(), "?user")
                .out("?hyper-log-log");

    Subquery uniques =
        new Subquery("?url", "?granularity", "?bucket", "?aggregate-hll")
            .predicate(hourlyUniques,"?url", "?hour-bucket", "?hourly-hll")
            .predicate(new EmitGranularities(), "?hour-bucket")
                .out("?granularity", "?bucket")
            .predicate(new MergeHyperLogLog(), "?hourly-hll")
                .out("?aggregate-hll");
    return uniques;
}
```

The first subquery determines hourly HyperLogLog sets for each URL.

The second subquery determines the HyperLogLog sets for all granularities.

It's also possible to create a function that abstracts away the parts common to the pageviews query and the unique-visitors query. We'll leave that as an exercise for the reader.

> ### Further optimizing the HyperLogLog batch view
>
> The implementation we've shown uses the same size for every HyperLogLog set: 1 KB. The HyperLogLog set needs to be that large in order to get a reasonably accurate answer for URLs that may receive millions or hundreds of millions of visits. But most websites using SuperWebAnalytics.com won't get nearly that many pageviews, so it's wasteful to use such a large HyperLogLog set size for them.
>
> For further optimization, you could look at the total pageview count for URLs on that domain and tune the size of the HyperLogLog set accordingly. Using this approach can vastly decrease the space needed for the batch view, at the cost of adding some complexity to the view-generation code.

9.7.3   Bounce-rate analysis

The last batch view computes the bounce rate for each URL. Let's take a look at the pipe diagram again in figure 9.8.

The key to this batch view is the AnalyzeVisits aggregator, which looks at all the pageviews a user has made on a domain and computes the number of visits and the number of those visits that were bounces. The easiest way to compute this is to look at the pageviews in sorted order. When more than 30 minutes have elapsed between

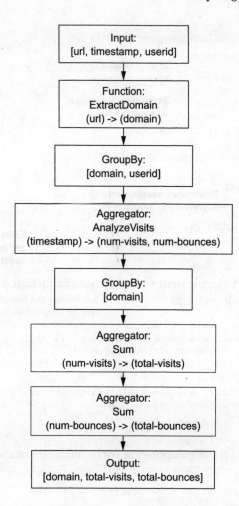

Figure 9.8   Bounce-rate-analysis pipe diagram

pageviews, a new visit has started. If a visit only contains a single pageview, then it counts as a bounce.

The following aggregator implements this logic. The surrounding query will ensure the input to this aggregator is provided in sorted order:

> Two successive pageviews belong to the same visit if they are separated by less than 30 minutes.

```
public static class AnalyzeVisits extends CascalogBuffer {
  private static final int VISIT_LENGTH_SECS = 60 * 30;

  public void operate(FlowProcess process, BufferCall call) {
    Iterator<TupleEntry> it = call.getArgumentsIterator();
    int bounces = 0;
    int visits = 0;
    Integer lastTime = null;
    int numInCurrVisit = 0;
```

Tracks the time of the previous pageview

Assumes that the pageviews are sorted chronologically

```
        while(it.hasNext()) {
          TupleEntry tuple = it.next();
          int timeSecs = tuple.getInteger(0);
          if(lastTime == null || (timeSecs-lastTime) > VISIT_LENGTH_SECS) {
            visits++;
            if(numInCurrVisit == 1) {
              bounces++;
            }
            numInCurrVisit = 0;
          }
          numInCurrVisit++;
        }
        if(numInCurrVisit==1) {
          bounces++;
        }
        call.getOutputCollector().add(new Tuple(visits, bounces));
      }
    }
```

Registers the beginning of a new visit ⟶ `visits++;`

Determines if previous visit was a bounce ⟵

Determines whether last pageview was a bounce ⟵

Emits visit and bounce counts ⟵

Before implementing the subquery, let's implement the next custom function needed for it. This function extracts a domain from a URL:

Uses Java native libraries to extract the domain ⟶

```
        public static class ExtractDomain extends CascalogFunction {
          public void operate(FlowProcess process, FunctionCall call) {
            String urlStr = call.getArguments().getString(0);
            try {
              URL url = new URL(urlStr);
              call.getOutputCollector().add(new Tuple(url.getAuthority()));
            } catch(MalformedURLException e) {}
          }
        }
```

Let's put everything together to produce the computation for bounce-rate analysis:

```
public static Subquery bouncesView() {
  Tap source = new PailTap("/tmp/swa/unique_pageviews");

  Subquery userVisits =
    new Subquery("?domain", "?user", "?num-user-visits",
                 "?num-user-bounces")
      .predicate(source, "?pageview")
      .predicate(new ExtractPageViewFields(), "?pageview")
        .out("?url", "?user", "?timestamp")
      .predicate(new ExtractDomain(), "?url")
        .out("?domain")
      .predicate(Option.SORT, "?timestamp")
      .predicate(new AnalyzeVisits(), "?timestamp")
        .out("?num-user-visits", "?num-user-bounces");

  Subquery bounces =
    new Subquery("?domain", "?num-visits", "?num-bounces")
      .predicate(userVisits, "?domain", "_",
                 "?num-user-visits", "?num-user-bounces")
      .predicate(new Sum(), "?num-user-visits")
        .out("?num-visits")
```

Sorts pageviews chronologically to analyze visits—the Option.SORT predicate allows you to control how each group is sorted before being fed to the aggregator operations ⟵

Bounces and visits are determined per user. ⟵

```
      .predicate(new Sum(), "?num-user-bounces")
         .out("?num-bounces");
   return bounces;
}
```

⟵━━━━━━━━ **Sum bounces and visits for all users to calculate the batch view**

Relax. Take a deep breath. After much time and effort, you've successfully completed the recomputation-based layer for SuperWebAnalytics.com!

9.8 Summary

The batch layer for SuperWebAnalytics.com is just a few hundred lines of code, yet the business logic involved is quite sophisticated. The various abstractions fit together well—there was a fairly direct mapping between what we wanted to accomplish at each step and how we accomplished it. Here and there, hairy details arose due to the nature of the toolset—notably Hadoop's small-files issue—but these were not difficult to overcome.

Although we've gone quite deep into the details of specific tooling in this chapter, it's important to step back and remember the overarching reasons for the batch layer. The immutability and recomputation aspects provide you with human-fault tolerance, a non-negotiable property of any data system. You saw how simple it is to write the code to produce the batch views—the hairy stuff like fault tolerance and concurrency is handled for you by the computation framework. The batch layer greatly simplifies the problem of producing realtime views because the realtime views only need to account for a very small portion of the full dataset. Later on, when you learn about the inherent complexities in realtime computation, you'll come to appreciate how the loose latency requirements in the batch layer allow the pieces of the batch layer to be much simpler to operate as well.

We'll next proceed to the serving layer so that the batch views can be quickly read in a random-access manner.

Part 2

Serving layer

Part 2 focuses on the serving layer of the Lambda Architecture. The serving layer consists of databases that index and serve the results of the batch layer. Part 2 is short because databases that don't require random writes are extraordinarily simple. Chapter 10 discusses the high-level concepts of the serving layer, while chapter 11 shows an example serving layer database called ElephantDB.

Serving layer

10

This chapter covers

- Tailoring batch views to the queries they serve
- A new answer to the data-normalization versus denormalization debate
- Advantages of batch-writable, random-read, and no random-write databases
- Contrasting a Lambda Architecture solution with a fully incremental solution

At this point you've learned how to precompute arbitrary views of any dataset by making use of batch computation. For the views to be useful, you must be able to access their contents with low latency, and as shown in figure 10.1, this is the role of the serving layer. The serving layer indexes the views and provides interfaces so that the precomputed data can be quickly queried.

The serving layer is the last component of the batch section of the Lambda Architecture. It's tightly tied to the batch layer because the batch layer is responsible for continually updating the serving layer views. These views will always be out of date due to the high-latency nature of batch computation. But this is not a concern, because the speed layer will be responsible for any data not yet available in the serving layer.

179

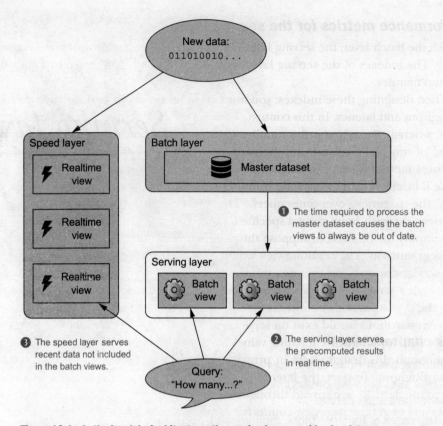

Figure 10.1   In the Lambda Architecture, the serving layer provides low-latency access to the results of calculations performed on the master dataset. The serving layer views are slightly out of date due to the time required for batch computation.

Unfortunately, the serving layer is an area where the tooling lags behind the theory. It wouldn't be hard to build a general-purpose serving layer implementation—in fact, it would be significantly easier than building any of the currently existing NoSQL databases. We'll present the full theory behind creating a simple, scalable, fault-tolerant, and general-purpose serving layer, and then we'll use the best tooling available to demonstrate the underlying concepts.

While investigating the serving layer, you'll learn the following:

- Indexing strategies to minimize latency, resource usage, and variance
- The requirements for the serving layer in the Lambda Architecture
- How the serving layer solves the long-debated normalization versus denormalization problem

We'll begin by examining the key issues you'll face when structuring a serving layer view.

10.1 *Performance metrics for the serving layer*

As with the batch layer, the serving layer is distributed among many machines for scalability. The indexes of the serving layer are created, loaded, and served in a fully distributed manner.

When designing these indexes, you must consider two main performance metrics: throughput and latency. In this context, *latency* is the time required to answer a single query, whereas *throughput* is the number of queries that can be served within a given period of time. The relationship between the structure of the serving layer indexcs and these metrics is best explained via an example.

We'll briefly return to our long-running SuperWebAnalytics.com example—specifically, the pageviews-over-time query. The objective is to serve the number of pageviews for each hour given a specific URL and a particular range of hours. To further simplify the discussion, suppose the pageview counts are only produced using an hourly granularity. The resulting view would look similar to figure 10.2.

A straightforward way to index this view would be to use a key/value strategy with [URL, hour] pairs as keys and pageviews as values. The index would be partitioned using the key, so pageview counts for the same URL would reside on different partitions. Different partitions would exist on separate servers, so retrieving a range of hours for a single URL would involve fetching values from multiple servers in your serving layer.

Although this design works in principle, it faces serious issues with both latency and throughput. To start, the latency would be consistently high. Because the values for a particular URL are spread throughout your cluster, you'll need to query numerous servers to get the pageview counts for a large range of hours. The key observation is that the response times of servers vary. For instance, one server may be slightly more loaded than the others; another may be performing garbage collection at the time. Even if you parallelize the fetch requests, the overall query response time is limited by the speed of the slowest server.

To illustrate this point, suppose a query requires fetching data from three servers. A representative sample of the distribution of response times is shown in figure 10.3.

URL	Bucket	Pageviews
foo.com/blog/1	0	10
foo.com/blog/1	1	21
foo.com/blog/1	2	7
foo.com/blog/1	3	38
foo.com/blog/1	4	29
bar.com/post/a	0	178
bar.com/post/a	1	91
bar.com/post/a	2	568

Figure 10.2 The pageviews-over-time batch view with hourly granularity

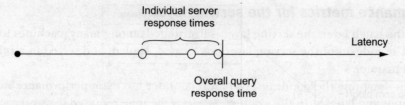

Figure 10.3   When distributing a task over multiple servers, the overall latency is determined by the slowest server response time.

For comparison, suppose the query hits 20 servers. A typical distribution of latencies would look like figure 10.4.

In general, the more servers a query touches, the higher the overall latency of the query. This is due to the simple fact that involving more servers increases the likelihood that at least one will respond slowly. Consequently, the variance of server response times turns the worst-case performance of one server into the common-case performance of queries. This is a serious problem for achieving good latency for the pageviews-over-time query.

Another problem with this key/value strategy is poor throughput, particularly if your servers use disks and not solid-state drives. Retrieving a value for a single key requires a disk seek, and a single query may fetch values for dozens or more keys. Disk seeks are expensive operations for traditional hard drives. Because there's a finite number of disks in your cluster, there's a hard limit to the number of disk seeks that can be achieved per second. Suppose that on average a query fetches 20 keys per query, the cluster has 100 disks, and each disk can perform 500 seeks per second. In this case, your cluster can only serve 2,500 queries per second—a surprisingly small amount given the number of disks.

But all is not lost—a different indexing strategy has much better latency and throughput characteristics. The idea is to collocate the pageview information for a single URL on the same partition and store it sequentially. Fetching the pageviews will then only require a single seek and scan rather than numerous seeks. Scans are extremely cheap relative to seeks, so this is far more resource-efficient. Additionally, only a single server needs to be contacted per query, so you're no longer subject to the variance issues of the previous strategy. The layout of the index for this strategy is shown in figure 10.5.

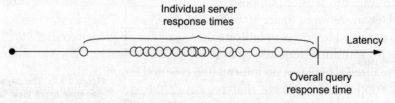

Figure 10.4   If you increase the number of servers involved in a distributed task, you also increase the likelihood that at least one will respond slowly.

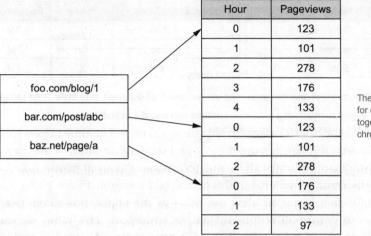

Hour	Pageviews
0	123
1	101
2	278
3	176
4	133
0	123
1	101
2	278
0	176
1	133
2	97

The pageview counts for each URL are stored together and sorted in chronological order.

Figure 10.5   A sorted index promotes scans and limits disk seeks to improve both latency and throughput.

These two examples demonstrate that the way you structure your serving layer indexes has dramatic effects on the performance of your queries. A vital advantage of the Lambda Architecture is that it allows you to tailor the serving layer for the queries it serves, to optimize efficiency.

10.2   The serving layer solution to the normalization/ denormalization problem

The serving layer solves one of the long-standing problems in the relational database world: the normalization versus denormalization dilemma. To grasp the solution and its implications, you first need to understand the underlying issues.

The normalization versus denormalization decision is ultimately a choice between unacceptable trade-offs. In the relational world, you want to store your data fully normalized; this involves defining relationships between independent datasets to minimize redundancy. Unfortunately, querying normalized data can be slow, so you may need to store some information redundantly to improve response times. This denormalization process increases performance, but it comes with the huge complexity of keeping the redundant data consistent.

To illustrate this tension, suppose you're storing user location information in relational tables, as shown in figure 10.6. Each location has an identifier, and each person uses one of those identifiers to indicate their location. A query to retrieve the location for a specific individual requires a join between the two tables. This is an example of a fully normalized schema, as no information is stored redundantly.

Now suppose you observe that retrieving the city and state for a user is an extremely common operation in your application. Joins are expensive, and you decide

User ID	Name	Location ID
1	Sally	3
2	George	1
3	Bob	3

Location ID	City	State	Population
1	New York	NY	8.2M
2	San Diego	CA	1.3M
3	Chicago	IL	2.7M

Figure 10.6   A normalized schema uses multiple independent datasets with little or no redundant data.

that you need better performance from this operation. The only means to avoid the join would be to redundantly store the city and state information in the user table.

This technique of redundantly storing information to avoid joins is called *denormalization*, and the resulting schema in this case would resemble figure 10.7.

Denormalization is not an ideal solution—as the application developer, it's your responsibility to ensure all redundant data is consistent. This raises uncomfortable questions, such as "What happens if the different copies of a field become inconsistent? What are the semantics of the data in this case?" Remember that mistakes are inevitable in long-lived systems, so given enough time, inconsistencies will occur.

Fortunately, the split between the master dataset and the serving layer in the Lambda Architecture solves the normalization versus denormalization problem. Within the batch layer you can normalize your master dataset to your heart's content. The computation on the batch layer reads the master dataset in bulk, so there's no need to design the schema to optimize for random-access reads. Complementarily, the serving layer is completely tailored to the queries it serves, so you can optimize as needed to attain maximal performance. These optimizations in the serving layer can go far beyond denormalization. In addition to prejoining data, you can perform additional aggregation and transformation to further improve efficiency.

As to the question of consistency in the Lambda Architecture, it's absolutely true that information will be redundantly stored between the batch and serving layers. The key distinction is that the serving layer is defined to be a function of the master dataset. If an error introduces inconsistencies, you can easily correct them by recomputing the serving layer from scratch.

User ID	Name	Location ID	City	State
1	Sally	3	Chicago	IL
2	George	1	New York	NY
3	Bob	3	Chicago	IL

Location ID	City	State	Population
1	New York	NY	8.2M
2	San Diego	CA	1.3M
3	Chicago	IL	2.7M

Figure 10.7   Denormalized tables store data redundantly to improve query performance.

10.3 *Requirements for a serving layer database*

The Lambda Architecture places a certain set of requirements on a serving layer database. But what is *not* required of a serving layer database is far more interesting than what is required. First, these are the requirements:

- *Batch writable*—The batch views for a serving layer are produced from scratch. When a new version of a view becomes available, it must be possible to completely swap out the older version with the updated view.
- *Scalable*—A serving layer database must be capable of handling views of arbitrary size. As with the distributed filesystems and batch computation framework previously discussed, this requires it to be distributed across multiple machines.
- *Random reads*—A serving layer database must support random reads, with indexes providing direct access to small portions of the view. This requirement is necessary to have low latency on queries.
- *Fault-tolerant*—Because a serving layer database is distributed, it must be tolerant of machine failures.

Hopefully, nothing on this list is a surprise. But a customary requirement that's missing from this list—one that's standard on all familiar databases—is *random writes*. Such functionality is completely irrelevant to the serving layer because the views are only produced in bulk. To be clear, random writes do exist in the Lambda Architecture, but they're isolated within the speed layer to achieve low-latency updates. Updates to the serving layer generate new views in their entirety, so a serving layer database does not need the ability to modify small portions of the current view.

This is an amazing result, because random writes are responsible for the majority of the complexity in databases—and even more complexity in distributed databases. Consider, for example, one of the nasty details discussed in chapter 1 of how random-write databases work: the need for compaction to reclaim unused space. An intensive operation, compaction occasionally sucks away many of the machine's resources. If it's not managed correctly, machines will become overloaded, and a cascading failure becomes likely as load gets shifted onto other machines.

Because the serving layer doesn't require random writes, it doesn't require online compaction, so this complexity, along with its associated operational burden, completely vanishes in the serving layer. The importance of this is magnified when you consider the relative sizes of your serving layer and speed layer clusters. The serving layer represents the views for the vast majority of your master dataset, likely well over 99%, so it requires the majority of the database resources. This means the vast majority of your database servers don't suffer from the operational burden of managing online compaction.

Online compaction is just one of the many complexities taken on by a database when it must support random writes. Another complexity is the need to synchronize reads and writes so that half-written values are never read. When a database doesn't have random writes, it can optimize the read path and get better performance than a random read/write database.

A rough but good indicator of the complexity can be seen in the size of the code-base. ElephantDB, a database built specifically as a serving layer database, is only a few thousand lines of code. HBase and Cassandra, two popular distributed read/write databases, are hundreds of thousands of lines long. The number of lines of code isn't normally a good complexity metric, but in this case the staggering difference should be telling.

A simpler database is more predictable because it does fewer things. It accordingly is less likely to have bugs and—as you saw with compaction—will be substantially easier to operate. Because the serving layer views contain the overwhelming majority of your queryable data, the serving layer's fundamental simplicity is a huge boon to the robustness of your overall architecture.

10.4   Designing a serving layer for SuperWebAnalytics.com

Let's now return to the SuperWebAnalytics.com example and design the ideal serving layer for it. When we last left off, we'd built a batch workflow for SuperWebAnalytics.com, producing batch views for three queries: pageviews over time, unique visitors over time, and bounce-rate analysis. The output of the batch layer is unindexed—it's the job of the serving layer to index those views and serve them with low latency.

It's our intention to focus on a serving layer design that would be ideal for Super-WebAnalytics.com. It's in the serving layer, more than anywhere else in the Lambda Architecture, that real-world tools lag behind the ideal tools. There is irony here, as serving layer databases are among the simplest and easiest to build of the tools required by a Lambda Architecture. We believe this is due to historical momentum—the majority of people build applications to be served by a single monolithic database cluster that is updated using realtime, incremental updates. But it's important to see what is ideally possible in order to provide a roadmap for future tooling. In practice, you may find yourself repurposing traditional databases for the serving layer.

Let's now see the ideal index types for each view for SuperWebAnalytics.com.

10.4.1 *Pageviews over time*

The pageviews-over-time query retrieves the pageview counts for a URL for a range of hours and sums them together. As already discussed, an ideal index for this query is key to a sorted map, as illustrated earlier in figure 10.5.

Recall that the batch view for pageviews over time computes the bucketed counts for not just the hourly granularity, but daily, weekly, monthly, and yearly granularities as well. This was done to minimize the total number of values that had to be retrieved to resolve a query—a one-year range would require retrieving thousands of hourly buckets, but only a handful of buckets when using the larger granularities. But if you use a key-to-sorted-map index type, it turns out that these higher granularities aren't needed. This is because when all the values for a range are stored sequentially, it's extremely cheap to read them all at once.

For example, let's suppose that every entry in the sorted map, a map from bucket to pageview counts, requires 12 bytes (4 bytes for the bucket number and 8 bytes for the value). Retrieving the bucket counts for a two-year period requires approximately 17,500 values. When you add everything up, this amounts to 205 KB that must be retrieved. This is a small amount, and it's better to optimize things so that only a single seek is needed even if more information overall needs to be read.

Of course, this analysis is specific to the characteristics of hard disks today. With SSDs or other tooling, your analysis may come to a different conclusion: that an index including granularities would be superior.

10.4.2 *Uniques over time*

Let's now discuss the ideal index for uniques over time (see figure 10.8). The uniques-over-time query is very similar to pageviews over time, retrieving a single combined value based on a range of values. One big difference, though, is that the HyperLogLog sets used for uniques over time are significantly larger than the values stored for buckets in pageviews over time. So if you made a sorted index containing only hourly granularities, and your HyperLogLog set size was 1024 bytes, then you'd have to retrieve about 17 MB of HyperLogLog information for a two-year query. If your hard disk can support a read throughput of 300 MB/s, just reading the information would take 60 ms (and this assumes totally ideal circumstances). In addition to that, merging HyperLogLog sets is more expensive than simply summing numbers, potentially adding even more latency to queries. Because uniques over time is inherently more expensive than pageviews over time, it seems that making use of the higher granularities would be better.

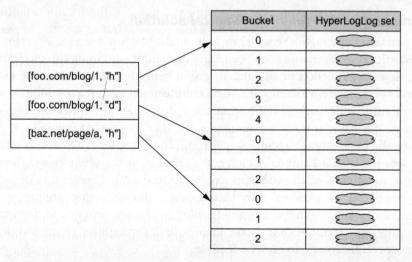

Figure 10.8   Index design for uniques over time. Although the index keys are a compound of URL and granularity, indexes are partitioned between servers solely by the URL.

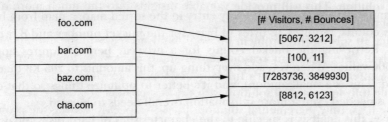

Figure 10.9   Implementing a bounce-rates view using a key/value index

In this case, an index like that represented in figure 10.8 seems optimal. It's the same key-to-sorted-map index as was used for pageviews over time, but with two differences:

- The key is a compound key of URL and granularity.
- The indexes are partitioned solely by the URL, not by both the URL and granularity. To retrieve a range of values for a URL and granularity, you'd use the URL to find the server containing the information you need, and then use both the URL and granularity to look up the values you're interested in. Partitioning by just the URL ensures that all buckets for a URL are collocated on the same server and avoids any variance issues from having to interact with many servers for a single query.

10.4.3   *Bounce-rate analysis*

The bounce-rate analysis view is a mapping from a domain to the number of visits and the number of bounces for that domain. This is the easiest view to support, since it only requires a key/value index, as shown in figure 10.9.

10.5   *Contrasting with a fully incremental solution*

In the past few chapters, you've seen how to build the batch and serving layers for Super-WebAnalytics.com. Everything has been fairly straightforward using this model of computing views as a function of all data. To gain a better appreciation for the excellent properties such a system exhibits, it's worth contrasting it against a traditional architecture built using fully incremental computation. A traditional architecture uses a large read/write database for state and maintains that state as new data comes in.

When the Lambda Architecture was introduced in chapter 1, we contrasted a traditional solution with a Lambda Architecture solution to the uniques-over-time problem. Now we've covered the concepts needed to look at that contrast in detail. Here we'll present the best-known, fully incremental solution to the uniques-over-time problem, and you'll see that the resulting solution is more complex to implement, is significantly less accurate, has worse latency and throughput characteristics, and requires special hardware to even be feasible.

10.5.1   *Fully incremental solution to uniques over time*

We'll build up to the best possible fully incremental solution step by step. To start this process, let's make the problem significantly easier by completely ignoring equivs in the initial solution. This will provide valuable insights into the much more difficult problem of uniques with equivs.

Note that in solving this problem we won't limit ourselves to the tooling available in the current landscape. Any reasonable variations of existing tooling are allowed. What we're interested in is what's fundamentally possible—how good or bad is the best possible fully incremental solution with the best possible tooling?

Because it's a fully incremental solution, the key aspect to solving the problem is determining what kind of database to use and how to maintain state in that database. For the first attempt, let's try using a key-to-set database. That is, the database implements an interface like the following:

```
interface KeyToSetDatabase {
    Set getSet(Object key);
    void addToSet(Object key, Object val);
}
```

Such a database can easily exist and be made distributed and fault tolerant. The reason for using this over something like a key/value database is to make the addToSet operation efficient. With a key/value database, you'd have to fetch the entire set, add the element, and then write the entire set back. By having the database inherently aware of the data structure it's storing, such an operation can be made much more efficient by only having to send over the element to be added to the set.

There are two pieces to any fully incremental approach: determining what happens when a new pageview is received (the write side), and determining what computation to do to resolve a query (the read side). For the write side, the key in the database will be set to the pair of [URL, hour bucket], and the value will be the set of all UserIDs to visit that URL in that hour bucket. Whenever a new pageview is received, that UserID is added to the appropriate bucket in the database. For the read side, queries are resolved by fetching all buckets in the range of the query, merging the sets together, and then computing the unique count of that set.

Although it's straightforward, there are a lot of problems with this approach:

- The database is very large space-wise, because effectively every pageview needs to be stored in the database.
- For a query over a large range, you have to do a very large number of database lookups. For example, a one-year period contains about 8,760 buckets. Having to fetch 8,760 buckets is not conducive to fast queries.
- For popular websites, even individual buckets could have tens of millions of elements in them (or more). Again, this is not conducive to very fast queries.

Let's take a different approach to greatly reduce the amount of work that needs to be done during queries. For the second approach to uniques over time, let's take advantage of HyperLogLog to approximate the set count and vastly decrease the amount of storage needed. In this attempt, a key-to-HyperLogLog database will be used. Again, there's no reason such a database couldn't exist in a distributed and fault-tolerant form—it would in fact be a minor variation on a database like Apache Cassandra.

As before, the key would be a pair of [URL, hour bucket] and the value would be a HyperLogLog set representing all UserIDs that visit that URL in that hour. The write side simply adds the UserID to the appropriate bucket's HyperLogLog set, and the read side fetches all HyperLogLog sets in that range, merges them together, and gets the count.

Because of the enormous space savings of HyperLogLog, everything about this approach is more efficient. Individual buckets are now guaranteed to be small, and the database as a whole is significantly more space-efficient. This is all achieved by making a very mild trade-off in accuracy on queries.

But this approach still has the problem of queries over large ranges requiring an unreasonable number of database lookups. You want queries over large ranges to be just as fast as queries over short ranges.

Fortunately, fixing this is fairly easy. For the last approach, let's again use a key-to-HyperLogLog database, but now change the key to be a triplet of [URL, hour bucket, granularity]. The idea is that rather than computing HyperLogLog sets just on an hour granularity, computing them on more coarse granularities like day, week, month, and year.

On the write side, whenever a new pageview comes in, that UserID is added to the HyperLogLog set for the appropriate hour, day, week, month, and year buckets. On the read side, the minimum number of buckets are read to compute the result. For example, for a query from December 1, 2013, to February 4, 2015, only the following buckets are needed:

- The month of December 2013
- The year of 2014
- The month of January 2015
- The days of February 1–3, 2014

This is a huge improvement over the thousands of buckets that needed to be read for large ranges in the previous attempt. This strategy is almost identical to the approaches taken in the batch layer for the SuperWebAnalytics.com views. As you've already seen, the storage costs for the extra granularities is minimal, so this mild increase in storage is well worth it to make all the queries run fast.

Overall, this is a very satisfactory approach to the problem: it's fast for all queries, space-efficient, easy to understand, and straightforward to implement. Let's now re-introduce equivs into the problem and see how everything gets turned on its head. Solving this problem in a fully incremental architecture is significantly more difficult, and you'll see that the resulting solution is not satisfactory.

As mentioned, what makes dealing with equivs tricky is that a new equiv can change the result for any possible query. For example, suppose you go back to the first attempt, where a set of UserIDs is stored for every [URL, hour bucket] pair. Suppose you intend to only ever store one UserID per person in the entire database, so whenever a new equiv comes in you have to make sure only one of that person's UserIDs exists in the entire database. Figure 10.10 shows an example of what the database might look like. Suppose a new equiv comes in between UserIDs A and C. In this example, that requires modifications to 75% of the buckets shown in the database! You don't know which buckets could be affected, so the only way to handle equivs in this approach is to iterate over the entire database for every equiv. This is obviously not reasonable.

One way you might try to optimize this approach is to maintain a second index from a UserID to the set of all buckets the UserID exists in. If a user only ever visited two buckets, then when an equiv comes in, you'd only have to fix the UserIDs in those two buckets rather than iterate over the entire database.

Key (URL, Hour bucket)	Set of UserIDs
"foo.com/page1", 0	A, B, C
"foo.com/page1", 1	A, D
"foo.com/page1", 2	A, C, F
"foo.com/page1", 102	A, B, C, G

Figure 10.10 Equivs could affect any bucket in the database.

Unfortunately, this approach is plagued with problems. What if there's a search engine bot that visits every URL every hour? That UserID's bucket list will contain every bucket in your database, which is highly impractical. There are many reasonable datasets for which performance will be erratic due to either individual UserIDs having enormous bucket lists or occasionally needing to iterate over large swaths of the database. In addition to the performance problems, there are complexity problems. The information about what UserID belongs to what bucket is stored in multiple places, which opens the door for the database to become inconsistent.

It should also be apparent that there's no way to use HyperLogLog when dealing with equivs. A HyperLogLog set doesn't know what elements are within it, which makes it impossible to apply equivs to remove redundant UserIDs. This is a terrible result, because HyperLogLog was such a massive optimization.

So far we've glossed over the problem of analyzing equivs to select a single UserID to represent each person. This is a fairly tricky problem on its own and rather complex to implement incrementally. But because this algorithm isn't required to understand the complexities of fully incremental architectures, we'll just assume that this problem is completely solved. The result of this solution is an index from userid to personid, where personid is the identifier selected to represent all the userids belonging to the same person.

What has made this problem difficult so far has been trying to handle equivs on the write side by "fixing" the database to ensure that two UserIDs connected by equivs don't simultaneously exist in the database. So let's take a different approach by moving the work of handling equivs to the read side of the query.

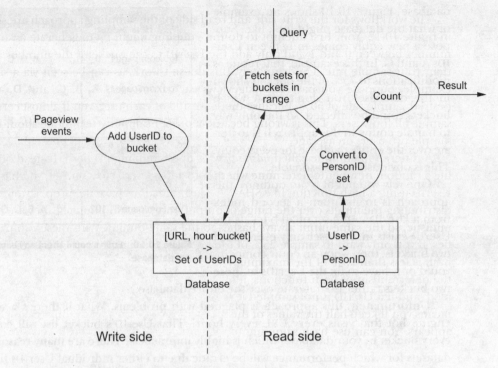

Figure 10.11 Handling equivs on the read-side workflow

In the first read-side attempt, illustrated in figure 10.11, the database will be a key-to-set database from `[URL, hour bucket]` to the set of all UserIDs to visit that URL in that hour. This time, multiple UserIDs for the same person are allowed to exist in the database, as handling that will be taken care of during reads. Reads work like this:

1 First, retrieve every UserID set for every hour in the range, and merge them.
2 Convert the set of UserIDs to a set of PersonIDs by using the UserID-to-PersonID index.
3 Return the count of the PersonID set.

Unfortunately, this approach isn't quite viable because it's far too expensive. Imagine a query that has 100 million uniques. That means you'd have to first fetch many gigabytes of information to get the UserID set, and then do 100 million lookups into the UserID-to-PersonID index. There's no way that work will ever complete in just a few milliseconds.

The prior approach can be modified slightly to become viable by using an approximation to drastically reduce storage and computation costs. The main idea is that rather than store the entire set of UserIDs for every bucket, you instead store a sample of the UserIDs for every bucket. If you only store 5% of the UserIDs, that's 95% less work to fetch the UserID sets and up to 95% less work to convert the UserIDs to PersonIDs. By dividing the count of the sampled PersonID set by the sample rate, you get an estimate for the count of the non-sampled set.

The workflows for the write side and read side of the sampling approach are shown in figure 10.12. Your first attempt to do the sampling might be to generate a random number between 0 and 1 and only add the UserID to the bucket if the number is less than your sample rate. Unfortunately, this doesn't work, as can be seen via a simple example. Suppose you have 100 pageviews each from users A, B, C, and D, and a desired sample rate of 50%. Because there are 100 of each user, you'll almost certainly sample all four users. This is wrong because a proper sampling technique should only sample two users on average.

A different technique called *hash sampling* does sampling properly. Instead of picking a random number to determine whether to add a UserID to a bucket, you hash the UserID using a hash function like SHA-256. Hash functions have the property of evenly distributing the inputs over the range of output numbers. Additionally, they are deterministic, so the same input always hashes to the same output. With these two properties, if you only want to sample 25% of the UserIDs, you simply keep all UserIDs whose hash is less than 25% of the maximum output value of the hash function. Because of the determinism of hash functions, if a UserID is sampled once it will always be sampled, and if a UserID is not sampled it will never be sampled. So a sample rate of 50% means you'll keep half the values of the set, regardless of how many times each UserID appears. You can use hash sampling to vastly decrease the sizes of the sets stored for

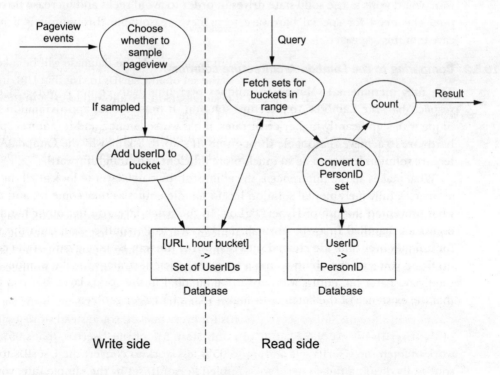

Figure 10.12 Adding sampling to the read-side workflow

each bucket, and the higher the sample rate you choose, the more accurate the results of queries will be.

The good news is that we finally have a viable approach to implementing this query that can be made performant. The bad news is that this comes with some caveats. First, the level of accuracy of the hash sampling approach is not nearly the same as HyperLogLog. For the same space usage as HyperLogLog, your average error will be at least 3x to 5x worse, depending on how large your UserIDs are.

Second, achieving good throughput with this approach requires special hardware for the UserID-to-PersonID index. To achieve reasonable error rates, your UserID sets will still need at least 100 elements in them. That means you need to do at least 100 lookups into your UserID-to-PersonID index during queries. Although it's a huge improvement over the potentially millions of lookups required in the non-sampled approach, this is still nothing to scoff at. If you're using hard disks to store your UserID-to-PersonID index, each lookup into the index requires at least one seek on your disks. You've seen how expensive disk seeks are, and having to do so many disk seeks for each query will vastly decrease query throughput.

There are two ways to get rid of this bottleneck. The first is to ensure that the UserID-to-PersonID index is kept completely in memory, avoiding the need to go to disk at all. Depending on the size of the index, this may or may not be feasible. Otherwise, you'd want to use solid-state drives in order to avoid seeks and increase throughput. The need for special hardware to achieve reasonable throughput is a major caveat of this approach.

10.5.2 *Comparing to the Lambda Architecture solution*

The fully incremental solution to uniques over time with equivs is worse in every respect than the Lambda Architecture solution. It must use an approximation technique with significantly higher error rates, it has worse latency, and it requires special hardware to achieve reasonable throughput. It's worth asking why the Lambda Architecture solution is able to be so much more efficient and straightforward.

What makes all the difference is the ability for the batch layer to look at all the data at once. A fully incremental solution has to handle equivs as they come in, and that's what prevented the use of HyperLogLog. In the batch layer, on the other hand, the equivs are handled first—by normalizing UserIDs to PersonIDs—and then the views for uniques over time are created with that out of the way. By taking care of the equivs up front, you gain the ability to use a far more efficient strategy for the uniques-over-time view. Later on, equivs will have to be handled in the speed layer, but you'll see that the existence of the batch layer makes that a far easier problem.

10.6 Summary

You saw in this chapter the fundamental concepts of the serving layer in the Lambda Architecture:

- The ability to tailor views to optimize latency and throughput
- The simplicity from not supporting random writes
- The capacity to store normalized data in the batch layer and denormalized data in the serving layer
- The inherent error-tolerance and correction of the serving layer, because it can be recomputed from the master dataset

The flexibility to completely tailor the serving layer views to the queries they serve is a great example of simplicity at work. In traditional data architectures, a single database is used as the master dataset, the historical store, and the realtime store. Having to handle all these roles at once forces you as the application developer to make unacceptable trade-offs, like how much you normalize or denormalize your schemas, and to take on major operational burdens, like dealing with compaction. In the Lambda Architecture, however, these roles are handled by separate components. Therefore, each role can be optimized much further and the system as a whole is much more robust.

In the next chapter you'll see an example of a practical serving layer database.

Serving layer: Illustration

This chapter covers

- ElephantDB as an example of a serving layer database
- Architecture of ElephantDB
- Drawbacks of ElephantDB
- Using ElephantDB for SuperWebAnalytics.com

Having covered the requirements of the serving layer, we can now consider an example of a database built specifically for use as a serving layer database. As with all the illustration chapters, no new theory is introduced in this chapter; it instead serves to map the concepts you've learned to the nuts and bolts of real tooling.

We've mentioned that the available tooling for the serving layer lags behind the ideal possibilities, and that fact will be evident as you build the serving layer for SuperWebAnalytics.com. You'll learn to use ElephantDB, a key/value serving layer database. Because it doesn't support index types beyond key/value, you'll have to diverge from the ideal index types described in the previous chapter.

We'll examine the basic architecture of ElephantDB to understand how it meets the requirements of the serving layer, and then we'll review its API to retrieve the contents of a batch view. Finally, you'll see how you can use ElephantDB to index and serve the batch views for SuperWebAnalytics.com.

11.1 Basics of ElephantDB

ElephantDB is a key/value database where both keys and values are stored as byte arrays. ElephantDB partitions the batch views over a fixed number of shards, and each ElephantDB server is responsible for some subset of those shards.

The function that assigns keys to shards is pluggable and is called a *sharding scheme*. One common scheme determines the target shard by taking the remainder of dividing the hash of a key by the total number of shards (the modulo operation). Informally we'll call this technique *hash modding*. It distributes the keys evenly among the shards and provides an easy means to determine which shard holds a given key. This is often the best choice, but you will see cases where you want to customize the sharding scheme. Once assigned to a shard, the key/value is stored in a local indexing engine. By default, this is BerkeleyDB, but the engine is configurable and could be any key/value indexing engine that runs on a single machine.

There are two aspects to ElephantDB: view creation and view serving. View creation occurs in a MapReduce job at the end of the batch layer workflow where the generated partitions are stored in the distributed filesystem. Views are then served by a dedicated ElephantDB cluster that loads the shards from the distributed filesystem and interacts with clients that support random read requests. We'll briefly discuss these two roles before finally diving into using ElephantDB.

11.1.1 View creation in ElephantDB

The ElephantDB shards are created by a MapReduce job whose input is a set of key/value pairs. The number of reducers is configured to be the number of ElephantDB shards, and the keys are partitioned to the reducers using the specified sharding scheme. Consequently, each reducer is responsible for producing exactly one shard of an ElephantDB view. Each shard is then indexed (such as into a BerkeleyDB index) and uploaded to the distributed filesystem.

Note that the view creation process doesn't directly send the shards to the ElephantDB servers. Such a design would be poor because the client-facing machines wouldn't control their own load and query performance could suffer. Instead, the ElephantDB servers pull the shards from the filesystem at a throttled rate that allows them to maintain their performance guarantees to clients.

11.1.2 View serving in ElephantDB

An ElephantDB cluster is composed of a number of machines that divide the work of serving the shards. To fairly share the load, the shards are evenly distributed among the servers.

ElephantDB also supports replication, where each shard is redundantly hosted across a predetermined number of servers. For example, with 40 shards, 8 servers, and a replication factor of 3, each server would host 15 shards, and each shard would exist on 3 different servers. This makes the cluster tolerant to machine failures, allowing full access to the entire view even when machines are lost. Of course, only so many machines can be lost before portions of the view become unavailable, but replication makes this possibility far less likely. Replication is illustrated in figure 11.1.

ElephantDB servers are responsible for retrieving their assigned shards from the distributed filesystem. When a server detects that a new version of a shard is available, it does a throttled download of the new partition. The download is controlled so as to not saturate the I/O of the machine and affect live reads. Upon completing the download, it switches to the new partition and deletes the old one.

After an ElephantDB server has downloaded its shards, the contents

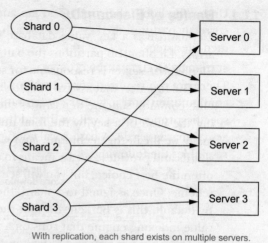

With replication, each shard exists on multiple servers.

Figure 11.1   Replication stores shards in multiple locations to increase tolerance to individual machine failures.

of the batch views are accessible via a basic API. We earlier mentioned that there's no general-purpose serving layer database—this is where the limitations of ElephantDB become apparent. Because ElephantDB uses a key/indexing model, the API only allows for the retrieval of values for specified keys. A general serving layer database would provide a richer API, such as the ability to scan over key ranges.

11.1.3 Using ElephantDB

The simplicity of ElephantDB makes it straightforward to use. There are three separate aspects to using ElephantDB: creating shards, setting up a cluster to serve requests, and using the client API to query the batch views. We'll step through each of these components.

CREATING ELEPHANTDB SHARDS

The tap abstraction makes it simple to create a set of ElephantDB shards using JCascalog. ElephantDB provides a tap to automate the shard-creation process. If you have a subquery that generates key/value pairs, creating the ElephantDB view is as simple as executing that subquery into the tap:

Applies hash mod partitioning as the sharding scheme

Directs the output of the subquery to the constructed tap

Uses BerkeleyDB as the local storage engine

Creates 32 shards at the given distributed filesystem path

```
public static elephantDbTapExample (Subquery subquery) {
    DomainSpec spec = new DomainSpec(new JavaBerkDB(),
                                     new HashModScheme());
    Object tap = EDB.makeKeyValTap("/output/path/on/dfs", spec, 32);
    Api.execute(tap, subquery);
}
```

Under the hood, the configured tap automatically configures the MapReduce job to correctly partition the keys, creates each index, and uploads each index to the distributed filesystem.

SETTING UP AN ELEPHANTDB CLUSTER

There are two required configurations for establishing an ElephantDB cluster: a local configuration and a global configuration. The local configuration contains server-specific properties as well as the addresses where the global configuration and the actual shards reside. A basic local configuration resides on each individual server and resembles the following:

The local directory to store downloaded shards

The address of the distributed filesystem that stores the shards

```
{:local-root "/data/elephantdb"          ◄──
 :hdfs-conf {"fs.default.name" "hdfs://namenode.domain.com:8020"}    ◄──
 :blob-conf {"fs.default.name" "hdfs://namenode.domain.com:8020"}}   ◄──
```

The address of the distributed filesystem hosting the global configuration

The global configuration contains information needed by every server in the cluster. This includes the replication factor, the TCP port that servers should use to accept requests, and the views served by this cluster. A single cluster can serve multiple domains, so the configuration contains a map from the domain names to their HDFS locations.

A basic global configuration would look like the following code:

The replication factor of all views for all servers

Host names of all servers in the cluster

The TCP port the server will use to accept requests

```
{:replication 1              ◄──
 :hosts ["edb1.domain.com" "edb2.domain.com" "edb3.domain.com"]   ◄──
 :port 3578
 :domains {"tweet-counts" "/data/output/tweet-counts-edb"
           "influenced-by" "/data/output/influenced-by-edb"
           "influencer-of" "/data/output/influencer-of-edb"}}   ◄──
```

Identifiers of all views and their locations on the distributed filesystem

These configurations are so simple they almost appear incomplete. For example, there's no explicit assignment from the servers to the specific shards they'll host. In this particular case, the servers use their position in the hosts list as input to a deterministic function to calculate the shards they should download. The simplicity of the configurations reflects the ease of using ElephantDB.

How do you actually start an ElephantDB server?

The process of launching an ElephantDB server follows standard Java practices, such as building a project uberjar and passing the configuration locations via a command-line statement. Rather than provide details that could quickly get out of date, we'll refer you to the project website (http://github.com/nathanmarz/elephantdb) for specifics.

QUERYING AN ELEPHANTDB CLUSTER

ElephantDB exposes a simple Thrift API for issuing queries. After connecting to any ElephantDB server, you can issue queries like so:

```
public static void clientQuery(ElephantDB.Client client,
                        String domain,
                        byte[] key) {
    client.get(domain, key);
}
```

If the connected server doesn't store the requested key locally, it will communicate with the other servers in the cluster to retrieve the desired values.

11.2   *Building the serving layer for SuperWebAnalytics.com*

Having covered the basics, you can now create the optimized ElephantDB views for each query in SuperWebAnalytics.com. First up is the pageviews-over-time view.

11.2.1 *Pageviews over time*

Recall that the ideal view for pageviews over time is an index from key to sorted map, illustrated again in figure 11.2. You saw how granularities beyond hours aren't needed due to each entry only requiring a few bytes of storage, so scanning over a multi-year range is fairly cheap.

Unfortunately, ElephantDB only supports key/value indexing, so this view is not possible with ElephantDB. Because each key needs to be retrieved separately, it's imperative to minimize the number of keys retrieved for each query. This implies that all the granularities should be indexed into the view. Let's see how you can use ElephantDB to implement this strategy.

At the end of chapter 8 you'd produced a view like that in figure 11.3. Recall that both the keys and values in ElephantDB are stored as byte arrays. For the pageviews-over-time view, you need to encode the URL, granularity, and time bucket into the key.

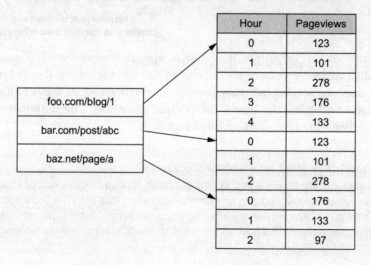

Figure 11.2   Ideal indexing strategy for pageviews over time

URL	Granularity	Bucket	Pageviews
foo.com/blog/1	h	0	10
foo.com/blog/1	h	1	21
foo.com/blog/1	h	2	7
foo.com/blog/1	w	0	38
foo.com/blog/1	m	0	38
bar.com/post/a	h	0	213
bar.com/post/a	h	1	178
bar.com/post/a	h	2	568

Figure 11.3 Pageviews-over-time batch view

The following JCascalog functions implement the required serializations for composite keys and the pageview values:

```
public static class ToUrlBucketedKey extends CascalogFunction {
  public void operate(FlowProcess process, FunctionCall call) {
    String url = call.getArguments().getString(0);
    String gran = call.getArguments().getString(1);
    Integer bucket = call.getArguments().getInteger(2);

    String keyStr = url + "/" + gran + "-" + bucket;          ← Concatenates the key components
    try {
      call.getOutputCollector()
          .add(new Tuple(keyStr.getBytes("UTF-8")));           ← Converts to bytes using UTF-8 encoding
    } catch(UnsupportedEncodingException e) {
      throw new RuntimeException(e);
    }
  }
}

public static class ToSerializedLong extends CascalogFunction {
  public void operate(FlowProcess process, FunctionCall call) {
    long val = call.getArguments().getLong(0);
    ByteBuffer buffer = ByteBuffer.allocate(8);               ← Configures ByteBuffer to hold a single long value
    buffer.putLong(val);
    call.getOutputCollector().add(new Tuple(buffer.array())); ← Extracts the byte array from the buffer
  }
}
```

The next step is to create the ElephantDB tap. To avoid the variance problem discussed at the beginning of the chapter, you can create a custom `ShardingScheme` to ensure that all key/value pairs for a single URL exist on the same shard. The following snippet accomplishes this by hash modding only the URL portion of the composite key:

```
private static String getUrlFromSerializedKey(byte[] ser) {
  try {
    String key = new String(ser, "UTF-8");
    return key.substring(0, key.lastIndexOf("/"));        ⟵ Extracts the URL from
  } catch(UnsupportedEncodingException e) {                   the composite key
    throw new RuntimeException(e);
  }
}

public static class UrlOnlyScheme implements ShardingScheme {
  public int shardIndex(byte[] shardKey, int shardCount) {
    String url = getUrlFromSerializedKey(shardKey);
    return url.hashCode() % shardCount;        ⟵ Returns the hash
  }                                                mod of the URL
}
```

The following JCascalog subquery puts the pieces together to transform the batch layer view into key/value pairs appropriate for ElephantDB:

The subquery must return only two fields corresponding to keys and values.

```
public static void pageviewElephantDB(Subquery batchView) {
  Subquery toEdb =
    new Subquery("?key", "?value")
      .predicate(batchView, "?url", "?gran", "?bucket", "?total-views")
      .predicate(new ToUrlBucketedKey(), "?url", "?gran", "?bucket")
        .out("?key")
      .predicate(new ToSerializedLong(), "?total-views")
        .out("?value");

  DomainSpec spec = new DomainSpec(new JavaBerkDB(),
                                   new UrlOnlyScheme(),
                                   32);
  Tap tap = EDB.makeKeyValTap("/outputs/edb/pageviews", spec);   ⟵
  Api.execute(tap, toEdb);
}
```

Defines the local storage engine, sharding scheme, and total number of shards

Specifies the HDFS location of the shards

Executes the transformation

Again, the pageviews-over-time view would benefit from a more-general serving layer database that could store the time buckets for each URL sequentially and in chronological order. This database would utilize disk scans and minimize expensive disk seeks.

Such a serving layer database doesn't exist at the time of this writing, though creating one would be much simpler than most currently available NoSQL databases. The approach shown here isn't much worse than the ideal serving layer database, though, as it's still able to ensure that all index retrievals for a single query only touch one node, and it only has to fetch a handful of values for any given query.

11.2.2 *Uniques over time*

The next query is the unique-pageviews-over-time query. Like pageviews over time, the lack of a key-to-sorted-map serving layer database prevents you from implementing the ideal index described in the previous chapter. But you can use a strategy similar to the one used by pageviews over time to produce a workable solution.

The only difference between the two queries is that uniques over time stores HyperLogLog sets. Like pageviews over time, the uniques over time can make use of the same sharding scheme in order to avoid the variance problem. Here is the code to produce the uniques-over-time view:

```
public static void uniquesElephantDB(Subquery uniquesView) {
  Subquery toEdb =
    new Subquery("?key", "?value")
      .predicate(uniquesView,"?url", "?gran", "?bucket", "?value")
      .predicate(new ToUrlBucketedKey(),"?url", "?gran", "?bucket")
        .out("?key");

  DomainSpec spec = new DomainSpec(new JavaBerkDB(),
                                   new UrlOnlyScheme(),
                                   32);
  Tap tap = EDB.makeKeyValTap("/outputs/edb/uniques", spec);
  Api.execute(tap, toEdb);
}
```

> Only the composite key needs to be serialized because the HyperLogLog sets are already serialized.

> Changes the output directory for the unique pageviews shards

An ideal serving layer database would know how to handle HyperLogLog sets natively and complete queries on the server. Instead of queries to the database returning HyperLogLog sets, the server would merge the sets and return only the cardinality of the HyperLogLog structure. This would maximize efficiency by avoiding the network transfer of any HyperLogLog sets during queries.

11.2.3   *Bounce-rate analysis*

The ideal bounce-rate-analysis view is a key/value index, so an ideal view can be produced with ElephantDB. The bounce-rate-analysis view is a map from each domain to the number of visits and the number of bounces.

You can reuse the framework from the previous queries, but you still need custom serialization code for the string keys and compound value:

```
public static class ToSerializedString extends CascalogFunction {
  public void operate(FlowProcess process, FunctionCall call) {
    String str = call.getArguments().getString(0);

    try {
      call.getOutputCollector().add(new Tuple(str.getBytes("UTF-8")));
    } catch(UnsupportedEncodingException e) {
      throw new RuntimeException(e);
    }
  }
}
```

> This serialization function is essentially identical to the one for the composite keys.

```
public static class ToSerializedLongPair extends CascalogFunction {
  public void operate(FlowProcess process, FunctionCall call) {
    long l1 = call.getArguments().getLong(0);
    long l2 = call.getArguments().getLong(1);
    ByteBuffer buffer = ByteBuffer.allocate(16);
    buffer.putLong(l1);
```

> Allocates space for two long values

```
        buffer.putLong(12);
        call.getOutputCollector().add(new Tuple(buffer.array()));
    }
}
```

Queries against this view will fetch only one domain at a time, so there are no concerns about variance in server response times. Normal hash mod sharding is therefore suitable for this case:

```
public static void bounceRateElephantDB(Subquery bounceView) {
    Subquery toEdb =
        new Subquery("?key", "?value")
            .predicate(bounceView, "?domain", "?bounces", "?total")
            .predicate(new ToSerializedString(), "?domain")
            .out("?key")
            .predicate(new ToSerializedLongPair(),"?bounces", "?total")
            .out("?value");

    DomainSpec spec = new DomainSpec(new JavaBerkDB(),
                                    new HashModScheme(),
                                    32);
    Tap tap = EDB.makeKeyValTap("/outputs/edb/bounces", spec);
    Api.execute(tap, toEdb);
}
```

Uses hash mod sharding scheme provided by ElephantDB

As you can see, integrating the batch views into the serving layer is almost no work at all.

11.3   Summary

ElephantDB is a database that can be used in the serving layer. You've seen how simple ElephantDB is to use and operate. We hope to see other serving layer databases created with different or more general indexing models, because the fundamental simplicity of the serving layer makes these databases easy to build.

Now that you understand the batch and serving layers, next up is learning the final piece of the Lambda Architecture: the speed layer. The speed layer will compensate for the high-latency updates of the serving layer and allow queries to access up-to-date data.

Part 3

Speed layer

Part 3 focuses on the speed layer of the Lambda Architecture. The speed layer compensates for the high latency of the batch layer to enable up-to-date results for queries.

Chapter 12 discusses realtime views versus batch views. The primary difference is a realtime view database must support random writes, which greatly increases the complexity of the database. You'll see that the existence of the batch layer eases the complexity of managing such a database. You'll also see that a speed layer can be implemented either synchronously or asynchronously. Chapter 13 illustrates realtime views using Apache Cassandra.

Synchronous architectures don't require any additional explanation, so chapter 14 begins the discussion of asynchronous architectures for the speed layer. It discusses the use of incremental computation using queues and stream processing. There are two main paradigms of stream processing, each with their own trade-offs: one-at-a-time and micro-batched. Chapter 14 explores the concept of one-at-a-time stream processing, and chapter 15 illustrates that model using Apache Kafka and Apache Storm.

Chapter 16 delves into the other paradigm: micro-batched stream processing. You'll see that by sacrificing some latency, you gain powerful new capabilities. Chapter 17 illustrates micro-batched stream processing using Trident.

Realtime views

12

This chapter covers

- The theoretical model of the speed layer
- How the batch layer eases the responsibilities of the speed layer
- Using random-write databases for realtime views
- The CAP theorem and its implications
- The challenges of incremental computation
- Expiring data from the speed layer

Up to this point, our discussion of the Lambda Architecture has revolved around the batch and serving layers—components that involve computing functions over every piece of data you have. These layers satisfy all the desirable properties of a data system save one: low-latency updates. The sole job of the speed layer is to satisfy this final requirement.

Running functions over the entire master dataset—potentially petabytes of data—is a resource-intensive operation. To lower the latency of updates as much as possible, the speed layer must take a fundamentally different approach than the batch and serving layers. As such, the speed layer is based on *incremental computation* instead of batch computation.

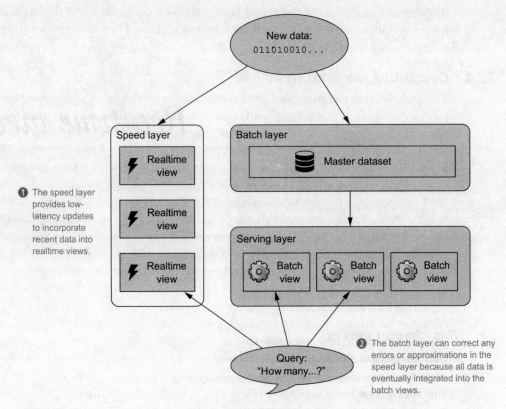

Figure 12.1   The speed layer allows the Lambda Architecture to serve low-latency queries over up-to-date data.

Incremental computation introduces many new challenges and is significantly more complex than batch computation. Fortunately, the narrow requirements of the speed layer provide two advantages. First, the speed layer is only responsible for data yet to be included in the serving layer views. This data is at most a few hours old and is vastly smaller than the master dataset. Processing data on a smaller scale allows for greater design flexibility. Second, the speed layer views are transient. Once the data is absorbed into the serving layer views, it can be discarded from the speed layer. Even though the speed layer is more complex and thus more prone to error, any errors are short-lived and will be automatically corrected through the simpler batch and serving layers.

As we've repeatedly stated, the power of the Lambda Architecture lies in the separation of roles in the different layers (as shown in figure 12.1). In traditional data architectures such as those based on relational databases, *all that exists is a speed layer.* These systems have limited options for battling the complexities of incremental computation.

There are two major facets of the speed layer: storing the realtime views and processing the incoming data stream so as to update those views. This chapter focuses on the structure and storage of realtime views. We'll begin with an overview of the theoretical foundation of the speed layer, and then continue on to the various challenges you'll encounter with incremental computation. Then we'll demonstrate how to expire data from the speed layer.

12.1 Computing realtime views

The basic objective of the speed layer is the same as for the batch and serving layers: to produce views that can be efficiently queried. The key differences are that the views only represent recent data and that they must be updated very shortly after new data arrives. What "very shortly" means varies per application, but it typically ranges from a few milliseconds to a few seconds. This requirement has far-reaching consequences on the computational approach to generating the speed layer views.

To understand the implications, consider one simple approach to the speed layer. Similar to the batch and serving layers producing views by computing a function on the entire master dataset, the speed layer could produce its views by running a function over all of the recent data (that is, data yet to be absorbed into the serving layer). This is attractive for both its simplicity and the consistency with how the batch layer works, as shown in figure 12.2.

Unfortunately, this scheme proves impractical for many applications once you consider its latency and resource-usage characteristics. Suppose your data system receives 32 GB of new data per day, and that new data gets into the serving layer within 6 hours of being received. The speed layer would be responsible for at most 6 hours of data—about 8 GB. While that's not a huge amount, 8 GB is substantial when attempting to achieve sub-second latencies. Additionally, running a function on 8 GB of data each time you receive a new piece of data will be extremely resource-intensive. If the average size of a data unit is 100 bytes, the 8 GB of recent data equates to approximately 86 million data units. Keeping the realtime views up to date would thus require an unreasonable amount of 86,000,000 × 8 GB worth of processing every 6 hours. You could reduce the resource usage by batching the updates, but this would greatly increase the update latency.

If your application can accept latency on the order of a few minutes, this simple strategy is a fine approach. But in general you'll need to produce realtime views in a resource-efficient manner with millisecond-level latencies. For the remainder of this chapter, we'll confine our discussion to this scenario.

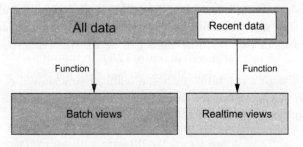

A simple strategy mirrors the batch/serving layer and computes the realtime views using all recent data as input.

Figure 12.2 Strategy: realtime view = function(recent data)

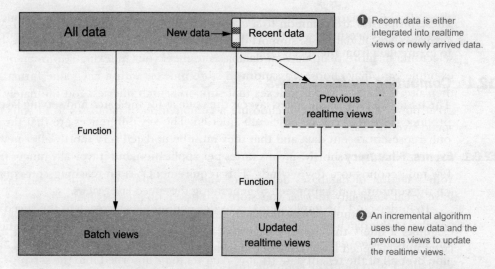

Figure 12.3   Incremental strategy: realtime view = function(new data, previous realtime view)

In general, any workable solution relies on using incremental algorithms, as depicted in figure 12.3. The idea is to update the realtime views as data comes in, thereby reusing the work that previously went into producing the views. This requires the use of random-read/random-write databases so that updates can be performed on existing views. In the next section we'll discuss these databases further, while delving into the details of storing the speed layer views.

12.2 *Storing realtime views*

The obligations of the speed layer views are quite demanding—the Lambda Architecture requires low-latency random reads, and using incremental algorithms necessitates low-latency random updates. The underlying storage layer must therefore meet the following requirements:

- *Random reads*—A realtime view should support fast random reads to answer queries quickly. This means the data it contains must be indexed.
- *Random writes*—To support incremental algorithms, it must also be possible to modify a realtime view with low latency.
- *Scalability*—As with the serving layer views, the realtime views should scale with the amount of data they store and the read/write rates required by the application. Typically this implies that realtime views can be distributed across many machines.
- *Fault tolerance*—If a disk or a machine crashes, a realtime view should continue to function normally. Fault tolerance is accomplished by replicating data across machines so there are backups should a single machine fail.

These properties are common to a class of databases that have been dubbed *NoSQL databases*. NoSQL databases support diverse data models and index types, so you can select one or more realtime view databases to meet your indexing requirements. For example, you may choose Cassandra to store indexes with a key/value format, and then use ElasticSearch for indexes that support search queries. You ultimately have great power and flexibility in choosing a combination of databases to fit your exact speed layer needs.

12.2.1 *Eventual accuracy*

Your selection of databases determines *how* the realtime views are stored, but you have great flexibility in *what* you store to answer queries. In many cases, the contents of your realtime views will exactly mirror the contents of your batch views. For example, a query that returns pageviews will store exact counts in both the batch layer and the speed layer. However, this need not be the case, because frequently it's difficult to incrementally compute functions that can be easily computed in batch. You've encountered this scenario before when determining unique counts. In batch this is easy to compute because you process the entire dataset at one time, but it's much harder in realtime because you need to store the entire set to correctly update the counts.

In these cases you can take a different approach in the speed layer and approximate the correct answer. Because all data is eventually represented in the batch and serving layer views, any approximations you make in the speed layer are continually corrected. This means any approximations are only temporary, and your queries exhibit eventual accuracy. This is a really powerful technique that gives you the best of all worlds: performance, accuracy, and timeliness. Eventually accurate approaches are common with sophisticated queries such as those that require realtime machine learning. Such views tend to correlate many kinds of data together and can't incrementally produce an exact answer in any reasonable way. You'll see examples that take advantage of eventual accuracy when we flesh out the speed layer for SuperWebAnalytics.com.

Again, we must emphasize that eventual accuracy is an *optional* technique that can be used to dramatically lower resource usage in the speed layer. It's an option available to you solely because the Lambda Architecture has two layers with distinct methods of computation. In a traditional architecture based on fully incremental computation, such a technique is not an option.

12.2.2 *Amount of state stored in the speed layer*

Speed layers store relatively small amounts of state because they only represent views on recent data. This is a benefit because realtime views are much more complex than serving layer views.

Let's briefly revisit the complexities of realtime views that are bypassed by the serving layer:

- *Online compaction*—As a read/write database receives updates, parts of the disk index become unused, wasted space. Periodically the database must perform compaction to reclaim space. Compaction is a resource-intensive process and could potentially starve the machine of resources needed to rapidly serve queries. Improper management of compaction can cause a cascading failure of the entire cluster.

- *Concurrency*—A read/write database can potentially receive many reads or writes for the same value at the same time. It therefore needs to coordinate these reads and writes to prevent returning stale or inconsistent values. Sharing mutable state across threads is a notoriously complex problem, and control strategies such as locking are notoriously bug-prone.

It's important to note that the speed layer is under less pressure because it stores considerably less data than the serving layer. The separation of roles and responsibilities within the Lambda Architecture limits complexity in the speed layer. Because the speed layer typically accounts for only a few hours of data, your random-read/random-write database cluster can be 100x smaller than it would be if you had a fully incremental architecture. Smaller clusters are a lot easier to manage.

Now that you understand the basics of the speed layer, let's look at the challenges you'll face when doing incremental computation as opposed to batch computation.

12.3 *Challenges of incremental computation*

In chapter 6 we discussed the differences between recomputation and incremental algorithms. To summarize, incremental algorithms are less general and less human-fault tolerant than recomputation algorithms, but they provide much higher performance. It's this higher performance that we're leveraging in the speed layer. But an additional challenge arises when using incremental algorithms in a realtime context: the interaction between incremental algorithms and something called the *CAP theorem*. This challenge can be particularly hairy and is important to understand.

The CAP theorem is about fundamental trade-offs between *consistency*, where reads are guaranteed to incorporate all previous writes, and *availability*, where every query returns an answer instead of erroring. Unfortunately, the theorem is often explained in a very misleading and inaccurate way. We'd normally avoid presenting an inaccurate explanation of anything, but this interpretation is so widespread it's necessary to discuss it to clarify the misconceptions.

CAP is typically stated as "you can have at most two of consistency, availability, and partition-tolerance." The problem with this explanation is that the CAP theorem is entirely about what happens to data systems when not all machines can communicate with each other. Saying a data system is consistent and available but not partition-tolerant makes no sense, because the theorem is entirely about what happens under partitions.

The proper way to present the CAP theorem is that "when a distributed data system is partitioned, it can be consistent or available but not both." Should you choose consistency, sometimes a query will receive an error instead of an answer. When you choose availability, reads may return stale results during network partitions. The best consistency property you can have in a highly available system is *eventual consistency*, where the system returns to consistency once the network partition ends.

12.3.1 *Validity of the CAP theorem*

It's fairly easy to understand why the CAP theorem is true. Say you have a simple distributed key/value database where every node in your cluster is responsible for a separate set of keys, meaning there is no replication. When you want to read or write data for a particular key, there is a single machine responsible for handling the request.

Now suppose you suddenly can't communicate with some of the machines in the distributed system. Obviously you can't read or write data to nodes that are inaccessible to you.

You can increase the fault tolerance of a distributed data system by replicating data across multiple servers. With a replication factor of three, every key would be replicated to three nodes. Now if you become partitioned from one replica, you can still retrieve the value from another location. But it's still possible to be partitioned from all replicas, though much less likely.

The real question is how to handle writes under partitions. There are a few options—for example, you could refuse to perform an update unless all replicas can be updated at once. With this policy, every read request is guaranteed to return the latest value. This is a consistent strategy, because clients partitioned from each other will always receive the same value (or get an error) when doing reads.

Alternatively, you can choose to update whatever replicas are available and synchronize with other replicas when the partition is resolved. This gets tricky when a scenario like that shown in figure 12.4 occurs. In this situation, clients are partitioned differently and communicate with different subgroups of machines. The replicas will diverge if you are willing to update a subset of the replicas, and merging is more complicated than simply picking the latest update.

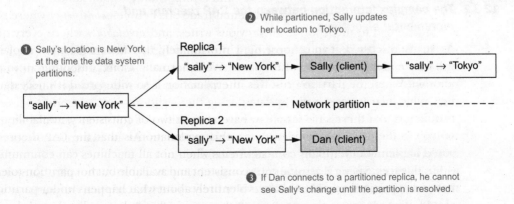

Figure 12.4   Replicas can diverge if updates are allowed under partitions.

With a partial update strategy, your data system is available but not consistent. In figure 12.4, Sally may update her location to Tokyo, but Dan's replica can't be updated, so he'll read an out-of-date value. This example demonstrates that it's impossible to have both availability and consistency during a partition, because there's no means to communicate with the replica that has the most recent information.

Extreme availability—sloppy quorums

Some distributed databases have an option called *sloppy quorums*, which provides availability in the extreme—writes are accepted even if replicas for that data aren't available. Instead, a temporary replica will be created and then merged into the official replicas once they become available. With sloppy quorums, the potential number of replicas for a piece of data is equal to the number of nodes in the cluster if every node is partitioned from every other node. While this can be useful, keep in mind that such an approach increases the incidental complexity of your system.

The batch and serving layers are distributed systems and are subject to the CAP theorem like any other system. The only writes in the batch layer are new pieces of immutable data. These writes don't require coordination between machines because every piece of data is independent. If data can't be written to the incoming data store in the batch layer, it can be buffered locally and retried later. As for the serving layer, reads are always stale due to the high latency of the batch layer. Not only is the serving layer not consistent, it's not even eventually consistent because it's always out of date. Accordingly, both the batch and serving layers choose availability over consistency.

Note that nothing complex was needed to determine these properties—the logic in the batch and serving layers is simple and easy to understand. Unfortunately this is *not* the case when striving for eventual consistency using incremental algorithms in a realtime context.

12.3.2 *The complex interaction between the CAP theorem and incremental algorithms*

As we just discussed, if you choose high availability for a distributed system, a partition will create multiple replicas of the same value that are updated independently of one another. When the partition resolves, the values must be merged together so that the new value incorporates every update during the partition—no more and no less. The problem is that there's no simple way to accomplish this for every use case, so it falls on you as the developer to identify a working strategy. As an example, consider how you'd implement eventually consistent counting.

In this scenario we'll assume you're only storing the count as the value. Suppose the network is partitioned, the replicas evolve independently, and then the partition is corrected. When it comes time to merge the replica values, you find that one replica has a count of 110 and another has a count of 105. What should the new value be? The cause of the confusion is that you're unsure at what point they began to diverge. If they diverged at the value 105, the updated count should be 110. If they diverged at 0, the right answer would be 215. All you know for certain is that the right answer is somewhere between these two bounds.

To implement eventually consistent counting correctly, you need to make use of structures called *conflict-free replicated data types* (commonly referred to as *CRDTs*). There are a number of CRDTs for a variety of values and operations: sets that support only addition, sets that support addition and removal, numbers that support increments, numbers that support increments and decrements, and so forth. The G-Counter is a CRDT that supports only incrementing, which is exactly what you need to solve the current counter issue. An example G-Counter is shown in figure 12.5.

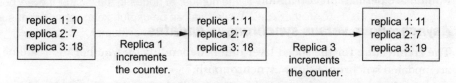

Figure 12.5   A G-Counter is a grow-only counter where a replica only increments its assigned counter. The overall value of the counter is the sum of the replica counts.

A G-Counter stores a different value per replica rather than a single value. The actual count is then the sum of the replica counts.

If a conflict between replicas is detected, the new G-Counter takes the max value for each replica. Because counts only increase, and only one server in the system will be updating the count for a given replica, the maximum value is guaranteed to be the correct one. This is illustrated in figure 12.6.

As you can see, implementing counting is far more complex in a realtime eventually consistent context. It's not sufficient to keep a simple count—you also need a strategy to repair values that diverge in a partition. The algorithms can also introduce

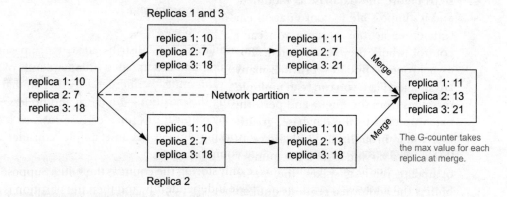

Figure 12.6   Merging G-Counters

further complexity. If you allow for decrements as well as increments, the data structure and merge algorithm become even more complicated. These merge algorithms—commonly called *read repair algorithms*—are huge sources of human error. This is not surprising given the complexity.

Unfortunately there's no escape from this complexity if you want eventual consistency in the speed layer. But you do have one thing going for you: the Lambda Architecture gives you inherent protection against making mistakes. If the realtime view becomes corrupted because you forgot an edge case or messed up the merge algorithm, the batch and serving layers will later automatically correct the mistake in the serving layer views. The worst possible outcome of a mistake is temporary corruption. Architectures without a batch layer backing up the realtime, incremental portions would have permanent corruption.

12.4 *Asynchronous versus synchronous updates*

The architecture for the speed layer differs depending on whether the realtime views are updated synchronously or asynchronously.

A synchronous update is something you've likely done a million times: the application issues a request directly to the database and blocks until the update is processed. For example, if a user registers an email address, you may choose to issue a synchronous update to the database to record the new information. Synchronous updates are fast because they communicate directly with the database, and they facilitate coordinating the update with other aspects of the application (such as displaying a spinning cursor while waiting for the update to complete).

The speed layer architecture for synchronous updates is illustrated in figure 12.7. Not surprisingly, the application simply issues updates directly to the database.

In contrast, asynchronous update requests are placed in a queue with the updates occurring at a later time. In the speed layer, this delay could range from a few milliseconds to a few seconds, but it could take even longer if there's an excess of requests. Asynchronous updates are slower than synchronous updates because they require additional steps before the database is modified, and it's impossible to coordinate them with other actions because you can't control when they're executed. But asynchronous updates provide many advantages. First, you can read multiple messages from the queue and perform batch updates to the database, greatly increasing throughput. They also readily handle a varying load: if the number of update requests spikes, the queue buffers the additional requests until all updates are executed. Conversely, a

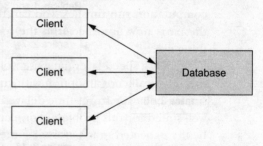

With synchronous updates, clients communicate directly with the database and block until the update is completed.

Figure 12.7   A simple speed layer architecture using synchronous updates

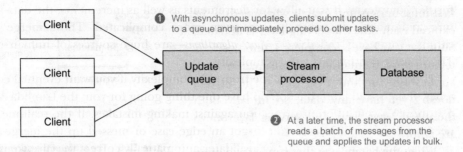

Figure 12.8 Asynchronous updates provide higher throughput and readily handle variable loads.

traffic spike with synchronous updates could overload the database, leading to dropped requests, timeouts, and other errors that disrupt your application.

The speed layer architecture for asynchronous updates is illustrated in figure 12.8. In the next chapter you'll learn about queues and stream processing in much more detail.

There are uses for both synchronous and asynchronous updates. Synchronous updates are typical among transactional systems that interact with users and require coordination with the user interface. Asynchronous updates are common for analytics-oriented workloads or workloads not requiring coordination. The architectural advantages of asynchronous updates—better throughput and better management of load spikes—suggest implementing asynchronous updates unless you have a good reason not to do so.

12.5 *Expiring realtime views*

Incremental algorithms and random-write databases make the speed layer far more complex than the batch and serving layers, but one of the key benefits of the Lambda Architecture is the transient nature of the speed layer. Because the simpler batch and serving layers continuously override the speed layer, the speed layer views only need to represent data yet to be processed by the batch computation workflow. Once a batch computation run finishes, you can then discard a portion of the speed layer views— the parts now absorbed into the serving layer—but obviously you must keep everything else.

Ideally a speed layer database would provide support to directly expire entries, but this is typically not an option with current databases. Tools like Memcached provide a similar behavior to set time-delayed expirations on key/value pairs, but they're not well suited for this problem. For example, you could set the expiration of an entry to be the expected time before it's integrated into the serving layer views (with perhaps extra time to serve as a buffer). But if for unexpected reasons the batch layer processing requires additional time, those speed layer entries would prematurely expire.

Instead, we'll present a generic approach for expiring speed layer views that works regardless of the speed layer databases being used. To understand this approach, you first must understand exactly what needs to be expired each time the serving layer is updated. Suppose you have a complete Lambda Architecture implementation and you turn on your application for the first time. The system doesn't yet have any data, so initially both the speed layer views and serving layer views are empty.

When the batch layer first runs, it will operate on no data. Say the batch layer computation takes 10 minutes due to the overhead of running jobs, creating empty indexes, and so forth. At the end of those 10 minutes, the serving layer views remain empty but the speed layer views now represent 10 minutes of data. This situation is illustrated in figure 12.9.

The second run of the batch layer immediately commences to process the 10 minutes of data that accumulated during the first run. For illustrative purposes, say the second run takes 15 minutes. When it finishes, the serving layer views will represent *the first 10 minutes* of data, whereas the speed layer views will represent all 25 minutes of data. The first 10 minutes can now be expired from the speed layer views, as shown in figure 12.10.

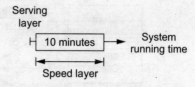

After the first batch computation run, the serving layer remains empty but the speed layer has processed recent data.

Figure 12.9   The state of the serving and speed layer views at the end of the first batch computation run

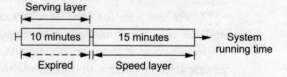

When the second batch computation run finishes, the first segment of data has been absorbed into the serving layer and can be expired from the speed layer views.

Figure 12.10   A portion of the realtime views can be expired after the second run completes.

Finally, suppose the third run of the batch layer takes 18 minutes. Consider the instant *before* the third run completes, as depicted in figure 12.11.

At this point, the serving layer still only represents 10 minutes of data, leaving the speed layer to handle the remaining 33 minutes of data. This figure demonstrates that the speed layer views compensate for between one and two runs of the batch layer, depending on how far the batch layer has progressed through its workflow. When a batch layer run finishes, data from three runs ago can safely be discarded from the speed layer.

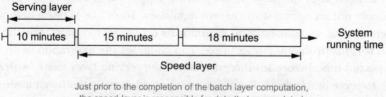

Just prior to the completion of the batch layer computation, the speed layer is responsible for data that accumulated during the prior two runs.

Figure 12.11   The serving and speed layer views immediately before the completion of the third batch computation run

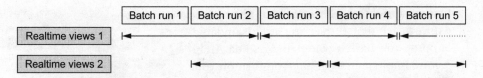

Figure 12.12 **Alternating clearing between two different sets of realtime views guarantees one set always contains the appropriate data for the speed layer.**

The simplest way to accomplish this task is to maintain *two sets* of realtime views and alternate clearing them after each batch layer run, as shown in figure 12.12. One of those sets of realtime views will exactly represent the data necessary to compensate for the serving layer views. After each batch layer run, the application should switch to reading from the realtime view with more data (and away from the one that was just cleared).

At a first glance, it may appear expensive to maintain two realtime views, since it essentially doubles the storage cost of the speed layer. The key is that the speed layer views only represent *a miniscule portion of your data*—at most a few hours' worth. Compared to potentially years of data represented by your serving layer, this can be less than 0.1% of all the data in your system. This scheme does introduce redundancy, but it's an acceptable price for a general solution to expire realtime views.

12.6 Summary

The speed layer is very different from the batch layer. Rather than compute functions on your entire dataset, you instead compute using more complex incremental algorithms on more complex forms of storage. But the Lambda Architecture allows you to keep the speed layer small and therefore more manageable.

You've learned the basic concepts of the speed layer and the details around managing realtime views. You saw two ways of updating realtime views, synchronously and asynchronously. There isn't much more to cover with synchronous speed layers, because you simply connect to the database and issue an update, but there's a lot more involved with asynchronous speed layers. Before getting to that, we'll first look at Cassandra, an example database that can be used for a speed layer view.

Realtime views: Illustration

This chapter covers

- Cassandra's data model
- Using Cassandra as a realtime view
- Controlling partitioning and ordering to support
  a wide range of view types

Now that you've learned the basics of the speed layer and realtime views, let's take a look at Cassandra, a database that can be used as a realtime view. Cassandra is not a general-purpose realtime view by any means—many systems require multiple databases to satisfy all of their indexing, consistency, and performance requirements. For our purposes, however, Cassandra serves to illustrate the concepts of realtime views, and it's the database that we'll use for the speed layer of SuperWebAnalytics.com later in the book. There are many publicly available resources to help you understand the inner workings of the database, so we'll focus on the properties of Cassandra from a user perspective.

13.1 Cassandra's data model

While many tout Cassandra as a column-oriented database, we find that terminology to be somewhat confusing. Instead, it's easier to consider the data model as a map with sorted maps as values (or optionally, a sorted map with sorted maps as values). Cassandra allows standard operations on the nested maps, such as adding key/value pairs, looking up by key, and getting ranges of keys.

To introduce the terminology, figure 13.1 illustrates the different aspects of the Cassandra data model. To expand upon the terms:

- *Column families*—Column families are analogous to tables in relational databases, and each column family stores a completely independent set of information.
- *Keys*—If you consider a column family as a giant map, keys are the top-level entries in that map. Cassandra uses the keys to partition a column family across a cluster.
- *Columns*—Each key points to another map of name/value pairs called *columns*. All columns for a key are physically stored together, making it inexpensive to access ranges of columns. Different keys can have different sets of columns, and it's possible to have thousands—or even millions—of columns for a given key.

To understand this model fully, let's return to the SuperWebAnalytics.com example. Specifically, let's see how you could model the pageviews-over-time view using Cassandra. For pageviews over time, you want to retrieve the pageviews for a particular URL and a particular granularity (hour, day, week, or four weeks) over a specific range of time buckets. To store this information in Cassandra, the key will be a [URL, granularity]

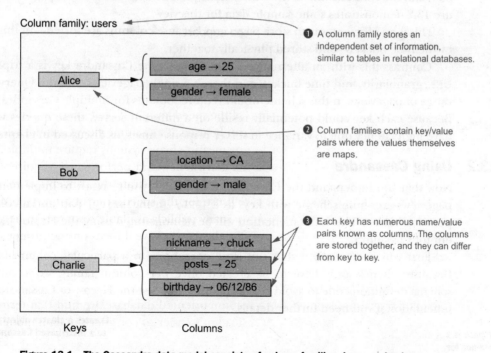

Figure 13.1 The Cassandra data model consists of column families, keys, and columns.

Column family: pageviews

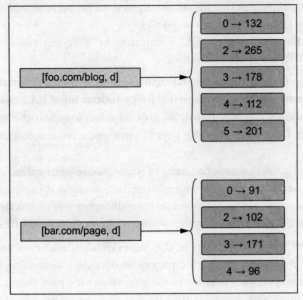

Figure 13.2   Pageviews over time represented in Cassandra

pair, and the columns will be the name/value pairs of time buckets and pageviews. Figure 13.2 demonstrates some sample data for this view.

This is an efficient way to store pageviews because columns are sorted—in this case by the time bucket—and stored physically together.

Contrast this with an alternative scheme where the Cassandra key is a triplet of URL, granularity, and time bucket, and there's a single pageviews column. Querying a range of pageviews in this scheme would require lookups for multiple Cassandra keys. Because each key could potentially reside on a different server, these queries would have high latency due to variance in server response times, as discussed in chapter 7.

13.2   *Using Cassandra*

Now that you understand the Cassandra data model, you're ready to implement the pageviews-over-time scheme with keys as a [URL, granularity] pair and a column-per-time bucket. This implementation will be demonstrated using the Hector Java client for Cassandra.

First you need a client that can issue operations to a particular column family. Because schemas only have to be created once per column family, we've omitted schema definition code to avoid cluttering the code. See the Hector or Cassandra documentation if you need further details.

A keyspace is a container for all the column families of an application.

Creates a cluster object to connect to a distributed Cassandra cluster

```
Cluster cluster = HFactory.getOrCreateCluster("mycluster","127.0.0.1");
Keyspace keyspace =
  HFactory.createKeyspace("superwebanalytics", cluster);
```

```
ColumnFamilyTemplate<String, Long> template =
   new ThriftColumnFamilyTemplate<String, Long> (keyspace,
                                                 "pageviews",
                                                 StringSerializer.get(),
                                                 LongSerializer.get());
```

A ColumnFamilyTemplate is used to issue operations to that column family for that keyspace.

Once you have a client to communicate with the cluster, you can retrieve the pageviews for a given URL and a given range of time buckets. The following code calculates total pageviews for foo.com/blog at a daily granularity for time buckets 20 to 55:

Creates a range template for a Cassandra query

```
SliceQuery<String, Long, Long> slice =
   HFactory.createSliceQuery(keyspace,
                             StringSerializer.get(),
                             LongSerializer.get(),
                             LongSerializer.get());
slice.setColumnFamily("pageviews");
slice.setKey("foo.com/blog-d");
```

Assigns the column family and key for the query

The serializers are for the keys (url/ granularity), names (buckets), and values (pageviews), respectively.

```
ColumnSliceIterator<String, Long, Long> it =
   new ColumnSliceIterator<String, Long, Long>(slice,
      20L, 55L, false);
long total = 0;
while(it.hasNext()) {
   total += it.next().getValue();
}
```

Obtains a column iterator for the given range

Traverses the iterator and sum the pageviews to obtain the total

The `ColumnSliceIterator` traverses all columns in the given range. If the range is enormous (such as containing tens of thousands of columns), it will automatically buffer and batch those columns from the server so as not to run out of memory. Remember, because the columns are ordered and stored together, slice operations over a range of columns are very efficient.

Updates are equally easy. The following code adds 25 to the pageviews of foo.com/blog for time bucket 7 at daily granularity:

Retrieves the current value for the specified URL, granularity, and time bucket

```
long currVal;
HColumn<Long, Long> col =
   template.querySingleColumn("foo.com/blog-d",
                              7L,
                              LongSerializer.get());
if (col==null)
   currVal = 0;
else
   currVal = col.getValue();
```

If no value is recorded, there have been no pageviews.

Serializer for pageview value

```
ColumnFamilyUpdater<String, Long> updater =
   template.createUpdater("foo.com/blog-d");
updater.setLong(7L, currVal + 25L);
template.update(updater);
```

Increments the pageviews and performs the update

Creates an update template for the given key

For an analytics use case like pageviews over time, you'd normally batch updates for multiple time buckets to increase efficiency. We'll discuss this further when we cover stream processing in chapter 15.

13.2.1 *Advanced Cassandra*

It's worth mentioning a few advanced features of Cassandra that make it suitable for a broader range of realtime view types.

The first addresses how Cassandra partitions keys among nodes in the cluster. You can choose between two partitioner types: the `RandomPartitioner` and the `Order-PreservingPartitioner`.

The `RandomPartitioner` makes Cassandra act like a hashmap and assigns keys to partitions using the hash of the key. This results in the keys being uniformly distributed across the nodes in the cluster. In contrast, the `OrderPreservingPartitioner` stores the keys in order, causing Cassandra to behave like a sorted map. Keeping the keys sorted enables you to do efficient queries on ranges of keys.

Though there are advantages to keeping the keys sorted, there's a cost to using the `OrderPreservingPartitioner`. When preserving the order of the keys, Cassandra attempts to split the keys so that each partition contains approximately the same number of keys. Unfortunately, there's no good algorithm to determine balanced key ranges on the fly. In an incremental setting, clusters can become unbalanced with some servers being overloaded while others have virtually no data. This is another example of the complexity you face with realtime, incremental computation that you avoid with batch computation. In a batch context, you know all the keys beforehand, so you can evenly split keys among partitions as part of the computation.

Cassandra has another feature called *composite columns* that extends the sorted map idea even further. Composite columns let you nest the maps arbitrarily deep—for example, you could model your index as a map of sorted maps of sorted maps of sorted maps. This gives you great flexibility in the indexing model you choose.

13.3 *Summary*

We've shown the basics of using Cassandra. There are other features—like support for eventual consistency—that we haven't covered because they aren't needed for the SuperWebAnalytics.com example. There are plenty of other resources you can search to learn more about that.

As a random-read/random-write database, Cassandra is significantly harder to operate than a serving layer database. Online compaction and the need to rebalance key ranges (if using `OrderPreservingPartitioner`) can cause significant pain. Fortunately, the transience of the speed layer in the Lambda Architecture protects you to a great extent—if anything goes seriously wrong, you can discard the speed layer and rebuild it.

The next step is connecting the stream of data being generated with the realtime views. In the next chapter you'll see how to combine a database like Cassandra with a stream-processing engine to accomplish this feat.

14

Queuing and stream processing

This chapter covers

- Single-consumer versus multi-consumer queues
- One-at-a-time stream processing
- Limitations of queues-and-workers approaches
  to stream processing

You've learned of two types of architectures for the speed layer: synchronous and asynchronous. With synchronous architectures, applications send update requests directly to the database and block until receiving a response. Such applications require the coordination of different tasks, but there's not much to add to the discussion from an architectural standpoint. Conversely, asynchronous architectures update the speed layer databases independently from the application that created the data. How you decide to persist and process the update requests directly affects the scalability and fault tolerance of your entire system.

This chapter covers the basics of queuing and stream processing, the two foundations of asynchronous architectures. You earlier saw that the key to batch processing is the ability to withstand failures and retry computations when necessary. The

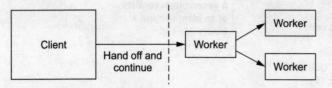

Figure 14.1   To implement asynchronous processing without queues, a client submits an event without monitoring whether its processing is successful.

same tenets carry over to the speed layer, as fault tolerance and retries are of the utmost importance in stream-processing systems. As usual, the incremental nature of the speed layer makes the story more complex, and there are many more trade-offs to keep in mind as you design applications.

After a discussion of the need for persistent queuing, we'll launch into an overview of the simplest kind of stream processing—one-at-a-time processing. You'll see how the fault-tolerance and retry story plays out for that kind of processing.

14.1   Queuing

To understand the need for persistent queuing in asynchronous systems, first consider an architecture without it. In such a system, events would simply be handed directly to workers that would process each event independently. This approach is illustrated in figure 14.1.

This fire-and-forget scheme can't guarantee that all the data is successfully processed. For example, if a worker dies before completing its assigned task, there's no mechanism to detect or correct the error. The architecture is also susceptible to bursts in traffic that exceed the resources of the processing cluster. In such a scenario, the cluster would be overwhelmed and messages could be lost.

Writing events to a persistent queue addresses both of these issues. Queues allow the system to retry events whenever a worker fails, and they provide a place for events to buffer when downstream workers hit their processing limits.

While it's now clear that an asynchronous architecture needs a queue to persist an event stream, the semantics of a good queue design require further discussion. A good place to begin are the queue interfaces you're already familiar with, such as the native `Queue` interface in Java. The methods from the interface that are relevant to this discussion are listed here:

```
interface Queue {
    void add(Object item);
    Object poll();
    Object peek();
}
```

Removes the item from the head of the queue → `Object poll();`

Adds new item to the queue → `void add(Object item);`

Inspects the item at the head of the queue without removing it → `Object peek();`

14.1.1   Single-consumer queue servers

The Java `Queue` interface is a natural starting point when designing a persistent queue for the speed layer. In fact, queue implementations such as Kestrel and RabbitMQ use a similar interface. They share the same single-consumer structure, as shown here:

```
                    struct Item {
                        long id;
                        byte[] item;
                    }

                    interface Queue {
                        Item get();
                        void ack(long id);
                        void fail(long id);
                    }
```

A generic Item consists of an identifier and a binary payload.

Retrieves an Item for processing

Acknowledges successful processing of an Item

Reports a failure when processing an Item

The single-consumer queue design is based on the idea that when you read an event from the queue, the event is not immediately removed. Instead, the item returned by the get function contains an identifier that you later use to acknowledge success (ack) or report failure (fail) for the processing of the event. Only when an event is acked will it be removed from the queue. If the event processing fails or a timeout occurs, the queue server will allow another client to retrieve the same event via a separate get call. An event may therefore be processed multiple times with this approach (for example, when a client processes an event but dies before acknowledging it), but each event is guaranteed to be processed at least once.

This all seems well and good, but there is actually a deep flaw in this queue design: what if multiple applications want to consume the same stream? This is quite common. For example, given a stream of pageviews, one application could build a view of pageviews over time while another could build a view of unique visitors over time.

One possible solution would be to wrap all the applications within the same consumer, as shown in figure 14.2.

When done this way, all the applications reside in the same codebase and run in the same workers. But this is a bad design as it eliminates any isolation among independent applications. Without isolation, if one application has a bug, it could potentially affect all the other applications running within the same consumer. This problem is exacerbated in larger organizations where multiple teams need to share

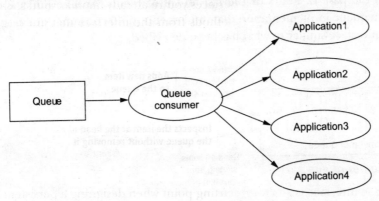

Figure 14.2 Multiple applications sharing a single queue consumer

the same stream. Without question, it's much better—and much saner—to isolate independent applications so that a broken application has no impact on others.

With the single-consumer queue design, the only way to achieve independence between applications is to maintain a separate queue for each consumer application. That is, if you have three applications, you must maintain three separate copies of the queue on the queue server. The obvious drawback is that this greatly increases the load on the queue server. Specifically, the load is now proportional to the number of applications multiplied by the number of incoming events, rather than just to the number of incoming events. It's entirely possible you'll want to build dozens of views using the same stream, and the queue server could potentially crash under the massive load.

Discussing the limitations of a single-consumer queue helps identify the desired properties for a queuing system. What you really want is a single queue that can be used by many consumers, where adding a consumer is simple and introduces a minimal increase in load. When you think about this further, the fundamental issue with a single-consumer queue is that the queue is responsible for keeping track of what's consumed. Because of the restrictive condition that an item is either "consumed" or "not consumed," the queue is unable to gracefully handle multiple clients wanting to consume the same item.

14.1.2   *Multi-consumer queues*

Thankfully there's an alternative queue design that doesn't suffer the problems associated with single-consumer queues. The idea is to shift the responsibility of tracking the consumed/unconsumed status of events from the queue to the applications themselves. If an application keeps track of the consumed events, it can then request the event stream to be replayed from any point in the stream history. This design is illustrated in figure 14.3.

Because the queue server doesn't know when all the consumers have processed any given item, it provides a service-level agreement (SLA) on the available events. That is, it will guarantee that a certain amount of the stream is available, such as all events from the past 12 hours or the last 50 GB of events. Apache Kafka is a good example of a queue implementation that implements multi-consumer queuing, and it exposes an interface similar to what has been described.

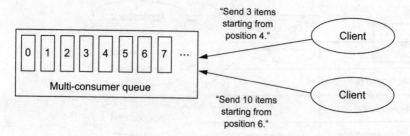

Figure 14.3   With a multi-consumer queue, applications request specific items from the queue and are responsible for tracking the successful processing of each event.

There's another notable difference between single-consumer and multi-consumer queues. With a single-consumer queue, a message is deleted once it has been acked and can no longer be replayed. As a result, a failed event can cause the event stream to be processed out of order. To understand this behavior, if the stream is consumed in parallel and an event fails, other events subsequent to the failed event may be processed successfully before a reattempt is made. In contrast, a multi-consumer queue allows you to rewind the stream and replay everything from the point of failure, ensuring that you process events in the order in which they originated. The ability to replay the event stream is great benefit of multi-consumer queues, and these queues don't have any drawbacks when compared to single-consumer queues. Accordingly, we highly recommend using multi-consumer queues such as Apache Kafka.

14.2 Stream processing

Once you have your incoming events feeding your multi-consumer queues, the next step is to process those events and update your realtime views. This practice is called *stream processing*, illustrated in figure 14.4.

Figure 14.4   Stream processing

Two models of stream processing have emerged in recent years: *one-at-a-time* and *micro-batched*. There are trade-offs to consider, since each has its strengths and weaknesses. They are very much complementary—some applications are better suited for one-at-a-time stream processing, and micro-batch stream processing is a better choice for others. Figure 14.5 summarizes the benefits of the two models. We'll focus on one-at-a-time stream processing in this chapter, and we'll cover micro-batch stream processing in the next.

A big advantage of one-at-a-time stream processing is that it can process streams with lower latency than micro-batched processing. Example applications that greatly benefit from this attribute include alerting and financial trading.

	One-at-a-time	Micro-batched
Lower latency	✓	
Higher throughput		✓
At-least-once semantics	✓	✓
Exactly-once semantics	In some cases	✓
Simpler programming model	✓	

Figure 14.5   Comparison of stream-processing paradigms

We'll start building a general model of one-at-a-time stream processing by first observing an antiquated approach: the *queues-and-workers* model. The problems plaguing this approach will motivate a more general way to accomplish this task.

14.2.1 *Queues and workers*

The queues-and-workers paradigm is a common means of achieving one-at-a-time stream processing. The basic idea is to divide your processing pipeline into worker processes, and place queues between them. With this structure, if a worker fails or the worker process restarts, it can simply continue where it left off by reading from its queue, as illustrated in figure 14.6.

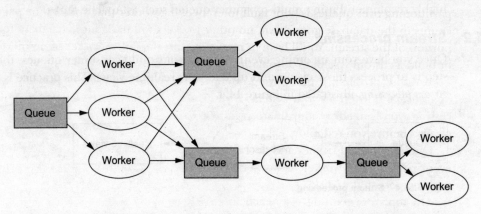

Figure 14.6   A representative system using a queues-and-workers architecture. The queues in the diagram could potentially be distributed queues as well.

For example, say you're implementing the pageviews-over-time view using the queues-and-workers approach, as illustrated in figure 14.7. The first set of workers reads pageview events from a set of queues, validates each pageview to filter out invalid URLs, and then passes the events to a second set of workers. The second set of workers then updates the pageview counts of the valid URLs.

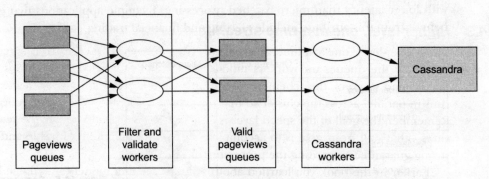

Figure 14.7   Computing pageviews over time with a queues-and-workers architecture

14.2.2 *Queues-and-workers pitfalls*

The queues-and-workers paradigm is straightforward but not necessarily simple.

One subtlety in this scheme is the need to ensure that multiple workers don't attempt to update the pageview count of the same URL at the same time. Otherwise, there would be potential race conditions where writes would be trampled in the database. To meet this guarantee, the first set of workers partitions its outgoing stream by the URL. With this partitioning, the entire set of URLs will still be spread among the queues, but pageview events for any given URL will always go to the same queue. A simple way to implement this is to choose the target queue by hashing the URL and modding the hash by the number of target queues. Unfortunately, a consequence of partitioning over queues is poor fault tolerance. If a worker that updates the pageview counts in the database goes down, no other workers will update the database for that portion of the stream. You'll have to manually start the failed worker somewhere else, or build a custom system to automatically do so.

Another problem is that having queues between every set of workers adds to the operational burden on your system. If you need to change the topology of your processing, you'll need to coordinate your actions so that the intermediate queues are cleared before you redeploy.

Queues also add latency and decrease the throughput of your system because each event passed from worker to worker is forced to go through a third party, where it must be persisted to disk.

On top of everything else, each intermediate queue needs to be managed and monitored and adds yet another layer that needs to be scaled.

Perhaps the biggest problem with the queues-and-workers approach is how tedious it is to build. Much of your code becomes dedicated to serialization and deserialization to pass objects through queues, routing logic to connect the worker pools, and instructions for deploying the workers over a cluster of servers. When all is said and done, your actual business logic ends up being a very small percentage of your codebase.

The fact that the workers work in tandem toward some higher goal while requiring highly detailed coordination is a strong indicator of the need for a higher-level abstraction.

14.3 *Higher-level, one-at-a-time stream processing*

The higher-level, one-at-a-time, stream-processing approach you'll learn is a generalization of the queues-and-workers model but without any of its complexities. Like queues and workers, the scheme processes tuples one tuple at a time, but the code runs in parallel across the cluster so that the system is scalable with high throughput. Remember, the goal of the speed layer is to process a stream and update the realtime views—that's all. Your goal is to accomplish that with a minimum of hassle and have strong guarantees regarding the processing of data.

Earlier in the book you learned about MapReduce as a model for scalable batch computation, with Hadoop being a specific implementation. Analogously, a model exists for one-at-a-time stream processing, but there isn't a short, catchy name. For our discussion we'll refer to it as the *Storm model* after the project that originated these techniques. Let's now go over this model and see how it alleviates the complexities of queues and workers.

14.3.1   *Storm model*

The Storm model represents the entire stream-processing pipeline as a graph of computation called a *topology*. Rather than write separate programs for each node of the topology and connect them manually, as required in the queues-and-workers schemes, the Storm model involves a single program that's deployed across a cluster. This flexible approach allows a single executable to filter data in one node, compute aggregates with a second node, and update realtime view databases with a third. Serialization, message passing, task discovery, and fault tolerance can be handled for you by the abstractions, and this can all be done while achieving very low latency (10 ms or less). Whereas previously you had to explicitly design and program for each of these features, you can now focus on your business logic.

Let's build the Storm model from the ground up. At the core of the Storm model are *streams*. A stream, illustrated in figure 14.8, is an infinite sequence of *tuples*, where a tuple is simply a named list of values. In essence, the Storm model is about transforming streams into new streams, potentially updating databases along the way.

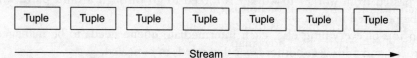

Figure 14.8   A stream is an infinite sequence of tuples.

The next abstraction in the Storm model is the *spout*. A spout is a source of streams in a topology (see figure 14.9). For example, a spout could read from a Kestrel or Kafka queue and turn the data into a tuple stream, or a timer spout could emit a tuple into its output stream every 10 seconds.

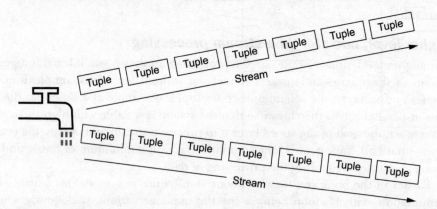

Figure 14.9   A spout is a source of streams in a topology.

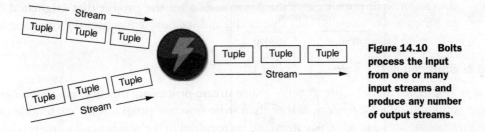

Figure 14.10   Bolts process the input from one or many input streams and produce any number of output streams.

While spouts are sources of streams, the *bolt* abstraction performs actions on streams. A bolt takes any number of streams as input and produces any number of streams as output (see figure 14.10). Bolts implement most of the logic in a topology—they run functions, filter data, compute aggregations, do streaming joins, update databases, and so forth.

Having defined these abstractions, a *topology* is therefore a network of spouts and bolts with each edge representing a bolt that processes the output stream of another spout or bolt (see figure 14.11).

Each instance of a spout or bolt is called a *task*. The key to the Storm model is that tasks are inher-

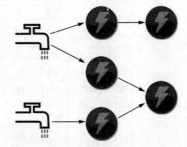

Figure 14.11   A topology connects spouts and bolts and defines how tuples flow through a Storm application.

ently parallel—exactly like how map and reduce tasks are inherently parallel in MapReduce. Figure 14.12 demonstrates the parallelism of tuples flowing through a topology.

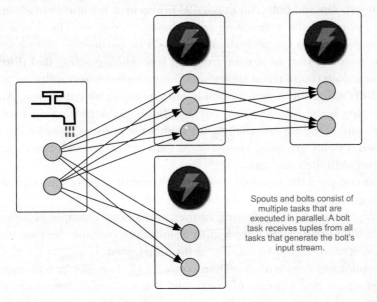

Spouts and bolts consist of multiple tasks that are executed in parallel. A bolt task receives tuples from all tasks that generate the bolt's input stream.

Figure 14.12   In a topology, the spouts and bolts have multiple instances running in parallel.

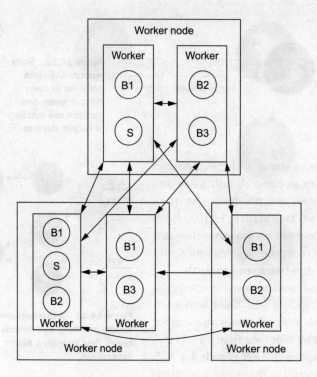

Figure 14.13   A physical view of how topology tasks could be distributed over three servers

Of course, all the tasks for a given spout or bolt will not necessarily run on the same machine. Instead they're spread among the different workers of the cluster. In contrast to the previous illustration, figure 14.13 depicts a topology grouped by physical machines.

The fact that spouts and bolts run in parallel brings up a key question: when a task emits a tuple, which of the consuming tasks should receive it? The Storm model requires *stream groupings* to specify how tuples should be partitioned among consuming tasks. The simplest kind of stream grouping is a *shuffle grouping* that distributes tuples using a random round-robin algorithm. This grouping evenly splits the processing load by distributing the tuples randomly but equally to all consumers. Another common grouping is the *fields grouping* that distributes tuples by hashing a subset of the tuple fields and modding the result by the number of consuming tasks. For example, if you used a fields grouping on the word field, all tuples with the same word would be delivered to the same task.

We can now complete the topology diagram by annotating every subscription edge with its stream grouping, as shown in figure 14.14.

Let's solidify this example by delving further into a basic example of a topology. Just as word count is the de facto introductory MapReduce example, let's see what the streaming version of word count looks like in the Storm model.

The word-count topology is illustrated in figure 14.15. The splitter bolt transforms a stream of sentences into a stream of words, and the word-count bolt consumes the words to compute the word counts. The key here is the fields grouping between the

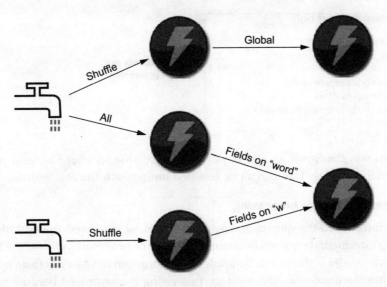

Figure 14.14   A topology with stream groupings

splitter bolt and the word-count bolt. That ensures that each word-count task sees every instance of every word they receive, making it possible for them to compute the correct count.

Now let's take a look at pseudo-code for the bolt implementations. First, the splitter bolt:

Bolts are defined as objects because they can keep internal state.

```
class SplitterBolt {
    function execute(sentence) {
        for(word in sentence.split(" ")) {
            emit(word)
        }
    }
}
```

Bolts receive tuples. In this case, this bolt receives a tuple with one field.

Emits a word to the output stream. Any subscribers to this bolt will receive the word.

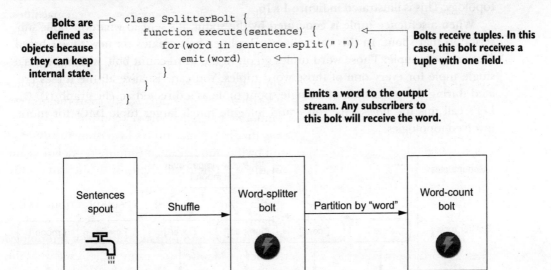

Figure 14.15   Word-count topology

Next, the word-count bolt:

```
class WordCountBolt {
    counts = Map(default=0)

    function execute(word) {
        counts[word]++
        emit(word, counts[word])
    }
}
```

Word counts are kept in memory.

As you can see, the Storm model requires no logic around where to send tuples or how to serialize tuples. That can all be handled underneath the abstractions.

14.3.2 *Guaranteeing message processing*

When we introduced the queues-and-workers model, we discussed at length the issues of keeping intermediate queues between every stage of processing. One of the beauties of the Storm model is that it can be implemented without any intermediate queues.

With intermediate queuing, message processing is guaranteed because messages aren't taken off the queue until they've been successfully processed by a worker. If the worker dies or has another sort of failure, it will retry the message. So intermediate queuing gives an at-least-once processing guarantee.

It turns out you can maintain that at-least-once guarantee without intermediate queues. Of course, it has to work differently—instead of retries happening wherever the failure occurred, retries happen from the root of the topology. To understand this, let's take a look at what the processing of a tuple looks like in the word-count topology. This is illustrated in figure 14.16.

When a sentence tuple is generated by the spout, it's sent to whatever bolts subscribe to that spout. In this case, the word-splitter bolt creates six new tuples based on that spout tuple. Those word tuples go on to the word-count bolt, which creates a single tuple for every one of those word tuples. You can visualize all the tuples created during the processing of a single spout tuple as a directed acyclic graph (DAG). Let's call this the *tuple DAG*. You could imagine much larger tuple DAGs for more-involved topologies.

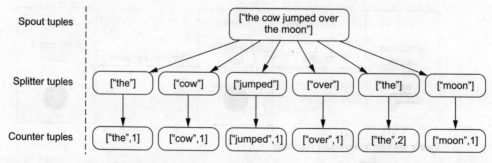

Figure 14.16   The tuple DAG for a single tuple emitted from the spout. The DAG size rapidly grows as the amount of processing increases.

Tracking tuple DAGs scalably and efficiently

You may be wondering how tuple DAGs can be tracked scalably and efficiently. A tuple DAG could contain millions of tuples, or more, and intuitively you might think that it would require an excessive amount of memory to track the status of each spout tuple. As it turns out, it's possible to track a tuple DAG without explicitly keeping track of the DAG—all you need is 20 bytes of space per spout tuple. This is true regardless of the size of the DAG—it could have trillions of tuples, and 20 bytes of space would still be sufficient. We won't get into the algorithm here (it's documented extensively in Apache Storm's online documentation). The important takeaway is that the algorithm is very efficient, and that efficiency makes it practical to track failures and initiate retries during stream processing.

It turns out there's an efficient and scalable algorithm for tracking tuple DAGs and retrying tuples from the spout if there's a failure anywhere downstream. Retrying tuples from the spout will cause the entire tuple DAG to be regenerated.

Retrying from the spout may seem a step backward—intermediate stages that had completed successfully will be tried again. But upon further inspection, this is actually no different than before. With queues and workers, a stage could succeed in processing, fail right before acknowledging the message and letting it be removed from the queue, and then be tried again. In both scenarios, the processing guarantee is still an at-least-once processing guarantee. Furthermore, as you'll see when you learn about micro-batch stream processing, exactly-once semantics can be achieved by building on top of this at-least-once guarantee, and at no point are intermediate queues needed.

Working with an at-least-once processing guarantee

In many cases, reprocessing tuples will have little or no effect. If the operations in a topology are idempotent—that is, if repeatedly applying the operation doesn't change the result—then the topology will have exactly-once semantics. An example of an idempotent operation is adding an element to a set. No matter how many times you perform the operation, you'll still get the same result.

Another point to keep in mind is that you might just not care about a little inaccuracy when you have non-idempotent operations. Failures are relatively rare, so any inaccuracy should be small. The serving layer replaces the speed layer anyway, so any inaccuracy will eventually be automatically corrected. Again, it's possible to achieve exactly-once semantics by sacrificing some latency, but if low latency is more important than temporary inaccuracy, then using non-idempotent operations with the Storm model is a fine trade-off.

Let's see how you can use the Storm model to implement part of the SuperWebAnalytics.com speed layer.

14.4   *SuperWebAnalytics.com speed layer*

Recall that there are three separate queries you're implementing for SuperWebAnalytics.com:

- Number of pageviews over a range of hours
- Unique number of visitors over a range of hours
- Bounce rate for a domain

We'll implement the unique-visitors query in this section and the remaining two in chapter 16.

The goal of this query is to be able to get the number of unique visitors for a URL over a range of hours. Recall that when implementing this query for the batch and serving layers, the HyperLogLog algorithm was used for efficiency: HyperLogLog produces a compact set representation that can be merged with other sets, making it possible to compute the uniques over a range of hours without having to store the set of visitors for every hour. The trade-off is that HyperLogLog is an approximate algorithm, so the counts will be off by a small percentage. The space savings are so enormous that it was an easy trade-off to make, because perfect accuracy is not needed for SuperWebAnalytics.com. The same trade-offs exist in the speed layer, so you can make use of HyperLogLog for the speed layer version of uniques over time.

Also recall that SuperWebAnalytics.com can track visitors using both IP addresses and account login information. If a user is logged in and uses both a phone and a computer to visit the same web page at approximately the same time, the user's actions should be recorded as a single visit. In the batch layer, this was accounted for by using the equiv edge relationships to keep track of which identifiers represented the same person, and then normalizing all identifiers for one person into a single identifier. Specifically, we could perform a complete equiv edge analysis before starting the uniques-over-time computation.

Handling the multiple identifier problem in the speed layer is much more complex. The difficulty arises because the multiple identifier relationship might be determined *after* the speed layer views are updated. For example, consider the following sequence of events:

1 IP address 11.11.11.111 visits foo.com/about at 1:30 pm.
2 User sally visits foo.com/about at 1:40 pm.
3 An equiv edge between 11.11.11.111 and sally is discovered at 2:00 pm.

Before the application learns of the equivalence relationship, the visits would be attributed to two distinct individuals. To have the most accurate stats possible, the speed layer must therefore reduce the [URL, hour] uniques count by one.

Let's consider what it would take to do this in real time. First, you'd need to track the equiv graph in real time, meaning the entire graph analysis from chapter 8 must be done incrementally. Second, you must be able to determine if the same visitor has been counted multiple times. This requires that you store the entire set of visitors for every hour. HyperLogLog is a compact representation and is unable to help with this, so handling the equiv problem precludes taking advantage of HyperLogLog in the first place. On top of everything else, the incremental algorithm to do the equiv graph analysis and adjust previously computed unique counts is rather complex.

Rather than striving to compute uniques over time perfectly, you can potentially trade off some accuracy. Remember, one of the benefits of the Lambda Architecture is that trading off accuracy in the speed layer is not trading off accuracy permanently—because the serving layer continuously overrides the speed layer, any inaccuracies are corrected and the system exhibits eventual accuracy. You can therefore consider alternative approaches and weigh the inaccuracies they introduce against their computational and complexity benefits.

The first alternative approach is to not perform the equiv analysis in real time. Instead, the results of the batch equiv analysis can be made available to the speed layer through a key/value serving layer database. In the speed layer, PersonIDs are first normalized through that database before the uniques-over-time computation is done. The benefit of this approach is that you can take advantage of HyperLogLog because you don't have to deal with realtime equivs. It's also significantly simpler to implement, and it's much less resource-intensive.

Now let's consider where this approach will be inaccurate. Because the precomputed equiv analysis is out of date by a few hours, any newly discovered equiv relationships aren't utilized. Thus, this strategy is inaccurate for cases where a user navigates to a page, registers for a UserID (upon which an equiv edge is captured), and then returns to the same page within the same hour but from a different IP address. Note that the inaccuracy only happens with *brand new* users—after the user registration has been processed by the batch equiv analysis, any subsequent visit by the user will be properly recorded. Overall this is a slight amount of inaccuracy to trade off for big savings.

You can potentially trade off additional accuracy. A second alternative is to ignore equivs completely and calculate realtime uniques solely based on whatever PersonID was in the pageview. In this case, even if an equiv was recorded between a UserID and an IP address many months ago, if that person were to visit a page, log in, and then revisit the same page, that would be recorded multiple times in the unique count for that hour.

The right thing to do is to run batch analyses to quantify the inaccuracy generated by each approach so you can make an informed decision on which strategy to take. Intuitively, it seems that ignoring equivs completely in the speed layer wouldn't introduce too much inaccuracy, so in the interest of keeping examples simple, that's the approach we'll demonstrate. Before moving on, we again emphasize that any inaccuracy in the speed layer is temporary—the entire system as a whole is eventually accurate.

14.4.1   *Topology structure*

Let's now design the uniques-over-time speed layer by ignoring equivs. This involves three steps:

1 Consume a stream of pageview events that contains a user identifier, a URL, and a timestamp.
2 Normalize URLs.
3 Update a database containing a nested map from URL to hour to a HyperLogLog set.

Figure 14.17 illustrates a topology structure to implement this approach.

Let's look at each piece in more detail:

- *Pageviews spout*—This spout reads from a queue and emits pageview events as they arrive.
- *Normalize URLs bolt*—This bolt normalizes URLs to their canonical form. You want this normalization algorithm to be the same as the one used in the batch layer, so it makes sense for this algorithm to be a shared library between the two layers. Additionally, this bolt could filter out any invalid URLs.
- *Update database bolt*—This bolt consumes the previous bolt's stream using a fields grouping on URL to ensure there are no race conditions updating the state for any URL. This bolt maintains HyperLogLog sets in a database that implements a key-to-sorted-map data structure. The key is the URL, the nested key is the hour bucket, and the nested value is the HyperLogLog set. Ideally the database would support HyperLogLog sets natively, so as to avoid having to retrieve the HyperLogLog sets from the database and then write them back.

That's all there is to it. By making an approximation in the speed layer by ignoring equivs, the logic of the speed layer is dramatically simplified.

It's important to emphasize that such an aggressive approximation can be made in the speed layer only because of the existence of a robust batch layer supporting it. In chapter 10 you saw a fully incremental solution to the uniques-over-time problem, and you saw how adding equivs to the mix made everything very difficult. A fully incremental solution just doesn't have the option of ignoring equivs because that would mean ignoring equivs for the entire view. As you've just seen, a Lambda Architecture has a lot more flexibility.

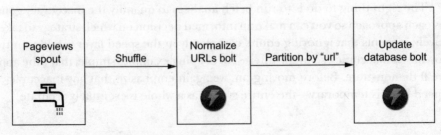

Figure 14.17   Uniques-over-time topology

14.5 Summary

You've seen how incremental processing with very tight latency constraints is inherently much more complex than batch processing. This is due to the inability to look at all your data at once and the inherent complexities of random-write databases (such as compaction). Most traditional architectures, however, use a single database to represent the master dataset, the historical indexes, and the realtime indexes. This is the very definition of complexity, as all these things should preferably be optimized differently, but intertwining them into a single system doesn't let you do so.

The SuperWebAnalytics.com uniques-over-time query perfectly illustrates this trichotomy. The master dataset is pageviews and equivs, so you store them in bulk in a distributed filesystem choosing a file format to get the right blend of space cost and read cost. The distributed filesystem doesn't burden you with unnecessary features like random writes, indexing, or compaction, giving you a simpler and more robust solution.

The historical views are computed using a batch-processing system that can compute functions of all data. It's able to analyze the equiv graph and fully correlate which pageviews belong to the same people even if the pageviews have different PersonIDs. The view is put into a database that doesn't support random writes, again avoiding any unnecessary complexity from features you don't need. Because the database isn't written to while it's being read, you don't have to worry about the operational burden from processes like online compaction.

Finally, the key properties desired in the realtime views are efficiency and low update latency. The speed layer achieves this by computing the realtime views incrementally, making an approximation by ignoring equivs to make things fast and simple to implement. Random-write databases are used to achieve the low latency required for the speed layer, but their complexity burden is greatly offset by the fact that realtime views are inherently small—most data is represented by the batch views.

In the next chapter you'll see how to implement the concepts of queuing and stream processing using real-world tools.

Queuing and stream processing: Illustration

This chapter covers

- Using Apache Storm
- Guaranteeing message processing
- Integrating Apache Kafka, Apache Storm, and Apache Cassandra
- Implementing the SuperWebAnalytics.com uniques-over-time speed layer

In the last chapter you learned about multi-consumer queues and the Storm model as a general approach to one-at-a-time stream processing. Let's now look at how you can apply these ideas in practice using the real-world tools Apache Storm and Apache Kafka. We'll conclude the chapter by implementing the speed layer for unique pageviews for SuperWebAnalytics.com.

15.1 Defining topologies with Apache Storm

Apache Storm is an open source project that implements (and originates) the Storm model. You've seen that the core concepts in the Storm model are tuples, streams,

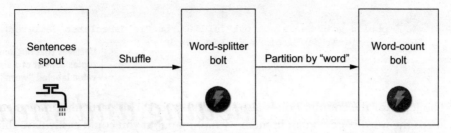

Figure 15.1 Word-count topology

spouts, bolts, and topologies. Let's now implement streaming word count using the Apache Storm API. For reference, the word-count topology is repeated in figure 15.1.

To begin, you first instantiate a `TopologyBuilder` object to define the application topology. The `TopologyBuilder` object exposes the API for specifying Storm topologies:

```
TopologyBuilder builder = new TopologyBuilder();
```

Next, you add a spout that emits a stream of sentences. This spout is named `sentence-spout` and is given a parallelism of 8, meaning 8 threads will be spawned across the cluster to execute the spout:

```
builder.setSpout("sentence-spout", new RandomSentenceSpout(), 8);
```

Now that you have a stream of sentences, you need a bolt that consumes the stream and transforms it into a stream of words. This bolt is called `splitter` and is given a parallelism of 12. Because there are no requirements on how the sentences are consumed, you use a shuffle grouping to evenly distribute the processing load across all 12 tasks:

```
builder.setBolt("splitter", new SplitSentence(), 12)
    .shuffleGrouping("sentence-spout");
```

The last bolt consumes the word stream and produces the desired stream of word counts. It's aptly called `counter` and also has a parallelism of 12. Note the use of fields grouping to ensure only one task is responsible for determining the total count of any particular word:

```
builder.setBolt("count", new WordCount(), 12)
    .fieldsGrouping("splitter", new Fields("word"));
```

With the topology defined, you can continue to the actual implementation of the spout and bolts. The implementation of the splitter bolt is extremely simple. It grabs the sentence from the first field of the incoming tuple and emits a new tuple for every word in the sentence:

```
                                public static class SplitSentence extends BaseBasicBolt {
Splits the sentence                 public void execute(Tuple tuple, BasicOutputCollector collector) {
and emits each                          String sentence = tuple.getString(0);        ◁──
word to the output                      for(String word: sentence.split(" ")) {          An incoming tuple contains
tuple stream                              collector.emit(new Values(word));              a single sentence.
                                        }
                                    }
                                }
```

```java
public void declareOutputFields(OutputFieldsDeclarer declarer) {
  declarer.declare(new Fields("word"));    ◄
}
}
```

Declares that outgoing tuples consist of a single value labeled "word"

The logic for the counter bolt is also straightforward. This particular implementation keeps the word counts in an in-memory hashmap, but you could easily have this communicate with a database instead.

An in-memory map stores the counts for all words received by the bolt.

Extracts the word from the incoming tuple

Initializes count if the word has not been previously observed

```java
public static class WordCount extends BaseBasicBolt {
  Map<String, Integer> counts =
    new HashMap<String, Integer>();    ◄

  public void execute(Tuple tuple, BasicOutputCollector collector) {
    String word = tuple.getString(0);
    Integer count = counts.get(word);    ◄
    if(count==null) count = 0;
    count++;
    counts.put(word, count);    ◄
    collector.emit(new Values(word, count));    ◄
  }

  public void declareOutputFields(OutputFieldsDeclarer declarer) {
    declarer.declare(new Fields("word", "count"));    ◄
  }
}
```

Retrieves the count for the current word

Stores the updated count

Emits the updated count for the given word

Declares outgoing tuples to consist of the word and its current count

All that remains is the spout implementation. Storm provides a number of prebuilt spouts like Kafka or Kestrel to read data from external queues, but the following code demonstrates how to build a custom spout. This spout randomly emits one of its sentences every 100 ms, creating an infinite stream of sentences:

Storm calls the nextTuple method in a loop.

An array of sentences to be emitted by the spout

Sleeps the current thread for 100 milliseconds

```java
public static class RandomSentenceSpout extends BaseRichSpout {
  SpoutOutputCollector _collector;
  Random _rand;

  public void open(Map conf, TopologyContext context,
                   SpoutOutputCollector collector) {
    _collector = collector;
    _rand = new Random();
  }

  public void nextTuple() {
    Utils.sleep(100);    ◄
    String[] sentences = new String[] {
      "the cow jumped over the moon",
      "an apple a day keeps the doctor away",
      "four score and seven years ago",
      "snow white and the seven dwarfs",
```

```
                  "i am at two with nature"};
                  String sentence = sentences[_rand.nextInt(sentences.length)];
                  _collector.emit(new Values(sentence));
               }

               public void declareOutputFields(OutputFieldsDeclarer declarer) {
                   declarer.declare(new Fields("sentence"));
               }
           }
```

Randomly emits one of the given sentences

Declares that outgoing tuples contain a single sentence

And that's it. Let's now see how Storm clusters work and how you can deploy to them.

15.2   Apache Storm clusters and deployment

The architecture of a Storm cluster is outlined in figure 15.2. Storm has a master node called *Nimbus* that manages running topologies. Nimbus accepts your requests to

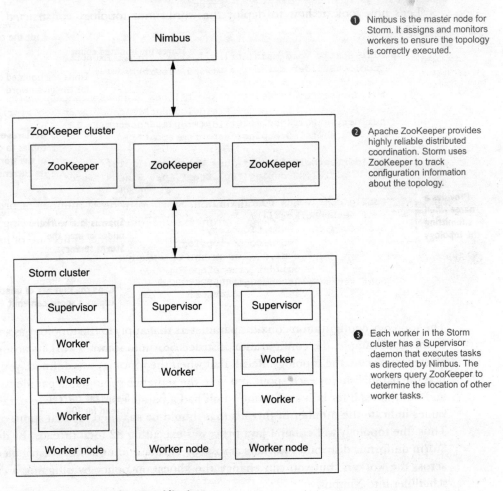

① Nimbus is the master node for Storm. It assigns and monitors workers to ensure the topology is correctly executed.

② Apache ZooKeeper provides highly reliable distributed coordination. Storm uses ZooKeeper to track configuration information about the topology.

③ Each worker in the Storm cluster has a Supervisor daemon that executes tasks as directed by Nimbus. The workers query ZooKeeper to determine the location of other worker tasks.

Figure 15.2   Apache Storm architecture

deploy a topology on Storm, and it assigns workers around the cluster to execute that topology. Nimbus is also responsible for detecting when workers die and reassigning them to other machines when necessary.

In the center of the architecture diagram is *Zookeeper.* Zookeeper is another Apache project that excels at keeping small amounts of state and has semantics perfect for cluster coordination. In a Storm architecture, Zookeeper tracks where workers are assigned and other topology configuration information. A typical Zookeeper cluster for Storm is three or five nodes.

The last group of nodes in a Storm cluster comprises your worker nodes. Each worker node runs a daemon called the *Supervisor* that communicates with Nimbus through Zookeeper to determine what should be running on the machine. The Supervisor then starts or stops the worker processes as necessary, as directed by Nimbus. Once running, worker processes discover the location of other workers through Zookeeper and pass messages to each other directly.

Let's now look at how to deploy the word-count topology constructed in section 15.1:

```
public static void main(String[] args) throws Exception {
    TopologyBuilder builder = new TopologyBuilder();

    builder.setSpout("sentence-spout", new RandomSentenceSpout(), 8);

    builder.setBolt("splitter", new SplitSentence(), 12)
            .shuffleGrouping("sentence-spout");

    builder.setBolt("count", new WordCount(), 12)
            .fieldsGrouping("splitter", new Fields("word"));

    Config conf = new Config();
    conf.setNumWorkers(4);
    StormSubmitter.submitTopology(
            "word-count-topology",
            conf,
            builder.createTopology());
    conf.setMaxSpoutPending(1000);
}
```

Provides a name when submitting the topology → (points to "word-count-topology")

Spawns four worker nodes among the Storm servers ← (points to conf.setNumWorkers(4))

Caps the number of unacked tuples a spout can emit ← (points to conf.setMaxSpoutPending(1000))

The topology configuration contains parameters that apply to the topology as a whole. In this code sample, the configuration instructs Storm to spawn 4 workers around the cluster to execute the topology. Recall that when the topology was defined, you specified the parallelism for each spout and bolt: the sentence spout had a parallelism of 8, and both the splitter bolt and counter bolt had a parallelism of 12. These parallelism values indicate the number of threads that should be spawned for that spout or bolt. Thus, the topology will entail 4 Java processes executing 32 total threads. By default, Storm uniformly distributes workers across the cluster and uniformly distributes tasks across the workers, but you can change the allocation policy by plugging a custom scheduler into Nimbus.

The code sample also has a second topology-wide configuration setting for handling spikes in incoming data. If there is a burst of incoming events, it's important that your stream processor not become overwhelmed and fail due to the increased load (such as by running out of memory). Storm has a simple mechanism for managing flow control based on its guaranteed message-processing features. The *topology max spout pending* setting controls the maximum number of tuples that can be emitted from a spout that are not yet fully processed by the topology. Once this limit is reached, spout tasks will stop emitting tuples until tuples either are acked, fail, or time out. In the preceding example, the code tells Storm that the largest number of pending tuples for any one spout task is 1,000. Because the sentence spout has a parallelism of 8, the number of pending tuples in the entire topology is at most 8,000.

15.3 Guaranteeing message processing

In the last chapter you saw that it's possible to guarantee message processing with the Storm model without intermediate message queues. When a failure is detected downstream from the spout in the tuple DAG, tuples can be retried from the spout. Let's now go into the specifics of how that works with Apache Storm.

Storm considers a spout tuple successfully processed only when an entire tuple DAG has been exhausted and every node in it has been marked as completed. In addition, that entire process needs to happen within a specified timeout (30 seconds by default). The timeout ensures that failures will be detected no matter what happens downstream—whether a worker process hangs or a machine suddenly dies.

As a user, you have two responsibilities in order to take advantage of this message-processing guarantee. You must inform Storm whenever you create a dependency edge in the tuple DAG, and you must notify Storm when the processing of a tuple is finished. These two tasks are called *anchoring* and *acking*, respectively. Let's look again at the sentence-splitter code from the streaming word count with the tuple DAG logic in place:

```
public static class SplitExplicit extends BaseRichBolt {    ◁──┐
  OutputCollector _collector;

  public void prepare(Map conf, TopologyContext context,
                      OutputCollector collector) {
    _collector = collector;
  }

  public void execute(Tuple tuple) {
    String sentence = tuple.getString(0);
    for(String word: sentence.split(" ")) {
      _collector.emit(tuple, new Values(word));    ◁──
    }
    _collector.ack(tuple);    ◁──
  }
}
```

BaseRichBolt subclasses require you to explicitly handle anchoring and acking of tuples.

Anchors the outgoing word tuple to the incoming sentence tuple

Acknowledges that the sentence tuple was successfully processed

```
public void declareOutputFields(OutputFieldsDeclarer declarer) {
    declarer.declare(new Fields("word"));
  }
}
```

The semantics of this bolt are actually identical to the original implementation in the previous section. When a new word tuple is emitted, the sentence tuple is included as the first argument. This process anchors the word tuple to the sentence tuple. After the new tuples are emitted, the sentence tuple is then acked, because it's not needed for further processing. It's a very common pattern for bolts to anchor all outgoing tuples to the input tuple, and then ack the tuple at the end, as done in this bolt. To automate this behavior, Storm provides a `BaseBasicBolt` class that takes care of this style of anchoring/acking for you. The first implementation of the splitter bolt made use of `BaseBasicBolt`.

But the `BaseBasicBolt` pattern doesn't hold for all operations, particularly if you're aggregating or joining streams. For example, suppose you want to process 100 tuples at a time. In that case, you could store all incoming tuples in a buffer, anchor the output tuple to all 100 tuples, and then ack all the tuples in the buffer. The following code demonstrates this strategy by emitting the sum of every 100 tuples:

```
public static class MultiAnchorer extends BaseRichBolt {
    OutputCollector _collector;

    public void prepare(Map conf, TopologyContext context,
                        OutputCollector collector) {
      _collector = collector;
    }
```
> The MultiAnchorer bolt adds the values for 100 incoming tuples and emits the sum.

```
    List<Tuple> _buffer = new ArrayList<Tuple>();
    int _sum = 0;
```
Keeps a running sum of the incoming values →

```
    public void execute(Tuple tuple) {
      _sum += tuple.getInteger(0);
      if(_buffer.size() < 100) {
        _buffer.add(tuple);
```
> Adds to the buffer until the capacity is reached

```
      } else {
        _collector.emit(_buffer, new Values(_sum));
        for(Tuple _tuple : _buffer) {
          _collector.ack(_tuple);
        }
```
Acks all the tuples in the buffer →

> When the buffer is full, emits a tuple with the sum that is anchored to all tuples in the buffer

```
        _buffer.clear();
        _sum = 0;
```
> Clears the buffer

Resets the running sum →

```
      }
    }
```

```
    public void declareOutputFields(OutputFieldsDeclarer declarer) {
      declarer.declare(new Fields("sum"));
    }
  }
```

In this case, you can't use `BaseBasicBolt` because tuples aren't acked immediately after being processed by the `execute` function—they're buffered and acked at a later time.

Internally, Storm tracks tuple DAGs using a highly efficient algorithm that only requires about 20 bytes of space per spout tuple. This is true regardless of the size of the DAG—it could have trillions of tuples, and 20 bytes of space would still be sufficient. We won't get into the algorithm here, but it's documented extensively on Storm's website. The important takeaway is that the algorithm is very efficient, and that efficiency makes it practical to track failures and initiate retries during stream processing.

15.4 Implementing the SuperWebAnalytics.com uniques-over-time speed layer

In the last chapter you saw the design for the SuperWebAnalytics.com uniques-over-time speed layer. The main idea was to make an approximation by ignoring equivs, so as to greatly simplify the implementation. For reference, figure 15.3 shows the topology design for this speed layer. We'll now implement this topology using Apache Storm, Apache Kafka, and Apache Cassandra.

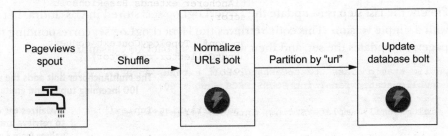

Figure 15.3   Uniques-over-time topology

To implement the topology, let's begin with the spout. The following code initializes a Kafka spout to read the pageviews from a cluster of Kafka servers. The pageviews are assumed to be stored on Kafka as the Thrift `Data` objects we defined in chapter 3.

```
                                                                   The address of the
                                                                   Zookeeper cluster
                                                                   and the namespace
     TopologyBuilder builder = new TopologyBuilder();              Kafka uses within
     SpoutConfig spoutConfig = new SpoutConfig(                    Zookeeper
The Kafka
topic for        new KafkaConfig.ZkHosts("zkserver:1234", "/kafka"),
the spout        "pageviews",
                 "/kafkastorm",              The Zookeeper
The ID for       "uniquesSpeedLayer");       namespace Storm
the spout                                     will use for the spout
                                                                   Sets the scheme to tell
     spoutConfig.scheme = new PageviewScheme();                    spout how to deserialize
     builder.setSpout("pageviews",                                 binary records into Data
Creates the              new KafkaSpout(spoutConfig), 16);         objects
spout with a
parallelism of 16
```

Most of this code is configuration: the details of the Kafka cluster and topic to use, and where in Zookeeper the spout should record what it has consumed so far.

The next step is to normalize the URLs in the pageview events:

```java
public static class NormalizeURLBolt extends BaseBasicBolt {
  public void execute(Tuple tuple, BasicOutputCollector collector) {
    PersonID user = (PersonID) tuple.getValue(0);
    String url = tuple.getString(1);
    int timestamp = tuple.getInteger(2);

    try {
      collector.emit(new Values(user,
                          normalizeURL(url),
                        timestamp ,
                        user));
    }
    catch(MalformedURLException e) {}
  }

  public void declareOutputFields(OutputFieldsDeclarer declarer) {
    declarer.declare(new Fields("user", "url", "timestamp"));
  }
}
```

Attempts to normalize the URL using a function that should be shared with the batch layer

If there's a failure normalizing the URL, filters the tuple by not emitting anything

Finally, the last step is to update the HyperLogLog sets stored in Cassandra. Let's start with a simple version. This code retrieves the HyperLogLog set corresponding to that pageview, updates the set, and then writes the set back to Cassandra:

```java
public static class UpdateCassandraBolt extends BaseBasicBolt {
  public static final int HOURS_SECS = 60 * 60;

  ColumnFamilyTemplate<String, Integer> _template;

  public void prepare(Map conf, TopologyContext context) {
    Cluster cluster =
      HFactory.getOrCreateCluster("mycluster", "127.0.0.1");

    Keyspace keyspace =
      HFactory.createKeyspace("superwebanalytics", cluster);

    _template =
      new ThriftColumnFamilyTemplate<String, Integer> (keyspace,
        "uniques", StringSerializer.get(), IntegerSerializer.get());
  }

  public void execute(Tuple tuple, BasicOutputCollector collector) {
    PersonID user = (PersonID) tuple.getValue(0);
    String url = tuple.getString(1);
    int bucket = tuple.getInteger(2) / HOURS_SECS;

    HColumn<Integer, byte[]> hcol =
    _template.querySingleColumn(url, bucket,
      BytesArraySerializer.get());
```

Initializes the classes to retrieve and stores values from Cassandra

Extracts the user, URL, and hour bucket from the incoming tuple

```
        HyperLogLog hll;
        try {
          if (hcol==null) hll = new HyperLogLog(800);
          else hll = HyperLogLog.Builder.build(hcol.getValue());  ⟵

          hll.offer(user);
          ColumnFamilyUpdater<String, Integer> updater =
            _template.createUpdater(url);
          updater.setByteArray(bucket, hll.getBytes());
          _template.update(updater);                              ⟵
        } catch(IOException e) { throw new RuntimeException(e); }
    }

    public void declareOutputFields(OutputFieldsDeclarer declarer) {
      // empty since the bolt does not emit an output stream
    }
}
```

> **Retrieves the HyperLogLog set from Cassandra, or initializes a new set if not found**

> **Adds the user to the HyperLogLog set and updates Cassandra**

For completeness, here's the code to wire the topology together:

```
public static void main(String[] args) {
  TopologyBuilder builder = new TopologyBuilder();
  SpoutConfig spoutConfig = new SpoutConfig(
    new KafkaConfig.ZkHosts("zkserver:1234", "/kafka"),
    "pageviews",
    "/kafkastorm",
    "uniquesSpeedLayer");

  spoutConfig.scheme = new PageviewScheme();
  builder.setSpout("pageviews",
                  new KafkaSpout(spoutConfig), 16);

  builder.setBolt("extract-filter", new NormalizeURLBolt(), 32)
         .shuffleGrouping("pageviews");
  builder.setBolt("cassandra", new UpdateCassandraBolt(), 16)
         .fieldsGrouping("extract-filter", new Fields("url"));
}
```

Note that the topology is completely fault tolerant. Because a spout tuple is only considered acked after the database has been updated, any failure will cause that spout tuple to be replayed. Failures and retries don't affect the accuracy of the system because adding to a HyperLogLog set is an idempotent operation.

The problem with the Cassandra code shown is that it requires a lot of overhead to retrieve sets from Cassandra and write them back. Ideally your database would support HyperLogLog natively, so you wouldn't have this overhead, but you don't have this feature with Cassandra.

You can still make things much more efficient by batching updates together, especially if the same set can be updated multiple times at once. The following code shows a template for this batching approach, writing to Cassandra every hundred tuples or once per second, whichever comes first:

```
public static class UpdateCassandraBoltBatched extends BaseRichBolt {
  public static final int HOURS_SECS = 60 * 60;

  List<Tuple> _buffer = new ArrayList();
  OutputCollector _collector;

  public void prepare(Map conf, TopologyContext context,
                      OutputCollector collector) {
    _collector = collector;
    // set up Cassandra client here
  }

  public Map getComponentConfiguration() {
    Config conf = new Config();
    conf.put(Config.TOPOLOGY_TICK_TUPLE_FREQ_SECS, 1);    ◄─┐
    return conf;
  }

  public void execute(Tuple tuple) {
    boolean flush = false;
    if(tuple.getSourceStreamId()
           .equals(Constants.SYSTEM_TICK_STREAM_ID)) {    ◄─┐
      flush = true;
    } else {
      _buffer.add(tuple);
      if(_buffer.size() >= 100) flush = true;    ◄─┐
    }

    if (flush) {
      // batch udpates to Cassandra here
      for(Tuple t: _buffer) {
        _collector.ack(t);
      }
      _buffer.clear();    ◄─┐
    }
  }

  public void declareOutputFields(OutputFieldsDeclarer declarer) {
    // empty since the bolt does not emit an output stream
  }
}
```

Emits a tick tuple every second to ensure at least once-per-second updates

Flushes if the current tuple is a tick tuple

If a regular tuple, adds to the buffer and flushes when the buffer is full

Acks all tuples and then clears the buffer

A key aspect of this code is that tuples are buffered and not acked until after the corresponding updates have been batched into Cassandra. This ensures that replays will happen if there are any failures. To ensure that updates occur at least once per second, a Storm feature called a *tick tuple* is used. A tick tuple is configured to the bolt once per second. When one of those tuples comes in, whatever is currently buffered is written to the database. We've left out the Cassandra portions of the code because it's somewhat hairy and distracts from the stream-processing aspects of the code.

There's a lot more that could be done to make this code even more efficient. Consider the following list of possible optimizations:

- A batch computation could potentially estimate the required size of the Hyper-LogLog sets of different domains (domains with more uniques need larger HyperLogLog sets). Most domains need very small HyperLogLog sets, and knowing this in advance could lead to considerable savings.
- You could implement a custom scheduler for your Storm cluster so that the Cassandra bolt tasks are collocated with the Cassandra partitions they update. This would eliminate network transfer between the updater tasks and Cassandra.
- As mentioned, if Cassandra could implement HyperLogLog natively, then the HyperLogLog sets wouldn't have to be transferred back and forth.

Implementing all these optimizations is beyond the scope of this book—these are just suggestions on techniques that could be used to improve this particular speed layer.

15.5 Summary

You should now have a good understanding of all the pieces of the speed layer—queues, stream processors, and realtime views. The speed layer is by far the most complex part of any architecture due to its incremental nature, and comparing the incremental code in this chapter with the batch code in previous chapters demonstrates this.

What's left in learning the speed layer is to learn about micro-batched stream processing, the other paradigm of stream processing. Micro-batched stream processing makes different trade-offs than one-at-a-time processing, such as sacrificing latency, but it enables some powerful things, such as exactly-once processing semantics for a more general set of operations.

16

Micro-batch
stream processing

This chapter covers

- Exactly-once processing semantics
- Micro-batch processing and its trade-offs
- Extending pipe diagrams for micro-batch stream processing

You've learned the main concepts of the speed layer in the last four chapters: realtime views, incremental algorithms, stream processing, and how all those fit together. There are no more fundamental concepts to learn about the speed layer—instead, in this chapter we'll focus on a different method of stream processing that makes certain trade-offs to get benefits like improved accuracy and higher throughput.

The one-at-a-time stream processing you've learned is very low latency and simple to understand. But it can only provide an at-least-once processing guarantee during failures. Although this doesn't affect accuracy for certain operations, like adding elements to a set, it does affect accuracy for other operations such as counting. In many cases, this inaccuracy is unimportant because the batch layer overrides the speed layer, making that inaccuracy temporary. But there are other cases where you want

254

full accuracy all of the time, and temporary inaccuracy is unacceptable. In those cases, micro-batch stream processing can give you the fault-tolerant accuracy you need, at the cost of higher latency on the order of hundreds of milliseconds to seconds.

After diving into the ideas underlying micro-batch stream processing, you'll see how the pipe diagrams used for batch processing can be extended to be used for micro-batch stream processing. Then those extended pipe diagrams will be used to finish the design of the SuperWebAnalytics.com speed layer.

16.1 Achieving exactly-once semantics

With one-at-a-time stream processing, tuples are processed independently of each other. Failures are tracked at an individual tuple level, and replays also happen at an individual tuple level.

The world of micro-batch processing is different. Small batches of tuples are processed at one time, and if anything in a batch fails, the entire batch is replayed. In addition, the batches are processed in a strict order. This approach allows you to make use of new techniques in order to achieve exactly-once semantics in your processing, rather than relying on inherently idempotent functions as one-at-a-time processing does.

Let's see how this works.

16.1.1 Strongly ordered processing

Suppose you just want to compute a count of all tuples in real time, and you want that count to be completely accurate regardless of how many failures you sustain during processing. To figure out how to do this, let's start with the one-at-a-time processing approach and see what it takes to give it exactly-once processing semantics.

The pseudo-code for one-at-a-time processing looks something like this:

```
process(tuple) {
    counter.increment()
}
```

As is, this code doesn't have exactly-once semantics. Think about what happens during failures. Tuples will be replayed, and when it comes time to increment the count, you have no idea if that tuple was processed already or not. It's possible you incremented the count but then crashed immediately before acking the tuple. The only way to know is if you were to store the ID of every tuple you've processed—but you'd be storing a huge amount of state instead of just a single number. So that's not a very viable solution.

The key to achieving exactly-once semantics is to enforce a strong ordering on the processing of the input stream. Let's see what happens when you only process one tuple at a time from the input stream, and you don't move on to the next tuple until the current one is successfully processed. Of course, this isn't a scalable solution, but it illustrates the core idea behind micro-batch processing. In addition, let's assume that every tuple has a unique ID associated with it that's always the same no matter how many times it's replayed.

The key idea is rather than just store a count, you store the count along with the ID of the latest tuple processed. Now, when you're updating the count, there are two cases:

- The stored ID is the same as the current tuple ID. In this case, you know that the count already reflects the current tuple, so you do nothing.
- The stored ID is different from the current tuple ID. In this case, you know that the count doesn't reflect the current tuple. So you increment the counter and update the stored ID. This works because tuples are processed in order, and the count and ID are updated atomically.

This update strategy is resilient to all failure scenarios. If the processing fails after updating the count, then the tuple will be replayed and the update will be skipped the second time around. If the processing fails before updating the count, then the update will occur the second time around.

16.1.2 Micro-batch stream processing

As mentioned, though, processing one tuple at a time is highly inefficient. A better approach is to process the tuples as discrete batches, as illustrated in figure 16.1. This is known as micro-batch stream processing.

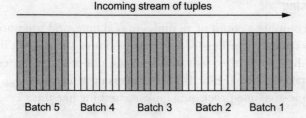

Incoming stream of tuples

Batch 5   Batch 4   Batch 3   Batch 2   Batch 1

Figure 16.1   Tuple stream divided into batches

The batches are processed in order, and each batch has a unique ID that's always the same on every replay. Because many tuples are processed per iteration rather than just one, the processing can be made scalable by parallelizing it. Batches must be processed to completion before moving on to the next batch.

Let's see how the global counting example works with micro-batch processing. Again, rather than just storing the count, you store the count along with the latest batch ID involved in updating that count. For example, suppose the current value of the stored state is as shown in figure 16.2.

Count	112
Batch ID	3

Figure 16.2   Count state including batch ID

Now suppose batch 4 comes in with 10 tuples. The state will be updated to look like figure 16.3.

Now let's say after the state in the database is updated, something fails in the stream processor and the message that the batch was finished is never received. The stream processor will timeout the batch and retry batch 4. When it comes time to update the state in the database, it sees that

Count	122
Batch ID	4

Figure 16.3   Result of updating count state

the state has already been updated by batch 4. So rather than increment the count again, it does nothing and moves on to the next batch.

Now let's look at a more complicated example than global counting to further drive home how micro-batch stream processing works.

16.1.3 *Micro-batch processing topologies*

Suppose you want to build a streaming application that consumes a massive stream of words and computes the top-three most frequently occurring words. Micro-batch processing can accomplish this task while being fully parallelized, fault tolerant, and accurate.

There are two tasks to accomplish for each batch of words. First, you have to keep state on the frequency of each word. This can be done using a key/value database. Second, if any of the words you just processed has a higher frequency than one of the current top-three most frequent words, the top-three list must be updated.

Let's start with updating the word frequencies. Just like how MapReduce and one-at-a-time stream processing partition data and process each partition in parallel, the same is done with micro-batched processing. Processing a batch of words looks like figure 16.4. As you can see, a single batch includes tuples from all partitions in the incoming stream.

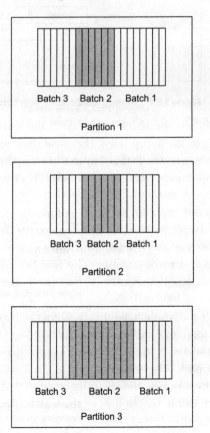

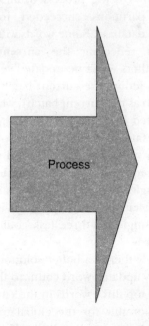

Figure 16.4 Each batch includes tuples from all partitions of the incoming stream.

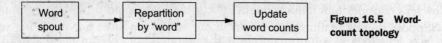

Figure 16.5   Word-count topology

To update the word frequencies, the words must be repartitioned so that the same word is always processed by the same task. This ensures that when the database updates, only one thread will be updating the values for that word, and there will be no race conditions. This is illustrated in figure 16.5.

Now you need to figure out what to store as the state for each word. In the same way that storing just a count wasn't enough for global counting, it's also not enough to store just a count for each word. If a batch is retried, you won't know if the current count reflects the current batch or not. So just as the solution for global counting was to store the batch ID with the count, the solution for the word counts is to store the batch ID with the count for each word, as illustrated in figure 16.6.

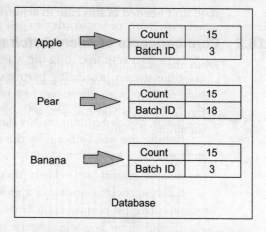

Figure 16.6   Storing word counts with batch IDs

Now let's consider a failure scenario. Suppose a machine dies in the cluster while a batch is being processed, and only some partitions succeeded in updating the database. Some words will have counts reflecting the current batch, and others won't be updated yet. When the batch is replayed, the words that have state including the current batch ID won't be updated (because they have the same batch ID as the current batch), whereas the words that haven't been updated yet will be updated like normal. Just like global counting, the processing is completely accurate and fault tolerant.

Let's now move on to the second part of the computation: computing the top-three most frequent words. One solution would be to send the new counts for every word to a single task, and have that task merge those word counts into its top-three list. The problem with this approach is that it's not scalable. The number of tuples sent to that single top-three task could be nearly the same size as the entire input stream of words.

Fortunately there's a better solution that doesn't have this bottleneck. Instead of sending every updated word count to the top-three task, each word-counting task can compute the top-three words in the current batch, and then send its top-three list to the task responsible for the global top-three. The global top-three task can then merge all those lists into its own list. Now the amount of data transferred to that global top-three task in each batch is proportional to the parallelism of the word-count tasks, not the entire input stream.

Now let's consider how failures might affect the top-three portion of the computation. Suppose there's a failure that results in one of the top-three lists not being sent to the global top-three task. In that case, the global top-three list will not be updated, and when the batch is replayed it will be updated normally.

Suppose there's a failure after the top-three list is updated (the message indicating the batch completed never gets through). In this case the batch will be replayed, and the same top-three lists will be received by the global top-three task. This time, the global top-three list already incorporates the current batch. But because merging those lists is an idempotent operation, remerging them into an already updated list won't change the results. So the trick used before of including the batch ID with the state isn't needed in this case to achieve fully accurate processing.

16.2 Core concepts of micro-batch stream processing

From the examples shown in the previous section, some core concepts should be emerging. There are two main aspects to micro-batch stream processing:

- *Batch-local computation*—There's computation that occurs solely within the batch, not dependent on any state being kept. This includes things like repartitioning the word stream by the word field and computing the count of all the tuples in a batch.
- *Stateful computation*—Then there's computation that keeps state across all batches, such as updating a global count, updating word counts, or storing a top-three list of most frequently used words. This is where you have to be really careful about how you do state updates so that processing is idempotent under failures and retries. The trick of storing the batch ID with the state is particularly useful here to add idempotence to non-idempotent operations.

Finally, micro-batch stream processing relies on a stream source that can replay a batch exactly as it was played before. It turns out that queues like Kafka, covered in the last chapter, have the perfect semantics for this. Because Kafka exposes an API very similar to files, when a batch is emitted the consumer can remember which offsets from which partitions were read for a particular batch. If a batch has to be replayed, the exact same batch can be emitted. These kinds of stream sources are called *transactional spouts*.

> **Beyond transactional spouts**
>
> There are also ways to achieve exactly-once processing semantics without transactional spouts. In a transactional spout, the exact same batch must be emitted on every replay. The problem with transactional spouts is that if a batch fails and a partition of the batch becomes unavailable, processing will be unable to continue because the batch can't be exactly replayed.
>
> A less restrictive kind of spout, called an *opaque spout*, must simply ensure that each tuple is successfully processed in only one batch. It allows for the following sequence of events:

(continued)

1   Batch A is emitted with tuples from partitions 1, 2, and 3.
2   Batch A fails to process.
3   Partition 3 becomes unavailable.
4   Batch A is replayed only with tuples from partitions 1 and 2.
5   Sometime later on, partition 3 becomes available.
6   Those tuples that were in a failed batch before succeed in a later batch.

In order to achieve exactly-once semantics with opaque spouts, more-complicated logic is needed when doing state updates. It's no longer sufficient to only store the batch ID with whatever state is being updated. A small amount of additional information must be tracked. You can find more information about opaque topologies in the documentation of Apache Storm.

The latency and throughput characteristics are different for micro-batch processing as compared to one-at-a-time processing. For any individual tuple, the latency from when it's added to the source queue to when it's fully processed is much higher in micro-batch processing. There's a small but significant amount of overhead to coordinating batches that increases latency, and instead of waiting for just one tuple to complete, processing needs to be done on many more tuples. In practice, this turns out to be latency on the order of hundreds of milliseconds to seconds.

But micro-batch processing can have higher throughput than one-at-a-time processing. Whereas one-at-a-time processing must do tracking on an individual tuple level, micro-batch processing only has to track at a batch level. This means fewer resources are needed on average per tuple, allowing micro-batch processing to have higher throughput than one-at-a-time processing.

16.3   *Extending pipe diagrams for micro-batch processing*

You've seen how pipe diagrams provide a very nice way to express batch-processing computations in a concise way without giving up any generality. It turns out that with a few extensions, you can use pipe diagrams to represent micro-batch stream processing computations as well.

The pipe diagrams you've seen so far are used to process a single batch one time. An easy way to interpret pipe diagrams in a micro-batch context is executing the pipe diagram on each batch independently. So things like aggregation and joining only happen within a batch—there's no computation that crosses batches.

Of course, processing each batch completely independently of each other isn't that useful. That handles batch-local computation, but you also need to be able to keep state between batches. Extensions to pipe diagrams are needed for this, and it's in these extensions that the batch ID logic for enabling exactly-once semantics exists.

These extensions will be introduced through an example. Let's take a look at implementing the streaming word count example again, except this time with micro-batch stream processing.

Figure 16.7 shows a pipe diagram that does this. You should interpret this pipe diagram just as you would those for regular batch processing. It processes to completion a batch of tuples containing a single field called sentence. Once the batch is complete, it moves on to the next batch of tuples.

As you can see, this is almost the same as the pipe diagram for the

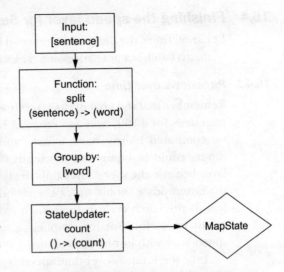

Figure 16.7 Micro-batch word-count pipe diagram

batch word count, except that instead of an Aggregator there's a StateUpdater that's connected to a MapState. The MapState represents a key/value datastore that could be either an external key/value database (like Cassandra) or state kept in memory on the processing tasks. StateUpdater functions are responsible for updating the state in a way that's idempotent under replays. In this case, the StateUpdater function applies the Count aggregator to update the count for each word in the MapState.

The beauty of this is that all the nitty-gritty details of storing and checking batch IDs to force idempotence can be automated for you underneath the abstractions. That means you don't have to think about this at all when making these pipe diagrams. You can pretend every tuple is processed exactly one time. Underneath the hood, the pipe diagrams get executed in a way that's fault tolerant and idempotent under replays.

You can store any kind of state in a pipe diagram—not just MapStates. The state represents whatever indexed data model you need to satisfy your realtime indexing requirements. For example, you might have a KeyToSortedMapState backed by a database that supports that data model, such as Apache Cassandra.

You saw how, in the batch-processing context, pipe diagrams were a complete replacement for MapReduce. The pipe diagrams could do everything MapReduce could do, with the same performance, but expressed much more elegantly. In the stream-processing context though, pipe diagrams are only a way to represent micro-batched computations and are not a replacement for one-at-a-time stream processing. Because micro-batched and one-at-a-time stream processing make different trade-offs between latency, throughput, and guaranteed message processing semantics, one is not best for all situations.

16.4 *Finishing the speed layer for SuperWebAnalytics.com*

Let's now finish the design for the speed layer of SuperWebAnalytics.com by making use of micro-batch stream processing. Let's start with the pageviews-over-time speed layer.

16.4.1 *Pageviews over time*

Remember that the goal of the pageviews-over-time query is to get the total number of pageviews for a URL over any range of hours. To make this query in the serving layer, we computed hourly, daily, weekly, and monthly rollups of pageviews so that large ranges could be computed efficiently. This optimization is not needed in the speed layer because the speed layer only deals with recent data—the time since the last serving layer update should only be a few hours, so keeping other rollups would be pointless. If the batch cycle is long, such as more than a day, then having a daily rollup might be useful. But for simplicity's sake, let's implement the pageviews-over-time speed layer with just hourly rollups.

Like the uniques-over-time speed layer from the previous two chapters, a realtime view implementing a key-to-sorted-map interface would work perfectly. And just like uniques over time, the key is a URL, the sorted map key is an hour bucket, and the sorted map value is the number of pageviews for that URL and hour bucket. Figure 16.8 shows a pipe diagram implementing the appropriate logic.

This pipe diagram uses a key-to-sorted-map state and updates it as pageviews come in. The UpdateInnerMap state updater is parameterized with the Count aggregator, so it knows how to apply updates to the state's inner maps that represent hour buckets to pageview counts.

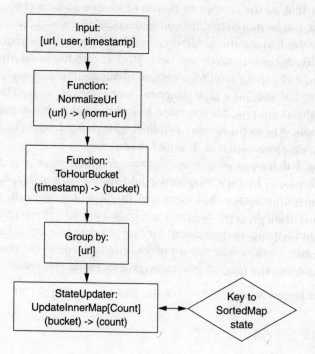

Figure 16.8 Micro-batched pageviews-over-time pipe diagram

16.4.2 Bounce-rate analysis

Let's now move on to the speed layer for computing bounce rates. Remember that a visit was defined as a bounce if the user visited a page and didn't visit another page on that domain within 30 minutes of the first visit. So a bounce occurring is based on an event not happening.

Like uniques over time, you have to take equivs into account to compute bounces completely accurately. If a user browses your website on their computer and then ten minutes later browses from their phone, that should be considered a single non-bouncing visit. If you didn't know those two user identifiers were the same person, then it should count as two bounced visits.

Like uniques over time, taking equivs into account massively complicates the computation. To see why, just consider what you need to do when you receive a new equiv. Here's an illustrative series of events:

1 Pageview received at minute 0 from `alice-computer`.
2 Pageview received at minute 10 from `alice-phone`.
3 Equiv received at minute 140 between `alice-computer` and `alice-phone`.

Before event 3, those two pageviews would have counted as two visits and two bounces. You didn't know they were equivalent, so there's nothing else you could possibly compute in real time. But event 3 changes everything. Now you have to go back and fix the bounce rates computed over two hours earlier.

The only way to do this is to retrieve all visits in the past for `alice-computer` and `alice-phone` and recompute the appropriate bounces. After comparing this with what was computed the first time around, the appropriate increments and decrements can be made to the database that stores bounce counts and visit counts. In addition to all this, the equiv graph analysis needs to be done in real time.

Besides being rather complicated to accomplish, taking equivs into account also massively increases storage costs for the speed layer. Rather than just storing bounce and visit counts per domain, you also need to be able to retrieve all the pageviews for a user since the last serving layer update. Because an equiv could come in at any time for any user, this means all speed layer pageviews need to be indexed. This is not infeasible, but it certainly is a lot more expensive.

Just like uniques over time, there's an easy way to simplify all this: just ignore equivs in the speed layer. It doesn't seem like this should create too much inaccuracy, and due to the fact that the batch and serving layers will automatically correct any speed layer inaccuracies, this seems like a great trade-off. So that's the approach we'll use. Of course, as always, you should verify the inaccuracy created by any approach by measuring it via offline analytics jobs.

There are three steps to doing the bounce-rate analysis in real time:

1 Consume a stream of pageview events that contains a user identifier, a URL, and a timestamp.

2 Identify bounces by detecting when a user has visited a single page on a domain and no other pages within 30 minutes.

3 Update a database containing a map from domain to bounce rate. The bounce rate will be stored as a pair of numbers [number of bounces, number of visits].

Like pageviews over time, bounce-rate analysis starts by consuming a stream of pageviews. Identifying bounces is more interesting, though, because it's a time-based event and not just a simple aggregation. At any given moment, a bounce could occur, and that would be based on pageviews from 30 minutes prior. Because in stream processing you only have access to events that have just occurred, to identify bounces you need to keep state about what has happened in the past 30 minutes.

The main idea is to track each *visit* (a [domain, user] pair) until that visit is complete. We've defined a visit to be complete when 30 minutes have elapsed with no further pageviews by that user on that domain. Once that visit is complete, the bounce-rate information for that domain can be updated. Each completed visit increments the number of visits by one, and the number of bounces is incremented if there was only one pageview in that visit. At the pipe diagram level, in order to track these visits we'll maintain a map from [domain, user] to the first time and the last time a pageview occurred in that visit. Once a minute, we'll iterate through the entire map to determine which visits have completed. Visits that have completed will be removed from the map and then be used to update the bounce-rate information for their corresponding domains.

This strategy requires tracking all visits in the last 30 minutes. If you're at large scale, this could be on the order of hundreds of millions or even billions of visits at once. If you figure tracking a visit requires about 100 bytes, what with the domain, user ID, timestamps, and memory usage by the map, the memory required will be on the order of a terabyte. This is doable, but expensive. After finishing the memory-based design, you'll see how this memory requirement can be reduced and even eliminated.

Windowed stream processing?

You may have heard the term *windowed stream processing* before, which refers to breaking an incoming stream into windows of time, such as 30 seconds, 1 minute, 5 minutes, or 30 minutes. Sometimes the window is "rolling" and always refers to the last *X* seconds of time. Other times the windows are fixed and occur right after one another.

At first glance, the bounce-rate analysis may seem like a good fit for windowed stream processing due to its time-oriented nature. But on a closer look, it doesn't fit windowed stream processing at all. Any particular visit could span an indefinite period of time. For example, if someone visits a page on a domain every 10 minutes for 16 hours, that visit must remain in the map for all 16 of those hours (until 30 minutes with no activity has elapsed). Windowed stream processing doesn't handle computations like this—it's meant to answer questions like "How many pageviews have I received in the last 15 minutes?"

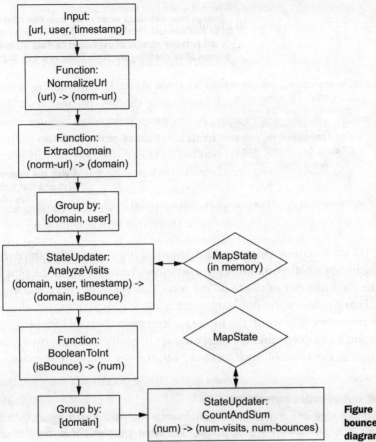

Figure 16.9 Micro-batched bounce-rate-analysis pipe diagram

The pipe diagram for bounce-rate analysis is shown in figure 16.9. The key to this pipe diagram is the `AnalyzeVisits` state updater, which determines when visits are complete and whether or not they were bounces. It keeps state on visits in an in-memory `MapState`.

Here is some pseudo-code for this state updater:

Stores a pair of timestamps [start-visit-time, last-visit-time] for each visit. The visit information is stored in a map with a key of a [domain, user] pair.

Gets the last time the visits were checked to see if any of them have completed (30 minutes since last visit). The visits will be swept over once a minute.

```
function AnalyzeVisits(mapstate, domain, user, timestamp) {
  THIRTY-MINUTES-SECS = 60 * 30

  update(mapstate,
      [domain, user],
      function(visit-info) {
        if(visit-info == null) [timestamp, timestamp]
        else [visit-info[0], timestamp]
      })
  last-sweep-time = get(state, "last-sweep", 0)
```

Sweeps over the visits when more than one minute has gone by since last checking. Note that this code depends on a steady stream of pageviews coming in, as it only sweeps after checking the timestamp of a new pageview.

When a visit is complete, emit the fact and stop tracking the visit in the map.

```
if(timestamp > last-sweep-time + 60) {
  for(entry in mapstate) {
    domain = entry.key[0]
    visit-info = entry.value
    if(timestamp > visit-info[1] + THIRTY-MINUTES-SECS) {
      emit(domain, visit-info[0] == visit-info[1])
      remove(mapstate, entry.key)
    }
  }
  put(mapstate, "last-sweep", timestamp)
}
}
}
```

A visit is a bounce if the first and last visit times are identical.

AnalyzeVisits emits a stream of visit information: a 2-tuple containing the domain and a Boolean signifying whether that visit was a bounce. The next part of the pipe diagram computes the total number of visits and the total number of bounces, storing them in a MapState. First it converts the Boolean to either a 0 or 1, depending on whether it was false or true, respectively. It counts the tuples to determine the total number of visits and sums the 0's and 1's to determine the total number of bounces. These two numbers are stored together as the value of the MapState, with the key being the domain.

Time and out-of-order messages

One of the assumptions made in the bounce-rate-analysis pipe diagram is that the timestamps in tuples are always increasing. But what if tuples come in out of order?

This is not just a hypothetical question—tuples are being generated all over the cluster and then placed together on your queue servers. It's very likely tuples won't be in perfect order. Beyond that, if you have network partitions or errors and tasks get delayed writing their tuples to your queues, tuples could be out of order by much longer, even on the order of minutes.

For many computations, such as pageviews over time, this doesn't matter. But for the bounce-rate analysis, which uses time to trigger checking for completed visits, this does matter. For example, a pageview for a visit could come in after you've checked for completed visits, and that pageview could turn a completed visit into a still active visit.

The way to deal with out-of-order tuples is to introduce latency into your computations. With the bounce-rate-analysis code, you could change the definition of a completed visit to "more than 45 minutes has passed since the last visit, and there are no additional pageviews in the 30 minutes after the last pageview." This strategy will handle out-of-order tuples that come up to 15 minutes late.

Of course, there's no perfect way to deal with out-of-order tuples. You could theoretically receive a tuple that was generated two days ago, but it's not reasonable for your bounce-rate-analysis code to wait indefinitely to see if there are any out-of-order tuples. Otherwise your code wouldn't be able to make any progress. You have to place a limit on how long you're willing to wait. As usual, it's prudent to do measurements to determine the distribution and rate of out-of-order tuples.

Like many things in the speed layer, this is another example of something that's fundamentally difficult to deal with in real time, but not a problem in batch. Because the Lambda Architecture has a batch layer that overrides the speed layer, any inaccuracy introduced by out-of-order tuples is weeded out over time.

There's a weakness to this design, though—all the state is kept in memory in the tasks executing the pipe diagram. Earlier we computed that memory on the order of a terabyte is required for very large scales. Although it's certainly possible to have a cluster with this much memory, it turns out there's another approach that doesn't require any memory at all.

16.5 Another look at the bounce-rate-analysis example

Let's see how you can completely eliminate the memory requirement for bounce-rate analysis. The trick is taking a step back and looking at the problem again. Visits are not complete until 30 minutes have passed without activity on that visit. That you have to wait 30 minutes to determine the status of a visit means that bounce-rate analysis is fundamentally not a realtime problem. Latency is not that much of a constraint, so you're not forced to use a memory-focused stream-processing system at all.

For this problem, using a batch-processing system for the speed layer is absolutely viable. The logic of the workflow doesn't change—you still maintain a map from visits to information about the visits, mark visits as bounces or not bounces after 30 minutes of inactivity have passed, and then aggregate the bounce and visit information into a key/ value database. The difference is that the underlying technologies change: for the computation system, you might use Hadoop. And for storing the speed layer view, you could use a serving layer database like ElephantDB. Finally, for the intermediate key/value state, you could also use something like ElephantDB. This is illustrated in figure 16.10.

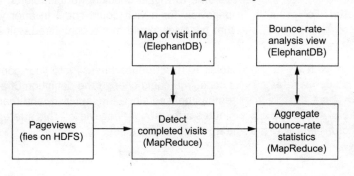

Figure 16.10 Bounce-rate analysis using incremental batch processing

So far we've only discussed using batch computation to do full recomputations, where you consume all the data at once to produce a view from scratch. Incremental batch processing works differently, where you consume new data and produce new views based on the last version of your views. This is different than stream processing, which mutates your views in place. The views produced by incremental batch-processing workflows are brand new and never modified after creation. We'll talk more about incremental batch processing in the final chapter.

16.6   Summary

You've seen how by sacrificing some latency, you can go beyond the at-least-once semantics of one-at-a-time stream processing and achieve exactly-once processing semantics. Whereas one-at-a-time stream processing has exactly-once semantics only with inherently idempotent operations, micro-batch processing can achieve it for nearly any computation.

It should also be apparent that the speed layer doesn't necessarily mean real time, nor does it necessarily entail stream processing. The speed layer is about accounting for recent data—you saw in the bounce-rate-analysis example that the definition of the problem is inherently not realtime. Accounting for recent data allows for other approaches, like incremental batch processing.

Now that you have an understanding of the concepts of micro-batch processing, you're ready to see how to apply the technique in practice.

Micro-batch stream processing: Illustration

In the last chapter you learned the core concepts of micro-batch processing. By processing tuples in a series of small batches, you can achieve exactly-once processing semantics. By maintaining a strong ordering on the processing of batches and storing the batch ID information with your state, you can know whether or not the batch has been processed before. This allows you to avoid ever applying updates multiple times, thereby achieving exactly-once semantics.

You saw how with some minor extensions pipe diagrams could be used to represent micro-batch streaming computations. These pipe diagrams let you think about your computations as if every tuple is processed exactly once, while they compile to code that automatically handles the nitty-gritty details of failures, retries, and all the batch ID logic.

Now you'll learn about Trident, Apache Storm's micro-batching API, which provides an implementation of these extended pipe diagrams. You'll see how similar it is to normal batch processing. You'll see how to integrate it with stream sources like Kafka and state providers like Cassandra.

17.1 Using Trident

Trident is a Java API that translates micro-batch processing topologies into the spouts and bolts of Storm. Trident looks very similar to the batch processing idioms you're already familiar with—it has joins, aggregations, grouping, functions, and filters. In addition to that, it adds abstractions for doing stateful processing across batches using any database or persistence store.

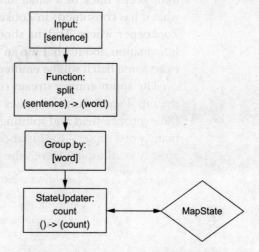

Recall the pipe diagram for streaming word count, which looks like figure 17.1. Let's look at how you can implement this with Trident.

For the purposes of illustration, this example will read an infinite stream of sentences from the following source:

Figure 17.1   Micro-batched word-count pipe diagram

```
FixedBatchSpout spout = new FixedBatchSpout(
        new Fields("sentence"),
        3, // number of tuples in each batch
        new Values("the cow jumped over the moon"),
        new Values("the man went to the store"),
        new Values("four score and seven years ago"),
        new Values("how many apples can you eat"),
        new Values("to be or not to be the person"));
spout.setCycle(true); // repeats these tuples forever
```

This spout emits three sentences every batch and cycles through the sentences ad infinitum.

Here's the definition of a Trident topology that implements word count:

```
TridentTopology topology = new TridentTopology();
topology.newStream("spout1", spout)
        .each(new Fields("sentence"),
                new Split(),
                new Fields("word"))
        .groupBy(new Fields("word"))
        .persistentAggregate(
                new MemoryMapState.Factory(),
                new Count(),
                new Fields("count"));
```

Let's go through the code line by line. First, a `TridentTopology` object is created. `TridentTopology` exposes the interface for constructing Trident computations. `TridentTopology` has a method called `newStream` that connects the topology to an input source. In this case, the input source is just the `FixedBatchSpout` defined before. If you wanted to read from Kafka, you'd instead use a Trident Kafka spout. Trident keeps track of a small amount of state for each input source (metadata about what it has consumed) in Zookeeper, and the `spout1` string here specifies the node in Zookeeper where Trident should keep that metadata. This metadata contains the information about what was in each batch, so that if a batch has to be replayed, the exact same batch will be emitted the next time.

The spout emits a stream containing one field called `sentence`. The next line of the topology definition applies the `Split` function to each tuple in the stream, taking the `sentence` field and splitting it into words. Each sentence tuple creates potentially many word tuples—for instance, the sentence "the cow jumped over the moon" creates six word tuples. Here's the definition of `Split`:

```
public static class Split extends BaseFunction {
    public void execute(TridentTuple tuple,
                        TridentCollector collector) {
        String sentence = tuple.getString(0);
        for(String word: sentence.split(" ")) {
            collector.emit(new Values(word));
        }
    }
}
```

Unlike Storm bolts, which take in entire tuples as input and produce entire tuples as output, Trident operations take in partial tuples as input and have their output values appended to the input tuple—which is exactly how pipe diagram operations are supposed to work. Behind the scenes, Trident compiles as many operations as possible together into single bolts.

You saw how pipe diagrams were extended with a `StateUpdater` operation that communicates with a `State` object to keep persistent state between batches. Trident has a `StateUpdater` interface that looks like this:

```
public interface StateUpdater<S extends State>
  extends Operation {
    void updateState(
      S state,
      List<TridentTuple> tuples,
      TridentCollector collector);
}
```

It takes in a batch of tuples and is expected to perform the appropriate logic to update that state.

Trident provides two methods for inserting a `StateUpdater` into your topology. The first is `partitionPersist`, which takes in an implementation of this `StateUpdater` interface. The second is `persistentAggregate`, which takes in an `Aggregator`.

Aggregators have no concept of state in them, so `persistentAggregate` will convert the `Aggregator` into a `StateUpdater` for you. For example, the `Count` aggregator will be converted to add the count of the current batch into the count stored in the state. This is often very convenient.

To complete the word-count example, the rest of the topology computes word count and keeps the results persistently stored. First, the stream is grouped by the word field. Then, each group is persistently aggregated using the `Count` aggregator and `persistentAggregate`. In this example, the word counts are kept in memory, but swapping this to use Memcached, Cassandra, or any other persistent store is trivial.

Let's see how you could get this code to store the word counts in Cassandra instead. Here's the code to do so:

```
CassandraState.Options opts =
        new CassandraState.Options();
opts.globalCol = "COUNT";
opts.keySerializer = StringSerializer.get();
opts.colSerializer = StringSerializer.get();

stream.groupBy(new Fields("word"))
    .persistentAggregate(
        CassandraState.transactional(
                "127.0.0.1",
                "mykeyspace",
                "mycolumnfamily"),
        new Count(),
        new Fields("count"));
```

This `CassandraState` implementation allows grouped aggregation to be done with either 1-tuple groups or 2-tuple groups. The 1-tuple case treats Cassandra as a key/value database, whereas the 2-tuple case treats Cassandra as a key-to-map database. In the 1-tuple case, as shown in the preceding example, the value in that tuple corresponds to the Cassandra key, and the column used will be the `globalCol` specified in the options. With 2-tuple groups, the first element of the grouping tuple is the Cassandra key and the second is the Cassandra column.

> **More information on `CassandraState`**
>
> The accompanying source code for this book provides a simple implementation of `CassandraState`. It's not ideal, however, as it does database operations one at a time instead of batching them, so the potential throughput of this `CassandraState` is much lower than it could be. The code is much easier to follow this way, though, so we hope it can serve as a reference implementation for making states that interact with whatever database you choose to use.

Here is the definition of the `Count` aggregator:

```
public static class Count
        implements CombinerAggregator<Long> {
```

```
public Long init(TridentTuple tuple) {
    return 1L;
}

public Long combine(Long val1, Long val2) {
    return val1 + val2;
}

public Long zero() {
    return 0L;
}
}
```

As you can see, it's a straightforward implementation of Count, similar to how parallel aggregators are defined in JCascalog. Notice in particular that nowhere in all this code is the tricky batch ID logic to achieve exactly-once semantics. Trident takes care of that behind the scenes automatically. In this case, it automatically stores the batch ID with the count, and if it detects that the stored batch ID is the same as the current batch ID, it won't do any updates to the persistent store.

Portions of Trident that haven't been covered yet will be explained as we go along. To provide deeper information on the Trident API, we refer you to the Storm documentation available online. Our goal here is to show how micro-batch processing can be applied to practical problems, not to get lost in every last detail of how these APIs work.

17.2 Finishing the SuperWebAnalytics.com speed layer

Let's now translate the pipe diagrams from the previous chapter into working code using Trident. The two queries left to finish are pageviews over time and bounce-rate analysis.

17.2.1 Pageviews over time

The pipe diagram for pageviews over time is repeated in figure 17.2. To implement this, you must decide what specific technologies to use for the source stream and for the state.

The source stream is well handled by Apache Kafka. Remember that one of the keys to achieving exactly-once semantics during failures is to always replay a batch exactly as it was played before. Storm refers to this property of a source queue as *transactional semantics*. Kafka has this ability, making it a good choice for micro-batched processing.

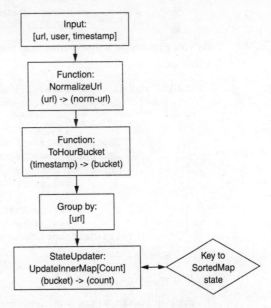

Figure 17.2   Micro-batched pageviews-over-time pipe diagram

As for the state, it requires a key-to-sorted-map index type. This is exactly the index type that Apache Cassandra provides, making it a good choice for this application.

To implement the topology, the first step is to define a spout to read the pageviews from Apache Kafka. The following code accomplishes this:

```
TridentTopology topology = new TridentTopology();
TridentKafkaConfig kafkaConfig =
        new TridentKafkaConfig(
                new KafkaConfig.ZkHosts(
                        "zkstr", "/kafka"),
                "pageviews"
                );
kafkaConfig.scheme = new PageviewScheme();
```

Configuring a Trident Kafka spout is similar to configuring a regular Storm Kafka spout, as shown in the last chapter. Note the setting of a scheme that will deserialize pageviews into three fields: url, user, and timestamp.

Here's the first part of the topology that normalizes URLs and converts timestamps into the appropriate hour bucket:

```
Stream stream =
    topology.newStream(
            "pageviewsOverTime",
            new TransactionalTridentKafkaSpout(
                    kafkaConfig))
            .each(new Fields("url"),
                    new NormalizeURL(),
                    new Fields("normurl"))
            .each(new Fields("timestamp"),
                    new ToHourBucket(),
                    new Fields("bucket"))
```

As you can see, it's just a function for each task. Here's the implementation of those functions:

```
    public static class NormalizeURL extends BaseFunction {
        public void execute(TridentTuple tuple,
                            TridentCollector collector) {
            try {
                String urlStr = tuple.getString(0);
                URL url = new URL(urlStr);
                collector.emit(new Values(
                        url.getProtocol() +
                        "://" +
                        url.getHost() +
                        url.getPath())));
            } catch(MalformedURLException e) {
            }
        }
    }


    public static class ToHourBucket extends BaseFunction {
        private static final int HOUR_SECS = 60 * 60;
```

```
public void execute(TridentTuple tuple,
                    TridentCollector collector) {
    int secs = tuple.getInteger(0);
    int hourBucket = secs / HOUR_SECS;
    collector.emit(new Values(hourBucket));
  }
}
```

The logic is no different than what was used in the batch layer, and it would be superior to just share code between the layers (it's duplicated here only so it's easier to follow).

Finally, all that's left is rolling up the pageview counts into Cassandra and ensuring this is done in an idempotent manner. First, let's configure the `CassandraState`:

```
CassandraState.Options opts =
        new CassandraState.Options();
opts.keySerializer = StringSerializer.get();
opts.colSerializer = IntegerSerializer.get();

StateFactory state =
        CassandraState.transactional(
            "127.0.0.1",
            "superwebanalytics",
            "pageviewsOverTime",
            opts);
```

The appropriate serializers are set for the keys (URLs) and columns (time buckets). Then the state is configured to point at the appropriate cluster, keyspace, and column family.

Here's the definition of the remainder of the topology:

```
stream.groupBy(new Fields("normurl", "bucket"))
    .persistentAggregate(
            state,
        new Count(),
        new Fields("count"));
```

In the pipe diagram, the `UpdateInnerMap` state updater was used with the `Count` aggregator to express the desired state transformation. In this code, though, there is no reference to `UpdateInnerMap`. This is entirely due to how `CassandraState` works. When a grouping is done with two keys, the second key is interpreted by `CassandraState` as the inner map key, which means `UpdaterInnerMap` is implicit in this topology definition.

In this case, the grouping key contains two fields, the `url` and the `bucket`. The `persistentAggregate` method is used to apply the built-in `Count` aggregator to roll up the counts. Trident automatically stores the batch ID with each count so that any failures and retries can be done in an idempotent manner.

That completes the implementation for the pageviews-over-time speed layer. As you can see, it's very concise and straightforward.

17.2.2 Bounce-rate analysis

Let's now see how you can implement bounce-rate analysis using Trident. For reference, the pipe diagram is repeated in figure 17.3.

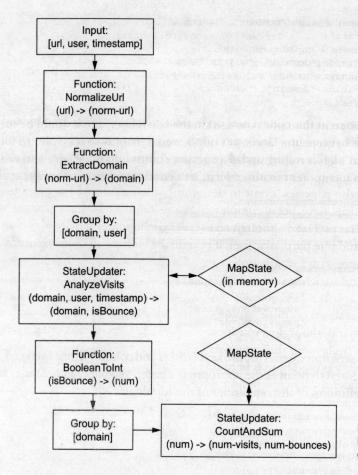

Figure 17.3 Micro-batched bounce-rate-analysis pipe diagram

This is a more involved topology, so let's go through it piece by piece. The topology mirrors the pipe diagram almost exactly.

The beginning of the topology looks like this:

```
topology.newStream(
        "bounceRate",
        new TransactionalTridentKafkaSpout(kafkaConfig))
        .each(new Fields("url"),
              new NormalizeURL(),
              new Fields("normurl"))
        .each(new Fields("normurl"),
              new ExtractDomain(),
              new Fields("domain"))
```

There's nothing new here. It consumes the stream of pageviews from Kafka and runs a couple of functions to extract the domain from the URL.

Here's the next part of the topology, which analyzes visits and determines when bounces occur:

```
.partitionBy(new Fields("domain", "user"))
.partitionPersist(
        new MemoryMapState.Factory(),
        new Fields("domain", "user", "timestamp"),
        new AnalyzeVisits(),
        new Fields("domain", "isBounce"))
.newValuesStream()
```

You should notice in this code a new operation: `partitionBy`. To understand why this is needed, let's recap how `AnalyzeVisits` works. `AnalyzeVisits` looks at a single pageview event at a time and updates state as to how long that user has been visiting that domain. `AnalyzeVisits` also sweeps through all visits once a minute—using the timestamp in the pageview event to determine when a minute has passed—to determine if any visits have been completed (more than 30 minutes passing without a pageview by that user). So although `AnalyzeVisits` updates state based on one particular domain and one particular user, it potentially looks at all domain/user pairs in its state when processing a single tuple.

Now let's get back to `partitionBy`. Trident provides two ways of dividing up tuples: `partitionBy` and `groupBy`. `groupBy` lets you group together tuples with a common key and run aggregations on those groups independent of all other groups. `partitionBy`, on the other hand, simply lets you specify how tuples should be divided up by the processing tasks. Tuples with the same partitioning keys will go to the same task. The reason `partitionBy` is used here is because `AnalyzeVisits` doesn't process domain/user pairs independently. Once a minute it looks at all domain/user pairs it's currently storing in memory.

This topology would also be correct if only partitioned by the `domain` field. But that might lead to skew if you have just a few domains dominating the visits in your dataset. If you partition by `user` and `domain`, the distribution will almost certainly be even because it's extremely unlikely a single person is dominating the pageviews in your dataset.

Now let's take a look at the implementation of `AnalyzeVisits`. It keeps all of its state in an in-memory map via the `MemoryMapState` class. `MemoryMapState` is provided by Trident and it implements all of the batch ID logic to be idempotent under retries. So if there's a failure and a batch is reprocessed, the `MemoryMapState` implementation ensures that updates aren't applied more than once. The `AnalyzeVisits` code doesn't have to worry about any of that.

A few helper classes are needed before getting to the meat of `AnalyzeVisits`. These represent the keys and values kept in the state used by `AnalyzeVisits` to keep track of user visits:

```
static class Visit extends ArrayList {
    public Visit(String domain, PersonID user) {
        super();
        add(domain);
        add(user);
    }
}
```

```
static class VisitInfo {
    public int startTimestamp;
    public Integer lastVisitTimestamp;

    public VisitInfo(int startTimestamp) {
        this.startTimestamp = startTimestamp;
        this.lastVisitTimestamp = startTimestamp;
    }

    public VisitInfo clone() {
        VisitInfo ret = new VisitInfo(this.startTimestamp);
        ret.lastVisitTimestamp = this.lastVisitTimestamp;
        return ret;
    }
}
```

And here is the implementation of `AnalyzeVisits`:

```
public static class AnalyzeVisits
    extends BaseStateUpdater<MemoryMapState> {

    static final String LAST_SWEEP_TIMESTAMP = "lastSweepTs";
    static final int THIRTY_MINUTES_SECS = 30 * 60;

    public void updateState(
            MemoryMapState state,
            List<TridentTuple> tuples,
            TridentCollector collector) {
        for(TridentTuple t: tuples) {
            final String domain = t.getString(0);
            final PersonID user = (PersonID) t.get(1);
            final int timestampSecs = t.getInteger(2);
            Visit v = new Visit(domain, user);
            update(state, v, new ValueUpdater<VisitInfo>() {
                public VisitInfo update(VisitInfo v) {
                    if(v==null) {
                        return new VisitInfo(timestampSecs);
                    } else {
                        VisitInfo ret = new VisitInfo(
                                        v.startTimestamp);
                        ret.lastVisitTimestamp = timestampSecs;
                        return ret;
                    }
                }
            });

            Integer lastSweep =
                (Integer) get(state, LAST_SWEEP_TIMESTAMP);
            if(lastSweep==null) lastSweep = 0;

            List<Visit> expired = new ArrayList();
            if(timestampSecs > lastSweep + 60) {
                Iterator<List<Object>> it = state.getTuples();
                while(it.hasNext()) {
                    List<Object> tuple = it.next();
                    Visit visit = (Visit) tuple.get(0);
                    VisitInfo info = (VisitInfo) tuple.get(1);
```

```
                        if(info.lastVisitTimestamp >
                              timestampSecs + THIRTY_MINUTES_SECS) {
                      expired.add(visit);
                      if(info.startTimestamp ==
                          info.lastVisitTimestamp) {
                          collector.emit(new Values(domain, true));
                      } else {
                          collector.emit(new Values(domain, false));
                      }
                  }
              }
              put(state, LAST_SWEEP_TIMESTAMP, timestampSecs);
        }

        for(Visit visit: expired) {
            remove(state, visit);
        }
    }
  }
}
```

The logic in this implementation is identical to the pseudo-code from the last chapter. The only difference is the Java syntax required to express it. This code uses a few helper functions for interacting with `MemoryMapState`, so for completeness these helpers are shown here:

```
private static Object update(MapState s,
                             Object key,
                             ValueUpdater updater) {
    List keys = new ArrayList();
    List updaters = new ArrayList();
    keys.add(new Values(key));
    updaters.add(updater);
    return s.multiUpdate(keys, updaters).get(0);
}

private static Object get(MapState s, Object key) {
    List keys = new ArrayList();
    keys.add(new Values(key));
    return s.multiGet(keys).get(0);
}

private static void put(MapState s, Object key, Object val) {
    List keys = new ArrayList();
    keys.add(new Values(key));
    List vals = new ArrayList();
    vals.add(val);
    s.multiPut(keys, vals);
}

private static void remove(MemoryMapState s, Object key) {
    List keys = new ArrayList();
    keys.add(new Values(key));
    s.multiRemove(keys);
}
```

With that complete, here's the rest of the topology definition:

```
.each(new Fields("isBounce"),
      new BooleanToInt(),
        new Fields("bint"))
.groupBy(new Fields("domain"))
.persistentAggregate(
        CassandraState.transactional(
                "127.0.0.1",
                "superwebanalytics",
                "bounceRate",
                opts),
        new Fields("bint"),
        new CombinedCombinerAggregator(
                new Count(),
                new Sum()),
        new Fields("count-sum"));
```

This part of the topology simply consumes the stream of ["domain", "isBounce"] and aggregates it into Cassandra to determine for each domain the number of visits and the number of bounces. First, isBounce is converted to a 0 if it's false and a 1 if it's true using the BooleanToInt function. Then, a standard persistentAggregate is done to update Cassandra.

You actually need to do two aggregations: a count to determine the number of visits, and a sum of the isBounce integers to determine the number of bounces. So the Count and Sum aggregators are combined into one using the CombinedCombinerAggregator utility. This utility is defined as follows:

```
public static class CombinedCombinerAggregator
        implements CombinerAggregator {

    CombinerAggregator[] _aggs;

    public CombinedCombinerAggregator(
            CombinerAggregator... aggs) {
        _aggs = aggs;
    }

    public Object init(TridentTuple tuple) {
        List<Object> ret = new ArrayList();
        for(CombinerAggregator agg: _aggs) {
            ret.add(agg.init(tuple));
        }
        return ret;
    }

    public Object combine(Object o1, Object o2) {
        List l1 = (List) o1;
        List l2 = (List) o2;
        List<Object> ret = new ArrayList();
        for(int i=0; i<_aggs.length; i++) {
            ret.add(
                _aggs[i].combine(
```

```
                          l1.get(i),
                          l2.get(i)));
    }
    return ret;
}

public Object zero() {
    List<Object> ret = new ArrayList();
    for(CombinerAggregator agg: _aggs) {
        ret.add(agg.zero());
    }
    return ret;
}
}
```

And that completes the implementation of the speed layer for bounce-rate analysis.

There's a problem with this implementation though. Although Trident and `MemoryMapState` ensure that updates aren't applied more than once, the state isn't persisted or replicated anywhere. So if a task carrying state dies, that state is lost.

One way to deal with this weakness is to just ignore it, accept the small amount of inaccuracy it introduces, and rely on the batch layer to correct that inaccuracy when it happens. Alternatively, it's possible to do stream processing with in-memory state that's tolerant to failures. Let's explore that now.

17.3 *Fully fault-tolerant, in-memory, micro-batch processing*

There are two ways to achieve local, in-memory state that can be recovered when workers die.

The first is to make use of the standard database technique of keeping a commit log in a replicated store. Good technologies for this are HDFS file appends or Kafka. Whenever you make an update to your state, you write what that update was to your log. Figure 17.4 illustrates what a commit log might look like.

When a task starts up, it replays the commit log to rebuild the internal state. Of course, the commit log grows indefinitely, so rebuilding state based on the log will get more and more expensive. You can fix this problem by periodically compacting the log. Compaction is the process of persisting the entire state itself, and then deleting all commit log elements

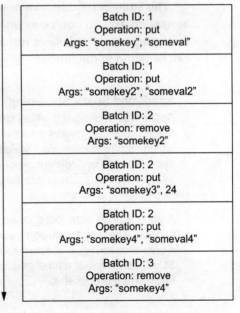

Figure 17.4   Commit log

involved in the construction of that state. A great technology for storing the state in its entirety is a distributed filesystem. Your strategy around compaction could be as simple as doing it once a minute, or after the commit log grows to a certain size.

There's another technique for accomplishing persistent, in-memory state that doesn't involve a commit log at all. Recall that the way Trident works is it processes batches in a strong order, and by keeping the batch ID stored with the state it can detect if a batch has been processed before and achieve exactly-once semantics. But what if your computation system could retry batches beyond just the last one—say, batches a few minutes in the past? This lets you do some cool new things.

The idea is to periodically checkpoint any state kept in memory by writing it out somewhere (like a distributed filesystem). You might checkpoint once a minute. The checkpoint also stores up to what point in the source stream that checkpoint represents.

Now let's say you have a failure 45 seconds later, and one of the tasks holding a partition of your state dies. At this point, the task that failed only has state current up to the batch from 45 seconds ago (when the last checkpoint was). All the other tasks are completely current because they haven't failed.

You can recover by rewinding the source stream to 45 seconds ago and replaying it. Although this would normally be very expensive, it can be made highly efficient because only one partition needs to be recovered. So during the recomputation, you can skip partitions for which you already have up-to-date state.

Like the commit log approach, this strategy requires the state to be periodically written out in full. However, it requires no commit log to be written out, making it a strictly better approach.

This strategy requires extensions to the micro-batch stream-processing model that Storm and Trident don't currently implement. Another system, however, called Spark Streaming, does implement this approach. More information about Spark Streaming can be found in the sidebar.

Spark and Spark Streaming

Spark was mentioned when talking about batch processing as an alternative to MapReduce that makes smart use of memory. Spark has another mode of operation called Spark Streaming, which implements the micro-batch stream-processing approach with periodic checkpointing of internal state. Whereas Trident is focused on integrating with external databases, Spark Streaming is focused on computing state to be kept in memory.

A good way to categorize computation systems is by the computation styles they support. The three main computation styles are batch processing, low latency one-at-a-time processing, and micro-batch processing. Hadoop does only batch processing, Storm does one-at-a-time and micro-batch processing, and Spark does batch and micro-batch processing.

17.4 *Summary*

You saw how to practically implement micro-batch stream processing using Storm's Trident API. There was a fairly direct mapping between the conceptual way of thinking about the data flow—the pipe diagrams—and the code to implement it. Although Trident has excellent support for storing state in external databases with exactly-once semantics, its support for local in-memory state isn't fully fault tolerant.

You've now explored every piece of the basic Lambda Architecture: a recomputation-based batch layer, a serving layer, and a speed layer. You've seen the intricacies of all these layers and a full-fledged example of implementing all these layers via SuperWeb-Analytics.com. With these basics down, let's now see how to go beyond the basic Lambda Architecture. There are many important variations that enable you to get better efficiency out of your data systems.

18

Lambda Architecture in depth

This chapter covers

- Revisiting the Lambda Architecture
- Incremental batch processing
- Efficiently managing resources in batch workflows
- Merging logic between batch and realtime views

In chapter 1 you were introduced to the Lambda Architecture and its general-purpose approach for implementing any data system. Every chapter since then has dived into the details of the various components of the Lambda Architecture. As you've seen, there's a lot involved in building Big Data systems that not only scale, but are robust and easy to understand as well.

Now that you've had a chance to dive into all the different layers of the Lambda Architecture, let's use that newfound knowledge to review the Lambda Architecture once more and achieve a better understanding of it. We'll fill in any remaining gaps and explore variations on the methodologies that have been discussed so far.

18.1 Defining data systems

We started with a simple question: "What does a data system do?" The answer was also simple: a data system answers questions based on data you've seen in the past. Or put more formally, a data system computes queries that are functions of all the data you've ever seen. This is an intuitive definition that clearly encapsulates any data system you'd ever want to build:

query = function(all data)

There are a number of properties you're concerned about with your queries:

- *Latency*—The time it takes to run a query. In many cases, your latency requirements will be very low—on the order of milliseconds. Other times it's okay for a query to take a few seconds. When doing ad hoc analysis, your latency requirements are often very lax, even on the order of hours.
- *Timeliness*—How up-to-date the query results are. A completely timely query takes into account all data ever seen in the past, whereas a less timely query may not include results from the recent minutes or hours.
- *Accuracy*—In many cases, in order to make queries performant or scalable, you must make approximations in your query implementations.

A huge part of building data systems is making them fault tolerant. You have to plan for how your system will behave when you encounter machine failures. Oftentimes this means making trade-offs with the preceding properties. For example, there's a fundamental tension between latency and timeliness. The CAP theorem shows that under partitions, a system can either be consistent (queries take into account all previous written data) or available (queries are answered at the moment). Consistency is just a form of timeliness, and availability just means the latency of the query is bounded. An eventually consistent system chooses latency over timeliness (queries are always answered, but may not take into account all prior data during failure scenarios).

Because data systems are dynamic, changing systems built by humans and with new features and analyses deployed all the time, humans are an integral part of any data system. And like machines, humans can and will fail. Humans will deploy bugs to production and make all manner of mistakes. So it's critical for data systems to be human-fault tolerant as well.

You saw how mutability—and associated concepts like CRUD—are fundamentally not human-fault tolerant. If a human can mutate data, then a mistake can mutate data. So allowing updates and deletes on your core data will inevitably lead to corruption.

The only solution is to make your core data *immutable*, with the only write operation allowed being appending new data to your ever-growing set of data. You can do things like set permissions on your core data to disallow deletes and updates—this redundancy ensures that mistakes can't corrupt existing data, so your system is far more robust.

This leads us to the basic model of data systems:

- A master dataset consisting of an ever-growing set of data
- Queries as functions that take in the entire master dataset as input

Anything you'd ever want to do with data can clearly be done this way, and such a system has at its core that crucial property of human-fault tolerance. If it were possible to implement, this would be the ideal data system. The Lambda Architecture emerges from making the fewest sacrifices possible to achieve this ideal of queries as functions of an ever-growing immutable dataset.

18.2   *Batch and serving layers*

Computing queries as functions of all data is not practical because it's not reasonable to expect queries on a multi-terabyte dataset, much less a multi-petabyte dataset, to return in a few milliseconds. And even if that were possible, queries would be unreasonably resource-intensive. The simplest modification you can make to such an architecture is to query precomputed views rather than the master dataset directly. These precomputed views can be tailored for the queries so that the queries are as fast as possible, whereas the views themselves are functions of the master dataset.

In chapters 2 through 9, you saw the details of implementing such a system. At the core is a batch-processing system that can compute those functions of all data in a scalable and fault-tolerant way—hence, this part of the Lambda Architecture is called the *batch layer*.

The goal of the batch layer is to produce views that are indexed so that queries on those views can be resolved with low latency. The indexing and serving of those views is done in the *serving layer*, which is tightly connected to the batch layer. In designing your batch and serving layers, you must strike a balance between the amount of precomputation done in the batch layer with the size of the views and the amount of computation needed at query time (discussed extensively in chapter 6).

Let's now go beyond this basic model of the batch and serving layers of the Lambda Architecture to explore more options you have available to you in designing them. A key performance metric of these layers is how long it takes to update the views. As the speed layer must compensate for all data not represented in the serving layer, the longer it takes the batch layer to run, the larger your speed layer views must be. Needing larger clusters of significantly more complex databases greatly increases your operational complexity. In addition, the longer it takes the batch layer to run, the longer it takes to recover from bugs that are accidentally deployed to production. One way to lower the latency of the batch layer is to incrementalize it.

18.2.1 *Incremental batch processing*

In chapter 6 we discussed the trade-offs between incremental algorithms and recomputation algorithms. You saw how one of the primary benefits of the batch layer is its ability to take advantage of recomputation algorithms, so you may be surprised at the suggestion to incrementalize the batch layer. Like all design issues, you must consider all the trade-offs in order to come to the best design.

Let's consider an extreme case, where the only view you're producing is a global count of all records in the master dataset. In this case, incrementalizing the batch layer is a clear win, as the incremental view is no bigger than a recomputation-based view (just a single number in both cases), and it's not complex to incrementalize the code. You save a huge amount of resources by not repeatedly recomputing over the entire master dataset. For instance, if your master dataset contains 100 terabytes of data, and each new batch of data contains 100 gigabytes, your batch layer will be orders of magnitude more efficient. Each iteration only has to deal with 100 gigabytes of data rather than 100 terabytes.

Now let's consider another example where the choice between incremental and recomputation algorithms is more difficult: the "birthday inference" problem. Imagine you're writing a web crawler that collects people's ages from their public profiles. The profile doesn't contain a birthday, but only what that person's age is at the moment you crawled that web page. Given this raw data of [age, timestamp] pairs, your goal is to deduce the birthday of each person.

The idea of the birthday-inference algorithm is illustrated in figure 18.1. Imagine you crawl the profile of Tom on January 4, 2012, and see his age is 23. Then you crawl his profile again on January 11, 2012, and see his age is 24. You can deduce that his birthday happened sometime between those two dates. Likewise, if you crawl the profile of Jill on October 20, 2013, and see she is 43, and then crawl it again on November 4, 2013, and see she is still 43, you know her birthday is not between those dates. The more age samples you have, the better you can infer that someone's birthday is within a small range of dates.

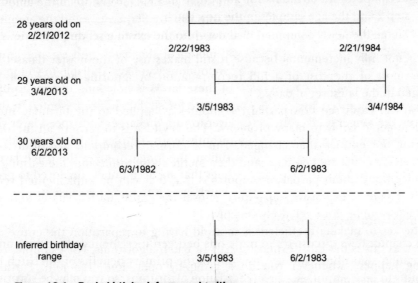

Figure 18.1 Basic birthday-inference algorithm

In the real world, of course, the data can get messy. Someone may have incorrectly entered their birthday and then changed it at a later date. This may cause your age inference algorithm to fail to produce a birthday because every day of the year has been eliminated as a possible birthday. You might modify your birthday inference algorithm to search for the smallest number of age samples it can ignore to produce the smallest range of possible birthdays. The algorithm might prefer to use recent age samples over older age samples.

If you implement a birthday-inference batch layer using recomputation, it's easy. Your algorithm can look at all age samples for a person at once and do everything necessary to deal with messy data and emit a single range of dates as output. But incrementalizing the birthday-inference batch layer is much trickier. It's hard to see how you can deal with the messy data problem without having access to the full range of age samples. Incrementalizing this algorithm fully would be considerably harder and may require a much larger and more involved view.

There's an alternative that blurs the line between incrementalization and recomputation and gets you the best of both worlds. This technique is called *partial recomputation*.

PARTIAL RECOMPUTATION

Recomputing every person's birthday from the age samples every single time the batch layer runs is wasteful. In particular, if a person has no new age samples since the last time the batch layer ran, then the inferred birthday for that person will not change at all. The idea behind a birthday inference batch layer based on partial recomputation is to do the following:

1 For the new batch of data, find all people who have a new age sample.
2 Retrieve all age samples from the master dataset for all people in step 1.
3 Recompute the birthdays for all people in step 1 using the age samples from step 2 and the age samples in the new batch.
4 Merge the newly computed birthdays into the existing serving layer views.

This is not fully incremental because it still makes use of the master dataset. But it avoids most of the cost of a full recomputation by ignoring anyone who hasn't changed in the latest set of data.

You can easily see how partial recomputes as applied to the birthday-inference problem could apply to many problems. The key idea is to retrieve all the relevant data for the entities that changed, run a normal recompute algorithm on the retrieved data plus the new data, and then merge those results into the existing views. The nice thing about partial recomputes is that they can be implemented very efficiently. The most expensive step—looking over the entire master dataset to find relevant data—can be done relatively cheaply.

The key to making it efficient is to avoid having to repartition the entire master dataset, as this is the most expensive part of batch algorithms. For example, repartitioning happens whenever you do a group-by operation or a join. Partitioning involves serialization/deserialization, network transfer, and possibly buffering on disk. In contrast, operations that don't require partitioning can quickly scan through the data and operate on each piece of data as it's seen. Retrieving relevant data for a partial recompute can be done using the latter method.

The first step to retrieving relevant data is to construct a set of all the entities for which you need relevant data. You then scan over the master dataset and only emit data for those entities that exist in the set (each task would have a copy of that set). In a batch-processing system like Hadoop, this would correspond to a map-only job.

You're limited by memory, so your set can only be so big. But a data structure called a *Bloom filter* can make this work for much larger sets of entities. A Bloom filter is a compact data structure that represents a set of elements and allows you to ask if it contains an element. A Bloom filter is much more compact than a set, but as a trade-off, query operations on it are probabilistic. A Bloom filter will sometimes incorrectly tell you that an element exists in the set, but it will never tell you an element that was added to the set is not in the set. So a Bloom filter has false positives but no false negatives.

Using a Bloom filter to optimize retrieving relevant data is illustrated in figure 18.2. If you use a Bloom filter to retrieve relevant data from the master dataset, you'll filter out the vast majority of the master dataset. Due to the false positives, though, some data will be emitted that you didn't want to retrieve. You can then do a join between the retrieved data and the list of desired entities to filter out the false positives. A join requires a partitioning, but because the vast majority of the master dataset was already filtered out, getting rid of the false positives is not an expensive operation.

Let's now make some estimates as to how much of a latency improvement an incremental batch layer based on partial recomputes offers compared to a fully recomputation-based batch layer. Let's say computing birthday inference requires one full MapReduce job with partitioning, and that the following facts exist about your cluster and your data:

- Your master dataset contains 100 terabytes of data.
- A partial recompute-based approach will have 50 gigabytes of new data each batch.
- A MapReduce job with partitioning takes 8 hours on the full master dataset.
- A map-only job (without any partitioning) takes 2 hours on the full master dataset (the 4x speed difference is typical in MapReduce clusters).
- Creating brand-new, serving layer views takes 2 hours in the full recompute.
- Updating the serving layer views takes 1 hour in the partial recompute.

With these numbers, recomputing all the birthday-inference views from scratch would take 8 hours for the computation plus 2 hours to build the serving layer views. That's 10 hours total. For a partial recompute, here are the figures:

- It takes 2 hours to get the relevant data from the master dataset.
- It takes a few minutes to compute the new birthdays for the entities in the current batch.
- It takes 1 hour to update the existing serving layer views with the newly computed birthdays.

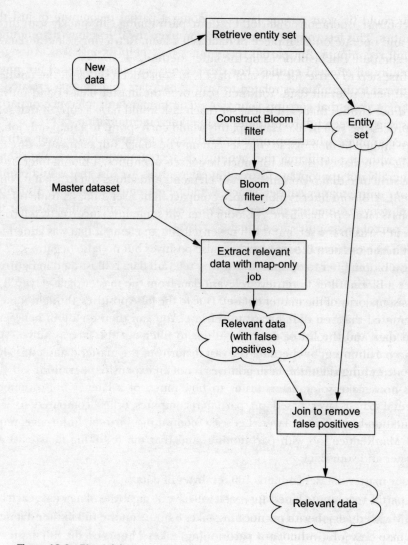

Figure 18.2 Bloom join

So the partial-recompute-based approach would only take about 3 hours, which is 70% faster than the full-recompute-based approach. These numbers are estimates, but it should give you a good idea of the kinds of performance improvements you could expect from a partial-recompute-based batch layer. For more-complex batch computations that require more than one partitioning step, the savings would be much greater. For instance, if the recomputation algorithm required four partitioning steps, the full recompute job would require 34 hours, while the partial recompute job would still only require about 3 hours.

Another benefit of partial recomputes is that they give you a certain amount of power to correct for human mistakes. If bad data is written that corrupts certain entities, you could fix your serving layers by doing a partial recompute of just the affected entities. This lets you get your application fixed in far less time than doing a complete, full recompute. But partial recomputes only help fix mistakes as long as you can identify all affected entities. For this reason, partial recomputes are much more effective at fixing mistakes related to writing bad data than mistakes related to deploying buggy code that corrupts your views. The human-fault tolerance of partial recomputes is in between full recomputes and full incrementalization.

Partial recomputes, when appropriate, enable you to have a batch layer with far less latency without sacrificing the benefits of recomputation-based algorithms. They're generally not appropriate for realtime algorithms because that would require indexing your entire master dataset, which would be extremely expensive. And, obviously, scanning over the entire master dataset in real time is impossible. But for the batch layer, partial recomputes are a great tool to have in your toolkit.

IMPLEMENTING AN INCREMENTAL BATCH LAYER

Whether you're doing fully incremental algorithms or partial recompute algorithms in your incremental batch layer, the main difference between an incremental batch layer and a recomputation-based batch layer is the need to update your serving layer views rather than create them from scratch.

It's absolutely viable to build the incremental batch layer similar to a speed layer, with the views being read/write databases that you modify in place. But this would negate the many advantages of serving layer databases (discussed in chapter 10) that result from not supporting random writes:

- *Robustness*—Not having random writes means the codebase is simpler and less likely to have bugs.
- *Easier to operate*—Fewer moving parts means there's less for you to worry about as an operator of these databases—less configuration and less that can go wrong.
- *More predictable performance*—By not having random writes that happen concurrently with reads, there's no need to worry about any sort of locking inside the database. Likewise, whereas a read/write database occasionally needs to perform compaction to reclaim unused parts of the index, which can significantly degrade performance, a database without random writes never needs to do this.

So let's focus on how to make serving layer databases that preserve these properties as much as possible. You saw one design for a serving layer database called ElephantDB in chapter 11.

The crux of how ElephantDB works is that the batch layer view is indexed and partitioned in a MapReduce job, and those indexes are stored on the distributed filesystem. An ElephantDB cluster periodically checks for new versions of the view and will hot-swap the new version once it's available. The key point here is that the creation and serving of views are completely independent and coordinated through a distributed filesystem.

The way to extend this design to enable incremental batch processing is to include the last version of the batch layer view as input to the job that creates the new version of the batch layer view. Then updates are applied to the old version, and the new version is written out to the distributed filesystem (ElephantDB implements this). For example, if you're using BerkeleyDB as your indexing system and storing word counts inside it, the job to create the new version of the view would work as follows. The task for a given partition of the view would download the appropriate partition from the distributed filesystem, open it locally, increment word counts for its batch of data, and then copy the updated view into the distributed filesystem under the folder for the new version. In a strategy like this, all the incrementalization happens on the view-creation side. Serving new versions of the view is no different than before.

A strategy like this saves you from redoing all the work that went into creating the prior version of the view. You can also take advantage of the higher latency of the batch layer to compact the indexes before writing them out to the distributed filesystem.

This strategy works better with moderate-to-smaller-sized views. If the views themselves are huge, the cost of the jobs may be dominated by reading and writing the entire view to and from the distributed filesystem. In these cases, incrementalization may not help very much. An alternative is to use a serving layer database design that ships "deltas" to the serving databases, and the serving databases merge them in on the fly. Of course, in that case you'd also have to do compaction while serving, so the serving layer would look more and more like a read/write database and have many of the associated complexities.

Fortunately, there's a way to minimize the size of your incremental batch layer views so that you're not forced to use the deltas strategy or a read/write database for your serving layer. Instead, you can keep the benefits of a serving layer where the creation and serving of views are completely independent. The idea is to have multiple batch layers.

MULTIPLE BATCH LAYERS

Instead of just having one batch layer and one speed layer that compensates for the latency of the batch layer, you can have multiple batch layers. For example, you could have one batch layer based on full recomputes that finishes once a month. Then you could have an incremental batch layer that only operates on data not represented in the full-recompute batch layer. That might run once every six hours. Then you would have a speed layer that compensates for all data not represented in the two batch layers.

In the basic Lambda Architecture, the batch layer loosens the performance requirements of the speed layer; similarly, with multiple batch layers, each layer loosens the requirements for the layer above it. In the example mentioned, the incremental batch layer only has to deal with two months of data. That means its views can be kept *much smaller* than if the views had to represent all data for all time. So techniques like making brand-new serving layer views based on the old serving layer views are feasible because the cost of copying the views won't dominate.

The other benefit to having multiple batch layers is that it helps you get the best of both worlds of incrementalization and recomputation. Incremental workflows can be much more performant but lack the ability to recover from mistakes that recomputation workflows give you. If recomputation is a constantly running part of your system, you know you can recover from any mistake.

The latency of each layer of your system directly affects the performance requirements of the layer above it. So it's incredibly important to have a good understanding of how the latency of each layer is affected by the efficiency of your code and the amount of resources you allocate to them. Let's see how that plays out.

18.2.2 *Measuring and optimizing batch layer resource usage*

There turns out to be a lot of counterintuitive dynamics at work in the performance of batch workflows. Consider these examples, which are based on real-world cases:

- After doubling the cluster size, the latency of a batch layer went down from 30 hours to 6 hours, an 80% improvement.
- An improper reconfiguration caused a Hadoop cluster to have 10% more task failure rates than before. This caused a batch workflow's runtime to go from 8 hours to 72 hours, a 9x degradation in performance.

It's hard at first to wrap your head around how this is possible, but the basic dynamic can be easily illustrated. Suppose you have a batch workflow that takes 12 hours to run, so it processes 12 hours of data each iteration. Now let's say you enhance the workflow to do some additional analysis, and you estimate the analysis will add two hours to the processing time of your current workflow. You've now increased the runtime of a workflow that operated on 12 hours of data to 14 hours. That means the next time the workflow runs, there will be 14 hours of data to process. Because the next iteration has more data, it will take longer to run, which means the next iteration will have even more data, and so on.

If and when the runtime stabilizes can be determined with some very simple math. First, let's write out the equation for the runtime of a single iteration of a batch workflow. The equation will make use of the following variables:

- T—The runtime of the workflow in hours.
- O—The overhead of the workflow in hours. This is the amount of time spent in the workflow that's independent of the data being processed. This can include things like setting up processes, copying code around the cluster, and so on.
- H—The number of hours of data being processed in the iteration. "Hours" are used here to measure the *amount* of data because it makes the resulting equations very simple. As part of this, it's assumed that the rate of incoming data is fairly constant. But the conclusions we'll make are not dependent on this.
- P—The dynamic processing time. This is the number of hours each hour of data adds to the processing time of the workflow. If each hour of data adds half an hour to the runtime, then P is 0.5.

Based on these definitions, the following equation is a natural expression of the run-time of a single iteration of a workflow:

$$T = O + P \times H$$

Of course, H will vary with every iteration of the workflow, because if the workflow takes shorter or longer to run than the last iteration, the next iteration will have less or more data to process, respectively. To determine the stable runtime of the workflow, you need to determine the point at which the runtime of the workflow is equal to the number of hours of data it processes. To do this, you simply plug in $T = H$ and solve for T:

$$T = O + P \times T$$
$$T = \frac{O}{(1 - P)}$$

As you can see, the stable runtime of a workflow is linearly proportional to the amount of overhead in the workflow. So if you're able to decrease overhead by 25%, your workflow runtime will also decrease by 25%. However, the stable runtime of a work-flow is non-linearly proportional with the dynamic processing time, P. One implica-tion of this is that there are diminishing returns on performance gains with each machine added to the cluster.

What happens if P is greater than or equal to 1?

You may be wondering what would happen if your dynamic processing time, P, is greater than or equal to 1. In this case, each iteration of the workflow will have more data than the iteration prior, so the batch layer will fall further and further behind, forever. It's incredibly important to keep P below 1.

Using this equation, the counterintuitive cases described earlier make a lot more sense. Let's start with what happens to your stable runtime when you double the size of your cluster. When that happens, your dynamic processing time, P, gets approx-imately in half, as you can now parallelize the processing twice as much (technically, your overhead to coordinate all those machines also increases slightly, but let's ignore that). If $T1$ is the stable runtime before doubling the cluster size, and $T2$ is the stable runtime afterward, you get these two equations:

$$T1 = \frac{O}{(1 - P)}$$
$$T2 = \frac{O}{(1 - P/2)}$$

Solving for the ratio $T2/T1$ nets you this equation:

$$\frac{T2}{T1} = \frac{1 - P}{(2 - P)}$$

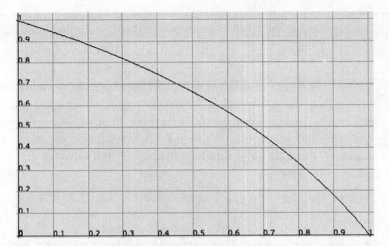

Figure 18.3 Performance effect of doubling cluster size

Plotting this, you get the graph in figure 18.3.

This graph says it all. If your *P* was really low, like 6 minutes of processing time per hour of data, then doubling the cluster size will barely affect the runtime. This makes sense because the runtime is dominated by overhead, which is unaffected by doubling the cluster size.

However, if your *P* was really high, say 54 minutes of dynamic time spent per hour of data, then doubling the cluster size will cause the new runtime to be 18% of the original runtime, a speedup of 82%! What happens in this case is the next iteration finishes much faster, causing the next iteration to have less data, upon which it will finish even faster. This positive loop eventually stabilizes at an 82% speedup.

Now let's consider the effect an increase in failure rates would have on your stable runtime. A 10% task failure rate means you'll need to execute about 11% more tasks to get your data processed. (If you had 100 tasks and 10 of them failed, you'd retry those 10 tasks. However, on average 1 of those will also fail, so you'll need to retry that one too.) Because tasks are dependent on the amount of data you have, this means your time to process one hour of data (*P*) will increase by 11%.

As in the last analysis, let's call *T*1 the runtime before the failures start happening and *T*2 the runtime afterward:

$$T1 = \frac{O}{(1 - P)}$$

$$T2 = \frac{O}{(1 - 1.11 \times P)}$$

The ratio *T*2/*T*1 is now given by the following equation:

$$\frac{T2}{T1} = \frac{(1 - P)}{(1 - 1.11 \times P)}$$

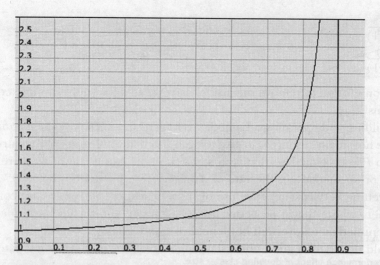

Figure 18.4   Performance effect of 10% increase in error rates

Plotting this, you get the graph in figure 18.4.

As you can see, the closer your P gets to 1, the more dramatic an increase in failure rates has on your stable runtime. This is how a 10% increase in failure rates can cause a 9x degradation in performance. It's important to keep your P away from 1 so that your runtime is stable in the face of the natural variations your cluster will experience. According to this graph, a P below 0.7 seems pretty safe.

By optimizing your code, you can control the values for O and P. In addition, you can control the value for P with the amount of resources (such as machines) you dedicate to your batch workflow. The magic number for P is 0.5. When P is above 0.5, adding 1% more machines will decrease latency by more than 1%, making it a cost-effective decision. When P is below 0.5, adding 1% more machines will decrease latency by less than 1%, making the cost-effectiveness more questionable.

To measure the values of O and P for your workflow, you may be tempted to run your workflow on zero data. This would give you the equation $T = O + P \times 0$, allowing you to easily solve for O. You could then use that value to solve for P in the equation $T = O / (1 - P)$. But this approach tends to be inaccurate. For example, on Hadoop, a job typically has many more tasks than there are task slots on the cluster. It can take a few minutes for a job to get going and achieve full velocity by utilizing all the available task slots on the cluster. The time it takes to get going is normally a constant amount of time and so is captured by the O variable. When you run a job with a tiny amount of data, the job will finish before utilizing the whole cluster, skewing your measurement of O.

A better way to measure O and P is to artificially introduce overhead into your workflow, such as by adding a `sleep(1 hour)` call in your code. Once the runtime of the workflow stabilizes, you'll now have two measurements, $T1$ and $T2$, for before and after you added the overhead. You end up with the following equations to give you your O and P values:

$$O = \frac{T1}{(T2 - T1)}$$
$$P = \frac{(1-1)}{(T2 - T1)}$$

Of course, don't forget to remove the artificial overhead once you've completed your measurements!

When building and operating a Lambda Architecture, you can use these equations to determine how many resources to give to each batch layer of your architecture. You want to keep P well below 1 so that your stable runtime is resilient to an increase in failure rates or an increase in the rate of data received. If your P is below 0.5, then you're not getting very cost-effective use of those machines, so you should consider allocating them where they'd be better used. If O seems abnormally high, then you may have identified an inadvertent bottleneck in your workflow.

You should now have a good understanding of building and operating batch layers in a Lambda Architecture. The design of a batch layer can be as simple as a recomputation-based batch layer, or you may find you can benefit from making an incremental batch layer that's possibly combined with a recomputation-based batch layer. Let's now move on to the speed layer of the Lambda Architecture.

18.3 Speed layer

Because the serving layer updates with high latency, it's always out of date by some number of hours. But the views in the serving layer represent the vast majority of the data you have—the only data not represented is the data that has arrived since the serving layer last updated. All that's left to make your queries realtime is to compensate for those last few hours of data. This is the purpose of the speed layer.

The speed layer is where you tend toward the side of performance in the trade-offs you make—incremental algorithms instead of recomputation algorithms and mutable read/write databases instead of the kinds of databases preferred in the serving layer. You need to do this because you need the low latency, and the lack of human-fault tolerance in these approaches doesn't ultimately matter. Because the serving layer constantly overrides the speed layer, mistakes in the speed layer are easily corrected.

Traditional architectures typically only have one layer, which is roughly comparable to the speed layer. But because there's no batch layer underpinning it, it's very vulnerable to mistakes that will cause data corruption. Additionally, the operational challenges of operating petabyte-scale read/write databases are enormous. The speed layer in the Lambda Architecture is largely free of these challenges, because the batch and serving layers loosen its requirements to an enormous extent. Because the speed layer only has to represent the most recent data, its views can be kept very small, avoiding the aforementioned operational challenges.

In chapters 12 through 17 you saw the intricacies and variations on building a speed layer, involving queuing, synchronous versus asynchronous speed layers, and one-at-a-time versus micro-batch stream processing. You saw how for difficult problems you can make approximations in the speed layer to reduce complexity, increase performance, or both.

18.4 *Query layer*

The last layer of the Lambda Architecture is the query layer, which is responsible for making use of your batch and realtime views to answer queries. It has to determine what to use from each view and how to merge them together to achieve the proper result. Each query is formulated as some function of batch views and realtime views.

The merge logic you use in your queries will vary from query to query. The different techniques you might use are best illustrated by a few examples.

Queries that are time-oriented have straightforward merging strategies, such as the pageviews-over-time query from SuperWebAnalytics.com. To execute the pageviews-over-time query, you get the sum of the pageviews up to the hour for which the batch layer has complete data. Then you retrieve the pageview counts from the speed views for all remaining hours in the query and sum them with the batch view counts. Any query that's naturally split on time like this will have a similar merge strategy.

You'd take a different approach for the birthday-inference problem introduced earlier in this chapter. One way to do it is as follows:

- The batch layer runs an algorithm that will appropriately deal with messy data and choose a single range of dates as output. Along with the range, it also emits the number of age samples that went into computing that range.
- The speed layer incrementally computes a range by narrowing the range with each age sample. If an age sample would eliminate all possible days as birthdays, it's ignored. This incremental strategy is fast and simple but doesn't deal with messy data well. That's fine, though, because that's handled by the batch layer. The speed layer also stores the number of samples that went into computing its range.
- To answer queries, the batch and speed ranges are retrieved with their associated sample counts. If the two ranges merge together without eliminating all possible days, then they're merged to the smallest possible range. Otherwise, the range with the higher sample count is used as the result.

This strategy for birthday inference keeps the views simple and handles all the appropriate cases. People that are new to the system will be appropriately served by the incremental algorithm used in the speed layer. It doesn't handle messy data as well as the batch layer, but it's good enough until the batch layer can do more involved analysis later. This strategy also handles bursts of new data well. If you suddenly add a bunch of age samples to the system, the speed layer result will be used over the batch layer result because it's based on more data. And of course, the batch layer is always recomputing birthday ranges, so the results get more accurate over time. There are variations on this implementation you might choose to use for birthday inference, but you should get the idea.

Something that should be apparent from these examples is that your views must be structured to be mergeable. This is natural for time-oriented queries like pageviews over time, but the birthday inference example specifically added sample counts into the views to help with merging. How you structure your views to make them mergeable is one of the design choices you must make in implementing a Lambda Architecture.

18.5 Summary

The Lambda Architecture is the result of starting from first principles—the general formulation of data problems as functions of all data you've ever seen—and making mandatory requirements like human-fault tolerance, horizontal scalability, low-latency reads, and low-latency updates. As we've explored the Lambda Architecture, we made use of many tools to provide practical examples of the core principles, such as Hadoop, JCascalog, Kafka, Cassandra, and Storm. We hope it's been clear that none of these tools is an essential part of the Lambda Architecture. We fully expect the tools to change and evolve over time, but the principles of the Lambda Architecture will always hold.

In many ways, the Lambda Architecture goes beyond the currently available tooling. Although implementing a Lambda Architecture is very doable today—something we tried to demonstrate by going deep into the details of implementing the various layers throughout this book—it certainly could be made even easier. There are only a few databases specifically designed to be used for the serving layer, and it would be great to have speed layer databases that can more easily handle the expiration of parts of the view that are no longer needed. Fortunately, building these tools is much easier than the wide variety of traditional read/write databases being built, so we expect these gaps will be filled as more people adopt the Lambda Architecture. In the meantime, you may find yourself repurposing traditional databases for these various roles in the Lambda Architecture, and doing some engineering yourself to make things fit.

When first encountering Big Data problems and the Big Data ecosystem of tools, it's easy to be confused and overwhelmed. It's understandable to yearn for the familiar world of relational databases that we as an industry have become so accustomed to over the past few decades. We hope that by learning the Lambda Architecture, you've learned that building Big Data systems can be far simpler than building systems based on traditional architectures. The Lambda Architecture completely solves the normalization versus denormalization problem, something that plagues traditional architectures, and it also has human-fault tolerance built in, something we consider to be non-negotiable. Additionally, it avoids the plethora of complexities brought on by architectures based on monolithic read/write databases. Because it's based on functions of all data, the Lambda Architecture is by nature general-purpose, giving you the confidence to attack any data problem.

index